# Psychobehavioral Counseling and Therapy

# Psychobehaviora

## an

### Integrating Behaviora

NEW YO

# Counseling
# Therapy

## and Insight Techniques

### Robert Henley Woody

Grand Valley State College
Psychobehavioral Institute for Human Resources
Washington School of Psychiatry

APPLETON-CENTURY-CROFTS
Educational Division
MEREDITH CORPORATION

Psychobehavioral Counseling and Therapy
*Integrating Behavioral and Insight Techniques*

Copyright © 1971 by

MEREDITH CORPORATION

751-1

Library of Congress Card Number: 75-152377

PRINTED IN THE UNITED STATES OF AMERICA

390-95795-X

Dedicated to
Jane Divita Woody, Mary Ann P. Dubner,
Paul G. Schauble, and Morris B. Parloff

# Contents

# Preface

The field of counseling and psychotherapy has witnessed numerous theoretical approaches emerge, produce a dazzling but short-lived presence, and fade into deserved obscurity. Some professionals have even asserted that this sort of grandiose debut is one of the pathological idiosyncrasies of the field: one psychologist, discussing new "Tinker Bell" therapies, stated that no sooner does a new approach appear than "a number of practitioners will offer to sustain its weak and flickering light by life-supporting shouts of 'I believe! I believe' "; a well-known theorist noted what he termed a "psychotic need to appear original."

With this kind of constant theoretical bubbling, it is not surprising that learning theory principles did not receive immediate, unreserved acceptance by clinicians. Rather, several decades passed before accumulated research in learning theory and its role in human behaviors and interactions made a significant impact in clinical services; but in the late 1950s, behavior therapy, based on learning theory principles, hit the field of counseling and psychotherapy with unprecedented force. Again, skeptics labeled behavior therapy a fad, comprising a few techniques but with an inadequate theoretical basis, that would enjoy a mere brief moment in the spotlight. The last decade, however, has witnessed a steady development of theoretical and technical principles of behavior therapy and an increasing application of these principles to varied clinical and applied settings; in the past five years, counselors and psychotherapists have started to incorporate behavioral modification procedures.

This book has three goals: to develop a rationale and offer guidelines for the integration of behavior therapy into insight-oriented counseling and psychotherapy; to present the basic technical aspects and the related research for behavior therapy techniques, in order to give the reader an introduction to behavioral modification and provide reference sources for those with special interests; to focus attention on the training implications of an integrated approach to counseling and psychotherapy, recognizing that the practice of any form of counseling or therapy is dependent to a large extent upon the knowledge and skills of the practitioner; specifically, trainee selection, program development, curriculum revision, academic knowledge, and the development of the "professional person" (i.e., the enhancing of functioning via melding the professional and the personal self-concepts) will be considered from the psychobehavioral viewpoint.

This is not a book on behavior therapy per se. In fact, the contents are directed much more at counselors and psychotherapists who are not behaviorists. It tries to prepare counselors and psychotherapists to understand and accept aspects of behavioral modification that can complement their insight- or psychodynamically-oriented approaches. One of the implicit assumptions is that the insight and behavioral approaches have the potential for a reciprocally beneficial integration; in other words, although the emphasis is on how behavioral techniques can contribute to the effectiveness of counseling and psychotherapy, it is also suggested that behavior therapy can be enhanced by the incorporation of insight techniques, e.g., a strong relationship between therapist and client. (This position is, of course, disputed by some behaviorists.)

There is no pretense of offering a new theory of counseling or psychotherapy. Rather, the concept of a psychobehavioral counselor-therapist denotes a technical frame of reference. It is designed to allow the counselor-therapist to maintain a theoretical posture based on any of the available comprehensive theories, but to augment it, in the quest for treatment efficacy, with behavioral modification procedures.

I believe that counseling represents a process more than a specialty or discipline. It can be performed by professionals in education, psychology (and any of its specialties), social work, medicine, nursing, or any number of other professions. Counseling does, however, require professional expertise. Counselors should be professionally prepared to assume the responsibility of being psychotherapeutic agents if their functions require it. Counselors, if they are performing true counseling, should potentially be psychotherapists. A distinction should be made between counseling and any guidance and advisement that might be given by professionals in the above-cited disciplines. There is also a real distinction to be made between counseling-therapy and the functions of other professions less related to mental health (e.g., religion, law, personnel management, and law enforcement) or the functions of paraprofessionals (e.g., youth leaders and mental health technicians). Thus, the focus, particularly in the training material, is to prepare counselors to perform therapy, and to give them an eclectic theoretical stance.

Underlying the entire book is a concern for the counselor's and psychotherapist's responsibility to clients and to society. To fulfill it, they must be prepared to deal with increasingly complex professional and societal issues; and trainers must therefore provide proper preparatory experiences and be prepared to enforce appropriate standards. These aspects of responsibility are present throughout the book.

There are several conditions that require consideration in professional training programs. One of the most visible, and one which has both direct and indirect implications for professional mental health workers, is the almost incomprehensible degree of complexity that has so rapidly evolved within our contemporary society. It is a commonplace to say that automation, population density and the resulting congestion, international relations, and domestic problems have created a highly stressed environment. One of the real threats from the composite of these conditions is that the complexity, the requisite blending of abstractions into the practical, and the unpredictability of many of the elements make necessary a constant effort to maintain personal identity and integrity. These sources of stress and the resulting anxiety from fear of loss or traumatic disintegration of human individuality are very much a part of the problems of our present society. We are all aware of the more spectacular manifestations of these problems. Among youth, we see drug abuse, a continuing search for new moral values and academic-vocational motivation, and the formation of seemingly illogical, possibly even self-destructive subcultures (e.g., the "hippie" trend); the violence, whether it be individual violations, "campus unrest," ghetto riots, the conflicts between racial and minority groups, and weakening of previously-held sources of identity, such as religion, sexual morality, economic ethics, and what seems most critical, the social institution of marriage and the family structure. These negative, destructive, and societally-

and personally-unproductive activities are signs of attempts to re-establish equilibrium for a faltering personal identity in the face of an overpowering environment. And the "capper" of evidence is witnessed by the ever-increasing demand for mental health services.

These comments, though apparently pessimistic, create a realistic backdrop for the societal roles played by mental health professionals. And this is where my professional and personal concerns join together, because I believe that the mental health services are not adequately meeting the needs and challenges presented by our contemporary society in many ways. My concerns center on the professions' (meaning all the mental health specialties) hesitation to acknowledge responsibility to society as well as to the individual patient or client, the perpetuation of outdated structures (such as role definitions and the contents of training programs), the difficulty of changing service roles and training models, the hesitancy to adopt well-documented theoretical principles and techniques in actual clinical-applied services, the neglect of preparing the personal elements along with the academic-professional elements of the would-be mental health worker, and the continuing self-defeating separation of specialties, even within a single discipline.

The theme of the 1964 Annual Meeting of the American Orthopsychiatric Association was "Orthopsychiatric Responsibility for Change," and Fried (1964) was invited to present a paper designed to "stimulate thought." He titled his presentation "Effects of Social Change on Mental Health," and in the course of it stated:

. . . *the acceptance of change requires a process of undoing, of giving up the past, of relinquishing previous modes of adaptation.* (p. 5)

In interpreting the long-term trends in social change, he said:

It suggests that *professional mental health services have become a more integral component of the social resources our society provides and accepts in dealing with problems of adaptation and adjustment.* (p. 7)

On the issue of the individual's right to be, he added:

. . . it becomes increasingly clear that *mental health does not inhere in the individual but in the relationship between the individual and his immediate environment.* Mental health appears to be a *process* that involves the fulfillment of individual needs, wishes and goals, but this also implies a *relationship* of interaction, participation and commitment with others whose needs, wishes and goals are fulfilled or frustrated by the reciprocal patterns of interpersonal and role contact. (p. 23)

From this, it is clear that counselors and psychotherapists are not dealing solely with the individual, nor is their responsibility only to the patient or client; the perimeter for both treatment and responsibility is the society.

Too often, it seems that professionals in the mental health fields and their ancillary units or persons (such as political, educational, and administrative systems) are hesitant to question existing structures. In fact, one often detects a blind dedication to ill-founded traditional structures and institutions, outdated by societal and human needs or by irrefutable evidence that a different system or structure would be of greater service. The issue is: should people (collectively or singly) owe allegiance to a given system-structure-institution, or should the latter exist solely to be of service to persons? That is why many of the actionist movements, even though one may disagree with their political or social objectives, must be interpreted as a positive sign. People are questioning, evaluating, and attempting to modify the so-called Establishment (which really means systems, structures, and institutions) in order to make it better serve humanity. These actionist movements make it mandatory that all persons, and certainly all professional mental health workers, do more than simply deny or decry actionist behaviors; they must assume the responsibility for asserting their own differing beliefs by taking actions of their own. But their actions must also be predicated on the basis of questioning, evaluating, and attempting to modify for the betterment of mankind.

And this brings us face to face with the dilemma of the mental health professions: there is a resistance to change. Berlin (1969) believes that our changing society necessitates more responsive models of theory and practice for mental health:

Mental health professionals resist change because such change may reduce their status, financial return, sense of personal satisfaction, and feeling of competency. Learning new methods of working, and especially using new models like public health concepts, are threatening to our established and already learned theoretical frameworks and practices. Community involvement because of crisis situations may force new learning upon mental health professionals. (p. 115)

Surely this kind of resistance to change is not truly professional! I am convinced that backing away from a distinct need because of personal fears and waiting for crisis situations to "force new learning" has led to just castigation of the mental health professions.

One of the areas in which change and the assumption of responsibility should start is the training programs. Too often, there is continuation of training practices without adequate reason. Hopefully, this is not due to conservatism for conservatism's sake, or resistance to change for fear of loss of status, for any such insecurity in what is supposed to be a profession is incongruous, and strips away the right to wear the cloak of professionalism. One of the major neglects, and this seems to be more true of educationally-oriented counselor training programs than of psychologically-oriented counselor-therapist training programs, is the failure to accept that counseling and psychotherapy represent more of a science than an art. Granted, there is an element of both—plus a few unclassifiable ingredients. The remedy would seem to be that training programs must encompass all of the behavioral sciences, and not be limited just to psychology or education. Thoresen (1969) views counseling as a "highly complex, social-psychological phenomenon" that makes it requisite that counselors be applied behavioral scientists:

Approaching counseling as an applied behavioral scientist will permit us to get on with the task of more effectively helping a wide variety of clients with their many different kinds of problems. For too long we have relied exclusively on one-to-one verbal interaction as the *sine qua non* of counseling. We desperately need some courageous souls who are willing to say, "I don't really know, but I can find out. I can explore. I can inquire. I can question. And I can create." Materlinck once said that for every progressive spirit there are a thousand men to guard the past. Let us permit the past to rest gently and get on here and now with the coming. (p. 847)

Although my views are less purely behavioral than his, I readily endorse Thoresen's view of the counselor as a "behavioral scientist"; but I would also want to add "humanist" to acknowledge the concept of "science for humanity." In this book, considerable attention is devoted to training the psychobehavioral counselor-therapist via a psycho-social behavioral-science model.

Compatible with such an interdisciplinary or multi-behavioral sciences viewpoint is my belief that effective counseling and psychotherapy can best be achieved by accepting an eclectic theoretical-technical position for service. At this time, eclecticism is best reflected in clinical services that combine behavioral techniques with insight counseling and psychotherapy. This integration is the crux of the psychobehavioral approach. This is the age of the loyalty oath, whether it be formal and tangible, as when one joins a university faculty or accepts a government position, or whether it be unspoken, as when one becomes a mental health professional and accepts, perhaps without cause, existing theories and identifies usually with one discipline, one specialty, and perhaps even one theoretical approach. In each of these instances, it should be noted that the loyalty oath gives primary emphasis to what you do not or should not believe in or practice, whereas it would seem more important to emphasize what you *do* believe in or practice. Throughout this book, the position maintained is that eclecticism is needed and cannot be sacrificed for isolated allegiance. (This may well be true for domestic, political, and professional issues alike.)

Cutting across the professional factors is the awareness that the handling of each of them is dependent upon the personal characteristics of the counselor-therapist. This is one area in which I differ from the "pure" behaviorists; that is, I believe that most straight-line behavior therapists do not give adequate consideration to the influence that personality and the therapist-client relationship have on the therapeutic processes. Any counseling or psychotherapeutic intervention has an undetermined degree of reliance upon the person, i.e., the idiosyncratic characteristics, of the counselor-therapist. I believe that too few training programs build in methods for developing self-understanding, that too little research has been done on the matters of how the therapist's characteristics influence therapeutic processes and how therapists can capitalize on their personal qualities for promoting therapeutic efficacy for the welfare of the client, that too little is known about how to foster and measure (or evaluate) self-understanding in professional mental health workers, and that too many counselors and therapists practice without having adequately resolved the potential or existing dissonance between the professional self- and the personal self-concepts.

A final concern is the separation of mental health disciplines.

There are desirable and necessary differences in training, skills, and role functions, but often one is struck by the illogical and unnecessary role distinctions, the staking out of exclusive rights to clinical service areas, the neglect of the resources of related disciplines and specialties, and the denouncing of the service intentions of mental health workers in other disciplines and specialties. In this day of insatiable demands for mental health services, this issue could almost be scoffed at and labeled "antiquated trivia" or "a thing of the past," except for the fact that such cleavages among the mental health professions still exist. The alarming thing is that these cleavages are not limited to different disciplines; taking my own discipline of psychology, it seems like a ridiculous waste of professional energy to have the different specialties battling or using passive-aggressive tactics, i.e., ignoring each other's existence and refusing to cooperate in training and research efforts. Earlier it was mentioned that separationism was "self-defeating," and indeed it will be unless steps are taken to eliminate it. There is a call for all mental health workers to confront this issue, and professional responsibility demands that the call be heeded. One of the areas most sensitive to these separationist actions is, of course, counseling and psychotherapy. Certainly no one specialty within psychology, and, moreover, no one mental health discipline, can justly lay claim to possessing the sole effective counseling and psychotherapy techniques. Obviously, there are skills and qualities that must be present for any professional, regardless of specialty or discipline, to offer himself as a counselor or therapist, but this should be a function of his characteristics and abilities, not of his discipline or specialty per se. Our society can ill-afford a continuation of cleavage among mental health professions. Thus, while this book is primarily directed to counselors and therapists from the discipline of psychology, and specifically to the specialties of clinical, counseling, and school psychology, in no way should this be interpreted as implying exclusion of other disciplines; it is done only because psychology is my discipline and the specialties of clinical, counseling, and school psychology are the ones from which I have formed my own frame of reference. I intend that the term "counselor" (or "counselor-therapist") should take on a generic meaning, encompassing medicine, social work, education, nursing, and any discipline or specialty that serves human development and any professional who has acquired or aspires to have the competencies necessary to do counseling and psychotherapy. For practical purposes, in most instances the term "counselor" or even "therapist" is interchangeable with the term "mental health specialist"; terminology receives further clarification in Chapter 1.

The materials within this book are suitable for use with graduate students in guidance, counseling, special education, human development, social work, psychiatry, and clinical, counseling, and school psychology. In view of the newness of applied behavioral techniques and the lack of behavioral-insight technical integration in day-to-day practice, the contents should be of value to students and professional practitioners alike. I believe that consideration of theoretical-technical integration should be a required part of the professional education of all counselors and psychotherapists.

An attempt has been made to maintain brevity and a practical flavor in the theoretical and technical discussions without sacrificing either academic scholarship or readability. To some, this style might evoke a feeling of incompleteness; an effort was made to counteract this possibility by including selected references. That is, this book is not designed to be an encyclopedia of research sources, but references have been included at strategic points to provide the reader with sources for elaboration on the points under discussion and to provide documentation when needed. In regard to the latter, the practical "guidebook" nature of this book in combination with the writing style may appear to convey a pontifical stance on aspects that are quite open to debate. If this impression is created, I apologize, because this was by no means a desired presentation mode. If documentation is not provided, and the material seems disputable to the reader, then it should be viewed as my own subjective opinion, which is based to a large extent on my clinical experiences and in no way is presented as irrefutable fact.

Increasing professional attention is being given to the use of paraprofessionals in mental health, professional versus academic training programs for clinicians, community mental health, mental health consultation, social systems analysis, and societal actions. It is hoped the reader will understand that considerations of space have prevented a more extensive treatment of these matters than is found in this book. It is also hoped that the relevant but limited information to be found here will lead the reader to further exploration of these important topics.*

My motivation for attempting to integrate behavioral and insight techniques has been stimulated by several sources. Foremost has been the reciprocal commitment to improvement that I have experienced with my clients; this has led me to explore a spectrum of theories and techniques. Second, the Washington School of Psychiatry (under the administration of Irving M. Ryckoff, M.D.) established an annual workshop in psychobehavioral therapy; preparing for and participating in this learning experience each year has been valuable. Finally, my colleagues associated with the Psychobehavioral Institute for Human Resources offer continuing personal support and professional challenge.

Appreciation is expressed to Dr. Morris B. Parloff for serving as the editorial consultant and to Dr. Paul G. Schauble for critiquing my ideas; both have had a significant influence on the formulation of my views, but in no way are they responsible for what might be shortcomings within the material. Special appreciation is extended to my wife, Dr. Jane Divita Woody, who devoted her literary skills and much time, at the expense of her own writing endeavors, to the editorial preparation of the manuscript (and to keeping our boistrous brood away from the piles of notes and reference cards).

R. H. W.

## REFERENCES

Berlin, I. N. Resistance to change in mental health professionals. *American Journal of Orthopsychiatry,* 1969, *39,* 109–115.

Fried, M. Effects of social change on mental health. *American Journal of Orthopsychiatry,* 1964, *34,* 3–28.

Thoresen, C. E. The counselor as an applied behavioral scientist. *Personnel and Guidance Journal,* 1969, *47,* 841–848.

Woody, R. H., and Woody, Jane D. (Eds.). *Clinical Assessment in Counseling and Psychotherapy.* New York: Appleton-Century-Crofts, 1972.

*A fuller analysis and discussion of these topics will be found in a forthcoming publication on clinical assessment by Woody and Woody, Appleton-Century-Crofts, 1972.

# I
# Theory, Techniques, and Application

# 1

# Psychobehavioral Counseling and Therapy: Theory and Rationale

Counselors and therapists have earned increasing acceptance from our society over the past two decades. Scarcely any public service institution would be structured without counseling services of some kind. Because of a wide range of employment settings, a variety of counseling and therapeutic subspecialties has developed. These are designed around the characteristics of the particular setting—schools, rehabilitation and community agencies, college personnel services, mental health facilities—but all share common behavioral science foundations: all incorporate aspects of personality theory, human development, social psychology, and interviewing and counseling-therapeutic techniques.

Because it is assumed that the reader will have academic familiarity with counseling and psychotherapy, a lengthy survey of definitions of counselor-therapist roles and functions seems unnecessary. However, the last part of this book deals with training, at which point these issues will be discussed (see Chapters 4, 5, and 6). Suffice it to say that the term "counselor" is used generically throughout this book, unless a specific context is presented. The use of the term "counselor-therapist" means that the functions under consideration should be performed by a professional who can move from counseling into psychotherapy.

The distinction between counseling and psychotherapy rests more on the personal-professional training or development and the characteristics of the practitioner and his employment setting than on theories and, to some degree, techniques and processes. For the most part, the materials in this book are designed for the professional or trainee who is or aspires to be able to perform both counseling and psychotherapy.

There is, then, a counseling-psychotherapy continuum. A given counselor-client relationship could begin as counseling and progress into psychotherapy, depending to a large extent on the needs of the client, the degree of affect or emotion involved, and the ability of the counselor-therapist to handle technically and personally the depth of the affectivity found in psychotherapy. This position is termed "therapeutic psychology," and is elaborated upon by Brammer and Shostrom (1968), among others. Likewise, the term "counselor" is used primarily within the framework of psychology; this usage is determined by the professional identity of the author, but in essentially all instances (except those that are clearly limited to the field of psychology), the terms "counselor," "therapist," and "counselor-therapist" could potentially be applied to all of the mental health specialties. Although there are distinctions in the training, theories, techniques, and service goals of the mental health specialties, it is believed that all should share a basic philosophy rooted in interpersonal dynamics, cultivate counseling-therapeutic skills, and appreciate a diversity of theories and techniques. There are some problems or types of clients that should not be dealt with by a particular counselor-therapist, but the distinction is more one of individual qualifications and conditions (barring, of course, medical treatment) than one of job title or disciplinary identification.

The evolution of counseling and psychotherapy has not always been smooth; in fact, there have been stormy periods; but, as is true of most professions, it has witnessed numerous theoretical battles. In the healthy scientific atmosphere that has encompassed the field, several theories have emerged and comparisons have subsequently been made between them in an attempt to establish respective soundness. This has occasionally resulted in a certain degree of estrangement, with counselors and therapists often tending to identify primarily with one theory.

Counseling-psychotherapy has achieved an important place in our society, has striven to develop a scientific rationale, has had specialized functions grow from the needs of particular employment settings, and has been dynamic to the point that a counselor-therapist can select from several theoretical approaches. The latter two points, if carried to the point of rigid adherence to the needs of one subspecialty, or to rigid subscription to one theoretical approach, could have a detrimental influence on the quality of counseling or psychotherapy: it is critical that counseling-psychotherapy retain a generic framework and that all relevant theoretical, technical, and practical factors be within the professional grasp of every counselor-therapist.

Unfortunately, this does not appear to be the present situation. London (1964) has indicated that approaches to counseling and psychotherapy can be dichotomized into Insight and Action. The insightists work to help their clients attain self-understanding or insight into their motives for behavior. Among insightists are such diverse theorists as Freud, Adler, and Rogers. The diversity among the insightists is not so great as one might think because they share the primary objective of insight, use verbal communication as the main instrument for therapeutic exploration, and allow the client to be responsible for the boundaries (within reason) of the counselor-client relationship and counseling-therapy goals. Actionists, or behaviorists, on the other hand, believe that problems represent maladaptive habits or stem from misinformation that can be counteracted by conditioning and reinforcement procedures; they believe that insight in and of itself is of little value for behavioral modification, and that the counselor has the responsibility to help the client achieve change, e.g., relief from his problem, by any professional means he determines. One of the major differences, as may be obvious, is that insightists believe that emotional or behavioral problems represent an underlying neurotic conflict that can only be resolved by understanding or insight, and that once insight allows resolution, behavioral change should follow. But the actionists or behaviorists believe that there need not be an underlying neurotic conflict, and that even if the client does have conflicting emotional or attitudinal concerns, the primary goal is to break habits, promote behavioral change, and learn or relearn nonproblem behaviors.

From this brief summary, it is apparent that a schism could develop, and indeed it seems that is *has* developed. One example may be found in writings dealing with the efficacy of a given approach to counseling-psychotherapy. One of the main arguments used is that theory $X$ is better than theory $Y$, and often $X$ and $Y$ represent insight versus action (or behaviorism). Proponents of a given theory frequently try to gain credence for their position by denouncing the opposition; this is easily seen both in professional meetings and in writings.

It is lamentable that the status of a theory should be derived from such comparisons, but the real misfortune is that such a schism should have developed at all, especially because, as we shall see, both the insightist and the behaviorist views have value. Establishing esteem for one view at the unnecessary expense of another is a price that the mental health professions can ill afford.

The advent of conditioning or behavior therapy has given impetus to the attempts to determine the effects of insight counseling and psychotherapy. In considering the research for the whole theoretical range of counseling and psychotherapy, be it measures of actualization from the client-centered school or measures of insight and neurotic conflict resolution from the psychoanalytically oriented school(s), it would seem that there are mixed results: it has been found that some investigations revealed significant benefits while others did not. In most instances, the degree of success did not appear to be related either to the theoretical position or to the type of problem being treated. These studies have been reviewed by Truax and Carkhuff (1967).

These contradicting results created professional concern, but even greater concern was provoked when studies were undertaken to compare the effects achieved by lay counselors as compared to those achieved by professional counselors. The consensus seems to be that with or without training and experience, lay counselors can help their clients as much (or more!) than professional counselors can help theirs (Carkhuff, 1968), at least according to some definitions or dimensions of counseling.

Relying heavily on the research and theory of Rogerian-style counseling, one approach to research on efficacy emphasizes that the primary ingredients for helping clients are *dimensions of the counselor-client relationship*. The forerunner of this view was, of course, Rogers, who stated:

If I can provide a certain type of relationship, the other person will discover within himself the capacity to use that relationship for growth, and change and personal development will occur. (Rogers, 1961, p. 33)

Rogers then set forth three attitudes or dimensions that the counselor must communicate to the client if constructive personality change is to occur: *unconditional positive regard*, i.e., the counselor's communicating nonpossessive, nonevaluative, unreserved caring for the client; *empathic understanding,* i.e., the counselor's communicating that he actually feels or senses the client's feelings; and *congruence,* i.e., the counselor's being genuine, being sincerely himself. Truax and Carkhuff (1967) conducted numerous investigations, and modified the attitudes or dimensions to be: *accurate empathy,* which is very similar to Rogerian empathy but also requires that the counselor must go beyond sensing the client's inner-world, that is, it ". . . involves both the therapist's *sensitivity to current feelings* and his *verbal facility to communicate this understanding* in a language attuned to the client's current feelings" (p. 46); *nonpossessive warmth,* essentially the same as Rogerian unconditional positive regard; and *genuineness,* replacing congruence. Carkhuff and Berenson (1967) proceed further, and take into account what happens between lay counselors and clients. They offer the following "dimension of human nourishment": empathic understanding, counselor respect, facilitative genuineness, personally relevant concreteness, and client self-exploration. Carkhuff and Berenson provide a compilation of research on the effectiveness of nonprofessional and professional counselors, and the research from which these dimensions were derived.

While it seems that there is ample support for facilitating conditions, there is not total accord. Gladstein (1970), for example, analyzes the available research on the relevance of empathy to counseling, and concludes that, contrary to expectations, there is reason to question whether empathy is actually important to counseling. He is opposed to the automatic assumption that empathy is important in producing counseling outcomes; rather, counselors should consider its relevance to the particular client and his problem. He states: "We might hypothesize, furthermore, that the more the counseling process deals with developmental concerns, the less need there is for empathy" (p. 826).

For the most part, research supports the position that there are identifiable dimensions that must be present in the counseling-therapeutic relationship if the counseling-therapy is to be effective, and much of the evidence seems indisputable. Of special importance is the possibility that these particular dimensions could, at least in part, depend on personal characteristics as much or more than on professional characteristics. Obviously, this is why lay counselors, some of whom are totally untrained, can equal the professional in effectiveness—at least in these dimensions. But the professional counselor-therapist has a reserve of "helping armament" to rely on that the lay counselor does not have. This armament is, of course, the scientific bases of the behavioral sciences and technical training. Indeed, this is why professional training programs exist, and to neglect these factors is to relegate counseling and therapy to a lay activity instead of according it the scientific professional stature of which it is capable and deserving.

Analysis of the counseling-psychotherapy research suggests two major points. First, the facilitating conditions or dimensions may very well contribute beneficially to counseling-therapeutic processes, but it has not been adequately established (via research) that they are enough to meet the challenges presented by the diverse problems and types of clients with which the professional counselor-therapist must be prepared to deal. Second, in view of the foregoing, the counselor-client relationship appears to be a necessary ingredient for both insight and behavior therapy. Of course, pure behavior therapists disagree with this, and have supposedly gone to some lengths to develop relationship-free techniques. Likewise, some insightists disagree with the proposition that their work could benefit from behavioristic supplements. These points, which will be repeatedly highlighted in subsequent sections, combine to support the belief that the properly trained counselor-therapist must be more than a "nice guy" who can exude prescribed interpersonal conditions—he must have an armamentarium of scientifically derived skills and techniques to supplement his effective interpersonal relations, and these come, in part, from behavior therapy (as well as from familiarity with the theories of counseling-psychotherapy).

It is this rationale that leads to the plea that counselor-therapists should be prepared, for the good of their clients, to escape the confines of a single theoretical approach or set of techniques, and to tailor their professional actions to the needs and characteristics of the client being treated. To do this, the counselor-therapist will have to be prepared academically to use a variety of techniques, some of which, particularly those aligned with conditioning or behavior therapy, have been vastly ignored or neglected in many training programs.

At this point, therefore, attention will focus on behaviorism. Special consideration will be given to causes of behavioral problems, the efficacy of treatment, the value of the therapeutic relationship, and the compounding factors involved in the effects supposedly attributable to conditioning processes. From this exploration, behaviorism and traditional insight counseling-psychotherapy will be synthesized into what will be termed a *psychobehavioral* approach to counseling and therapy.

## BEHAVIOR THERAPY

Since it seems wise to keep the theoretical in a practical perspective, behaviorism will be presented herein in its applied clinical form: behavior therapy. Behavior therapy, also called conditioning therapy, is closely related to both behavioral and psychobehavioral counseling and therapy. Behavior therapy and behavioral counseling are both based on learning theory, and both use conditioning techniques. They are distinguished primarily by the goals that they maintain. Behavioral counseling has been limited, at least at this point in time, to only a few counseling goals and techniques, namely verbal conditioning of clients' in-counseling comments, whereas behavior therapy has been directed at a wide variety of problem behaviors and uses diverse learning-theory-based techniques. It is probable that the scope of problems served and techniques employed in behavioral counseling will increase; this is one of the reasons why psychobehavioral counseling and therapy seems most appropriate: it is based on the premise that the counselor-therapist can integrate seemingly-disparate techniques in order to deal with a host of problems.

### Causes of Neurosis

Insight approaches to counseling and psychotherapy maintain that problem behaviors are manifestations of underlying neurotic conflicts, and that "cure" is achieved only when the conflicts are brought into consciousness, discussed and explored for meaning, and resolved to some degree. Behavior therapists, conversely, state that there is no underlying neurotic conflict, only a set of faulty or maladaptive learnings that become manifested as problem behaviors. "Cure" is attained by unlearning the unacceptable behavioral patterns and learning new acceptable ones (Eysenck and Rachman, 1965).

Needless to say, this difference in etiology leads to vehement denunciations from the opposing camps. There are, however, two questions within this matter: Are there really differences in the concepts of etiology? Is etiology really the central issue?

The intriguing thing is that on close analysis, there appears a certain amount of similarity between the insightists' and behaviorists' views on causation. For example, Dollard and Miller (1950) translate psychodynamic principles, primarily from a psychoanalytic orientation, into a learning theory system for psychotherapy. And Mowrer (1966) presents a convincing discussion on the striking theoretical similarities among Freudian psychoanalysis, Rogerian client-centered therapy, and Wolpean behavior therapy in regard to definitions of the origins of neurotic behavior; in fact, Mowrer (1964) points out that while the language is different, behavior therapy and psychoanalysis are quite compatible in terms of theoretical principles.

But of perhaps more importance is the question of whether causation is a valid point of departure. In some ways it seems that the real issue is what aspect of the problem should be treated, the manifest symptom or the dynamic bases for the symptom. The behavior therapist is concerned with reducing inappropriate anxiety, e.g., phobias, or eliciting anxiety, e.g., character disorders (drug addiction, alcoholism, sexual perversion). The classical psychotherapist is also concerned with bringing the client's feelings like fear, anxiety, and rage into awareness, the hypothesis being that these feelings have been repressed or suppressed or in some way kept out of the client's awareness, and that such repression leads to mental conflicts. The psychotherapist believes that unless the feelings are brought into awareness, the client's functioning will be limited and that he may experience problems; he tries to help the client gain this awareness by focusing upon the defense mechanisms. It would appear that the behavior therapist is not as concerned with unexpressed affect or with the inappropriate expression of affects other than anxiety. Both approaches are, in fact, concerned about anxiety, but they go about dealing with it differently. Logic would seem to support that attention should be paid to both positions.

Further support for an integrated approach to causation can be gained from looking at the effects of therapeutic interventions. Specifically, it appears that a behavioral intervention leads to psychodynamic changes. When studying systematic desensitization with phobics, Kamil (1970) found that there were also psychodynamic alterations, presumably because of the behavioral treatment. His interpretation of the evidence suggests that improved ego strength might have come from an increased "sense of mastery and competence stemming from the successful desensitization experience" (p. 204) and from "a quantum of ego energy freed for adaptive use by the reduction of fear" (p. 204). Similarly, Kraft (1969) maintains that while behavior therapy removes a particular target symptom, such a successful treatment also results in improvement of the client's general life adjustment; for example, he presents clinical cases illustrating that a client treated by behavior therapy loses the target problem behavior and that this change also results in a change in the relationship between the client and his spouse.

Thus there are sufficient differences between the insightists and the behaviorists, but both acknowledge a commonality for etiology in affect—it is simply a matter that anxiety reactions receive greater emphasis from the behavior therapists. If a comparative posture is assumed, the typically cited differences regarding etiology between the insight therapists and the behavior therapists seem spurious.

### Efficacy of Treatment

Open animosity has sometimes developed when behaviorists and insightists get together, and this is usually based on claims of efficacy. The behaviorists maintain that traditional insight counseling and psychotherapy, particularly psychoanalysis and client-centered therapy, contribute nothing more to mental health than does no treatment, and that "results" are really spontaneous remissions. Eysenck (1952, 1965) has published critiques of insight psychotherapy that cite percentages of cures, presenting evidence that approximately two-thirds of clients receiving psychotherapy are cured, but an approximately equal number who do not receive treatment (but who had needed it initially) are also cured just by the passage of time (presumably); and he points to the fact that approximately nine out of ten clients seen for behavior therapy are cured. In addition to Eysenck's critiques, similar and compatible comparative evaluations have been described by Eysenck and Rachman (1965), Lazarus (1963), and Wolpe (1964, 1969a). However, numerous critics have, in turn, contradicted the foregoing behaviorally-aligned critiques (e.g., Kiesler, 1966). Nonetheless, it should be acknowledged that there is still room for dispute regarding the efficacy of counseling and psychotherapy.

Length of treatment is another factor used to compare efficacies. The behaviorists point with pride to the fact that their conditioning procedures usually produce the desired therapeutic results in far less time than would counseling or psychotherapy (Wolpe, 1964)—when it is successful. To exemplify, Wolpe and Lazarus (1966) report that the mean number of sessions to treat phobic clients successfully via behavior therapy was 11.2 (the median number of sessions was 10.0); because in counseling and psychotherapy the phobia might not receive direct attention, and thus the treatment goal would be different, it is probably not possible to compute the average number of sessions required for successful treatment. In other words, the kinds of problems dealt with in behavior therapy may well differ significantly from those dealt with in counseling and psychotherapy, and thus the criterion of length of treatment per se is essentially meaningless. Indeed, Klein, Dittmann, Parloff, and Gill (1969) observed that there seems to be a trend toward behavior therapists' accepting more complex or seriously disturbed cases than in earlier years; relatedly, they note that there have been changes in the reported outcome rate; behavioral claims for cures have dropped from approximately 90 percent to approximately 80 percent and in some cases 70 percent, and there has been an increase in the average number of interviews needed for successful behavior therapy. Obviously, the insight and behavioral approaches place different amounts of importance on the time element and number of sessions. On the basis of a purist position, it could be asserted that the insightists give little if any consideration to duration of treatment, while to the behaviorists the principle of economy, defined in terms of time, suffering, and money, fully justifies primary emphasis. To be fair to counseling and psychotherapy, one must acknowledge that the practical position is probably quite different than the purist position; that is, from all indication of actual practice and in the increasing amount of research dealing with "short-term" or "brief" psychotherapy, it would appear that insightists are very much concerned with the principle of economy, but admittedly it has received scant attention in theoretical treatises.

One of the critical facts that is frequently overlooked is that the criteria for cure or improvement are different for behavior therapy and for insight counseling and psychotherapy. Counseling and psychotherapy, in accord with the insight frame of reference, view improvement as being reflected in the amount of self-understanding that the client achieves. In fact, it is theoretically possible that a client could still have an overt problem behavior after having had counseling-psychotherapy, but because he understands and accepts his "self" involvement in the problem, the counseling-psychotherapy might still be deemed successful. Behavior therapy and, consequently, behavioral counseling measure success by the presence or absence of the specific problem behaviors that brought the client for treatment. Again the distinction between a purist and a practical position for counseling and psychotherapy should be made. The actual practical situation is that insightists are typically dissatisfied with their success rates. In fact, if they were willing to base their rate of success on solely the theoretical criterion of increased self-understanding, the success rate would undoubtedly be higher. When making evaluations of the effects of their counseling-therapy, insightists do consider certain behavioral factors, such as symptomatic improvement and changes in social competence (Parloff, 1961). The differences between theory and practice have led to ambiguous efficacy studies for counseling and psychotherapy. Moreover, the differences in criteria for improvement, whether from a theoretical or practical viewpoint, negate the value of comparing efficacies on the basis of the percentages of clients who have lost their overt behavior problems. These and other differences in criteria and assessment of efficacy have been explored in more detail by Breger and McGaugh (1965), Gelder (1965), and Kiesler (1966).

It should be noted that the efficacy war between insight and behavior therapies, regardless of the limitations imposed by measurement procedures, is not as well-declared as any set of percentages might suggest. The fact is that comparison studies are few—at least there are few that actually merit being called comparison studies. Perhaps this is best illustrated by the fact that while there are numerous studies that profess superiority for one approach over the other, there are other studies that find that there is little or no difference; to take but one example of the latter, Marks, Sonoda, and Schalock (1968) found that both relationship (insight) therapy and reinforcement (behavior) therapy improved the functioning of

chronic schizophrenics, but that there was no systematic difference
in efficacy between the two treatment approaches. At this point in
the evolution of relevant research, claims for superiority by either
side seem unjustified.

In spite of the complexities involved in comparing the two
approaches and the fact that percentages do not tell the complete
story, it is very important to note that when behavioral or conditioning
techniques are applied to an overt behavior problem, there is generally a 90 percent chance (or slightly lower, if recent claims are
accepted) that the problem behavior can be eliminated (Wolpe,
1964, 1969a; Wolpe and Lazarus, 1966). This is important because
many of the clients seeking help from counselors and psychotherapists
do have specific overt behavior problems that they would like to have
treated. One can thus see the importance of the counselor-therapist's
being prepared to provide a treatment approach tailored to the needs
of a particular client, rather than requiring that the client adjust his
needs to the parameters of the theory espoused and practiced by the
counselor-therapist; this matter relates to responsibility, which will
receive attention at subsequent points in this book. Suffice it to say
at the present, the fact that behavioral techniques can so effectively
alleviate and eliminate problem behaviors justifies the view that
learning-oriented techniques merit and, moreover, demand inclusion
in the counselor-therapist's repertoire of professional skills.

### The Therapeutic Relationship

Behavior therapists place no importance on the therapist-client
relationship, which is, of course, of critical importance to insight approaches. Behavior therapists do not capitalize in any way on the
possible benefits of the therapist-client relationship. In behavior
therapy there is so little importance attached to the relationship that
there may even be several therapists working with the same client
(e.g., Geer, 1964; Geer and Katkin, 1966).

It is interesting to note that while behaviorists do not consider
the relationship to be influential, relationship factors are plainly
present in their therapy. Unfortunately there are few published accounts relevant to this matter. Personal observations of a number of
practicing behavior therapists in both the United States and Great
Britain reveal that in virtually every case there was a relationship

between the therapist and the client that could have contributed to the therapeutic outcome, albeit potentially negatively in some cases. Similar observations are reported by Klein, Dittmann, Parloff, and Gill (1969) as a result of their observation of the treatment services offered by Wolpe and Lazarus, two of the most prominent proponents of behavior therapy. These observers were struck by the amount of suggestion conveyed by the behavior therapist to the client that would feasibly prescribe the client's expectations and attitudes about making therapeutic improvement. This point is discussed more fully in the "Clinical Suggestion and Hypnosis" section of Chapter 2.

Related to these observations, Murray and Jacobson (in press) conclude that all therapies—behavior and insight—have their effectiveness rooted, at least in part, in the communication of the belief in the client's ability to change and providing the client with influences that will lead to general increase in self esteem. The behaviorists' use of multiple therapists with one client in no way changes the picture. For example, one client being treated via aversive therapy by three behavior therapists stated, "Dr. X seems cold and uninterested in me and Dr. Y seems to take delight in pushing the button to feed the electric shock to me, but Dr. Z is very nice, almost fatherly to me." This kind of statement readily reflects quite different relationships between the various behavior therapists and the client, but one must resort to speculation as to how each respective relationship contributed—positively or negatively—to the therapeutic outcome. Beech (1963) has indicated that the differences in success achieved by behavior therapists may be due to differences in their relationships with their clients. Wolpe and Lazarus (1966), although attributing their therapeutic effects solely to conditioning, state that the behavior therapy client "enjoys the nonjudgmental acceptance of a person whom he perceives as possessing the necessary skills and desire to be of service" (p. 10). This "nonjudgmental acceptance" in the Wolpe-Lazarus behavior therapy could easily promote many of the same effects as Rogerian nonpossessive acceptance and Truax-Carkhuff nonpossessive warmth. The point is that while the behaviorists claim the relationship between the counselor-therapist and the client is of no therapeutic value and that the effects of their behavior therapy are due to conditioning, there is ample evidence that the relationship is of definite therapeutic value, and that it operates in behavior therapy. Therefore, it may be asserted that the effects of behavior therapy are

contaminated by unmeasured influences from the relationship between the counselor-therapist and the client.

## Compounding Factors

The foregoing discussion of the therapeutic relationship and
how it is influential, in an unacknowledged and uncontrolled fashion,
in behavior therapy leads directly to a number of other sources of
contamination. Intrinsic to this section is the belief that the integration of insight and behavior therapy techniques cannot be a loose-knit
haphazard application of relevant principles, something that both
insightists and behaviorists have all too frequently allowed to occur
in their therapy. It must consist of conscious and explicit use of techniques and procedures. This section is directed at pinpointing some
of the obvious loopholes in application, the contaminations in behavior therapy research that result from the failure to account for
insight-related variables.

In view of the presence of relationship factors, one might question whether insight might also be involved in behavior therapy.
Numerous examples can be found in behavior therapy research in
which considerable time was spent discussing the client's feelings
about his problems (see, for example, Lazarus, 1964), and yet the
effects were attributed totally to conditioning. Similarly, one behavior therapy technique called "behavioral rehearsal" involves the
role-playing of coping behaviors; there is certainly reason to believe
that this approach could lead to increased understanding of motives,
much in the same manner as Moreno-style psychodrama. Further,
Wolpe and Lazarus (1966) state that the behavior therapist "may
find it desirable to offer advice, reassurance, support, encouragement
or clarification" (p. 27); here again it is clear that behavior therapy
draws on the beneficial dimensions of both the therapeutic relationship and client insight. There seems no denying that these actions
are quite similar to those of insight-oriented counselors and psychotherapists. These similarities lend support to the psychobehavioral
position, which finds insight and behavioral approaches compatible.
Parenthetically, it might be added that there is laboratory evidence
that insight can facilitate conditioning processes (Cole and Sipprelle,
1967; Heap and Sipprelle, 1966).

Suggestion, either planned or unplanned, constitutes another compounding factor in behavior therapy. Faith, hope, expectancy, or direct suggestion in the therapeutic relationship, regardless of the theoretical alignment of the therapist, is a reality, and behavior therapy is not exempt from these effects (Wilson, Hannon, and Evans, 1968). Moreover, there appears to be no clinical research study on behavior therapy that unquestionably documents that the behavior therapist is not giving, either verbally or by his covert and overt actions, suggestions to his clients that their therapy will be successful, or suggestions about how the clients can expect to react once the treatment has started. In fact it is common for behavior therapists to assure their clients that they can be cured. What this means is that the effects produced by the behavior therapy will be influenced by the suggestibility of the client. It should be emphasized that often these suggestions are uncontrolled; that is, the therapist may be making them unconsciously or in an unplanned fashion. The scientifically-ideal approach would be to acknowledge that suggestion does play a part in treatment, plan consciously how it can best used, and include it as one of the factors to be assessed when the outcomes of therapy are being measured and analyzed.

Clinical hypnosis, which can be described as induced relaxation to facilitate heightened suggestibility and the therapeutic offering of planned suggestions from the counselor-therapist, has been much used by behavior therapists. Again, however, the majority of behavioral studies make no mention of the effects of hypnosis on the therapy being investigated; but in subsequent or round-about sorts of ways it becomes evident that the behavior therapist does, in fact, often consciously apply hypnotic procedures. One example is that Wolpe and Lazarus (1966) report that they use hypnosis in about 33 percent of their desensitization cases, and Cautela (1966) states that in a personal communication, Wolpe acknowledges using hypnosis with 25 percent of his cases, and in a later source, Wolpe (1969a) indicates that 10 percent of his systematic desensitization cases involve hypnosis. Regardless of contradictory percentages, the results of desensitization research, including that of Wolpe and Lazarus, are attributed only to the reciprocal inhibition principle (see p. 68). The point here is not to criticize behavior therapists for using hypnosis; in fact, it is commendable that they feel free to select the technique that seems called for with a given client (which is probably the reason why hypnosis is used with only a percentage of the clients).

Rather, what is significant is that therapeutic effects attributed to a certain behavioral principle, such as the reciprocal inhibition principle, may be due only in part to that principle, with some of the effects being attributable to other processes, such as hypnotic phenomena. And it should be noted that the techniques used for so-called nonhypnotic behavior therapy (for example, inducing relaxation to use in conjunction with systematic desensitization or some other behavior therapy procedure) are essentially identical to those used to induce the hypnotic state. Cautela (1966) maintains that the commonly employed concept of hypnosis is not part of behavior therapy, but in view of the undeniable similarities, scientific skepticism seems appropriate.

To move beyond the issue of contamination, there is evidence that clinical hypnosis can enhance the overall efficacy of behavior therapy. Hussain (1964), for example, presents evidence that systematic desensitization is more effective when hypnosis is used than when it is not. Moreover, Wolpe and Lazarus (1966) cite several techniques with which hypnosis can be used, and they state that the well trained behavior therapist should have proficiency with hypnotic induction techniques and be knowledgeable about hypnotic phenomena. Again, as with previously discussed contaminating factors, it seems we must act to acknowledge, incorporate, and consciously direct the aspects of hypnosis that enter into therapeutic techniques.

## REINFORCEMENT IN COUNSELING AND PSYCHOTHERAPY

The preceding section has shown that certain factors intrinsic to insight counseling and psychotherapy are also to be found in behavior therapy, and that the effects attributed to the conditioning techniques of behavior therapy may represent compounded sources. It is both fair and necessary to add equal emphasis to the fact that certain aspects of behavior therapy, particularly reinforcement elements, are present in traditional insight counseling and psychotherapy (Woody, 1968b). These behavioral facets are occasionally planned, but are for the most part unacknowledged and uncontrolled.

### Selective Responding

Verbal conditioning is an important behavioral technique, in which the counselor-therapist uses his own responding as a way of influencing how the client responds. In other words, the counselor-therapist responds, either verbally or nonverbally, when the client makes some specified type of statement, but does not respond in any way when the client makes a statement outside of the specified type. This behavior tends to reinforce the occurrence of the specified type of statement, and as research (to be subsequently cited) shows, it is an efficient way of modifying the verbal behaviors in counseling and even the overt behaviors outside of the counseling interview. The significance of the counselor-therapist's responding behavior is clear-cut in such a situation: the counselor-therapist, regardless of his espoused theory, must know how to control and use his responses.

There is evidence, however, that counselor-therapists are not always in control of their selective reinforcement of client-responses. Murray (1956) analyzed a verbatim nondirective case of Carl R. Rogers, and found that the categories of verbal behavior that were approved by the therapist increased in frequency, but those categories disapproved decreased in frequency. In a similar study, Truax (1966a) analyzed audio recordings of psychotherapy sessions conducted by Rogers, and found that he reinforced certain classes of verbal responses from the client, but did not respond to (i.e., did not reinforce) other classes of responses. Analysis of subsequent sessions revealed that the client made a significantly greater number of statements in the reinforced classes and a significantly fewer number in those classes that received no counselor-therapist reinforcement. This reinforcement took place in the client-centered approach, which prides itself on being nondirective, but in fact, the counselor-therapist was being directive—he was conditioning the client to respond in the unconsciously-determined way the counselor-therapist wanted him to respond! Roberts and Renzaglia (1965) found that counselors varied their responses when they knew they were being monitored or recorded; that is, when their counseling sessions were recorded without their knowledge, they displayed different response styles than they did when they knew they were being recorded. Thus, what happens in actual sessions can only be assumed.

This evidence clearly indicates that counselors and psychotherapists must understand their responding behaviors, and to use their responses in a preplanned, controlled manner. That it is likely that selective responding will occur in traditional insight-oriented counseling-psychotherapy supports the position that reinforcement can be incorporated into any form of counseling-therapy. When in-

sightists denounce behaviorists for using reinforcement with their
clients, they should take stock of their own behaviors; it may well be
that they too are reinforcing but in a less professional manner than
the behaviorist. One might even wonder which is the most responsible
approach.

### Desensitization in Counseling and Psychotherapy

Just as reinforcement occurs in counseling and psychotherapy,
there is theoretical evidence that desensitization might also explain
part of the processes. The client, by exploring anxiety-laden areas
with the counselor-therapist, becomes increasingly able to deal with
anxiety, so that the longer the counseling-therapy lasts, the more
densensitized the client becomes to a given level of anxiety-provoking
stimuli, so that eventually he can deal with these stimuli without becoming anxious. This occurrence is often termed "getting down to
gut-level," or "moving into affective material." This is also similar
to psychoanalytically-oriented "working through" (Auld, 1968). In
other words, when a client becomes more able to deal with affect and
the accompanying anxiety, it may be because he has become desensitized, since he was able to experience lower levels of anxiety, explore them, and survive psychologically.

### The Counselor-Therapist as a Reinforcer

If selective responding occurs, and if counseling and psychotherapeutic processes fit a desensitization model, and both seem to be
true, then the counselor-therapist may be called a "reinforcer." Truax
(1966b) considers the three Rogerian-type dimensions or attitudes
for the therapeutic relationship:

It might be tentatively proposed that these three "therapeutic conditions"
have their direct and indirect effects upon patient change in the following
four modalities: (1) they serve to reinforce positive aspects of the patient's
self-concept, modifying the existing self-concept, thus leading to changes
in the patient's own self-reinforcement system; (2) They serve to reinforce
self-exploratory behavior, thus eliciting self-concepts and anxiety-laden
material which can then be potentially modified; (3) they serve to extinguish anxiety or fear responses associated with specific cues, both
those elicited by the relationship with the therapist and those elicited by

patient self-exploration; and, (4) they serve to reinforce human relating, encountering or interacting and to extinguish fear or avoidance learning associated with human relating. (p. 162)

Subsequently, Truax (1968), in an investigation of mental patients (predominantly diagnosed as schizophrenics) receiving group counseling or psychotherapy, found that when the therapist offered high levels of differential reinforcement (that is, the dimensions of accurate empathy, nonpossessive warmth, and genuineness were viewed as reinforcers) for self-exploration, the patients showed a greater amount of self-exploration and therapeutic involvement than those who received a low level or negative reinforcement. This altering of dimensions need not be considered undesirable unless, of course, it was unplanned or uncontrolled. On this point, it bears emphasizing that there is evidence that traditional insight counseling and psychotherapy involve reinforcement, and if such reinforcement is inadvertent and haphazard, it can result in deterioration rather than improvement in a client's behavior (Wilson, Hannon, and Evans, 1968). There seems to be virtually no doubt that the counselor-therapist's responses, the dimensions of the relationship, and the desensitization inherent to the processes provide both positive and negative reinforcement to the client.

## RESPONSIBILITY TO THE CLIENT

The ultimate charge to the professional counselor-therapist is the responsibility to help the client. How he interprets this depends on his theoretical position, but there are parameters that seem to cut across all theoretical boundaries. This brief discussion could not possibly cover in depth all of the ramifications of "responsibility to the client," but it can emphasize some of the major concerns.

All theories of counseling and psychotherapy emphasize that the counselor-therapist has the responsibility of working with the client until adequate resolution has been reached. Most of the insight approaches allow the client to determine, within certain limits, what constitutes an adequate resolution, and even the behavioral-action approaches use the client's initial definition, that is, his objective for seeking treatment, as the primary determinant of an appropriate termination point. Insightists maintain that self-understanding of motives is the crucial end goal, while behaviorists maintain that the elimination or at least the alleviation of specific problem behaviors constitutes the main end goal; thus it is not surprising that there is disagreement about the meaning of "resolution."

It is probable that this disagreement is not as extensive as it seems. Insightists and behaviorists are both concerned with the client's perceiving a solution or resolution of his reasons for seeking treatment. Both want the client to perceive positive changes, and though overt behavioral changes receive less emphasis from the insightists than from the behaviorists, there is universal agreement that behaviors should be modified on both covert and overt levels.

Assuming that behavior change is part of responsibility, the counselor-therapist must then attempt to provide services that will best achieve this objective. Schmidt (1965) points out that accepting a client means that the counselor has the obligation to help the person "through at least some initial or contributing solution to his difficulty, no matter how unpleasant or stressful the situation may become" (p. 379), and he indicates that this often involves making professional judgments that may have great consequences for both the client and the counselor. In other words, *the counselor has the responsibility to be responsible.* Similarly, Krumboltz (1965) states that the behavioral counselor must help the client resolve the problems for which he seeks counseling, and that if the initial problem remains, the counselor has failed; solving the problem or planning a course of action that will lead to modification of the initial problem provides the basis for success. Krumboltz indicates that in behavioral counseling the client is allowed a certain amount of freedom to dictate the criteria for success, but this freedom never usurps the counselor's professional responsibility and control; that is, the counselor encourages the client to specify his expectations for the counseling goals, but the counselor has the prerogative of imposing limitations on the basis of his own counseling interests, his competency limits as a counselor, and his ethical standards.

Accepting this challenging responsibility means, of course, that the counselor must feel free to act, and action is a crucial component of behavioral and psychobehavioral counseling-therapy. Kanfer (1966) underscores this point:

Recent developments in the field of psychotherapy suggest that in addition to warmth, understanding and compassion we should also train the clinician so that he possesses the technical skills to *do* something about the patient's misery. (p. 176)

In other words, "listening and understanding impose a heavy moral burden on the listener. They obligate him to action" (Kanfer, 1966, p. 176).

In order to fulfill his responsibility to the client, the counselor-therapist must be personally and professionally equipped to assume a sincere helping responsibility, and this definitely involves a willingness and ability to take prescriptive professional actions that will be beneficial to the client. This does not negate the dimensions of traditional counseling-psychotherapy, not even client-centered counseling and therapy, but it does require that certain aspects commonly associated with behaviorism be incorporated. More extensive consideration will be devoted to therapeutic responsibility and responsible actions in Chapter 6.

## PSYCHOBEHAVIORAL COUNSELING AND THERAPY

*Psychobehavioral counseling and therapy* does not represent a theory of counseling or therapy; it fails to fulfill such important criteria as offering a theory of personality or views on the nature of man. What it does offer is a frame of reference for the integration of behavioral techniques into insight-oriented counseling and psychotherapy. It allows the counselor-therapist to accept either the psychodynamic viewpoint of the insightists or the conditioning viewpoint of the actionists or behaviorists, thereby offering no boundaries to personality theory or other aspects requisite for a full-blown theory of counseling or therapy. Therefore, *psychobehavioral counseling and therapy* denotes a technical eclecticism, with special emphasis on the use of both conditioning and insight techniques and the role of the counselor-therapist as the person significantly responsible for the counseling-therapeutic action. Such technical eclecticism has been demonstrated to be effective in a variety of clinical and experimental situations; these will be subsequently exemplified. Of key importance is the blending, with some logical and theoretical justification, of what may seem to be diverse or contradictory techniques.

The value of an eclectic stance seems clearcut. Brammer (1969) points out the need for an eclectic position "that avoids indiscriminate picking and choosing and leads to a consistent and comprehensive synthesis of theory unique to the individual counselor" (p. 193). Achievement of this posture largely depends on the counselor's ability to resist "emphasizing theory exclusively" and instead to adopt "a behavioristic stance in the broad meaning of the word." In responding to Brammer's (1969) position on eclecticism, Shoben (1969) believes that consideration of eclecticism for the creation of a therapeutic style:

is all the more appropriate since eclecticism is a primary route by which we all form and re-form the stylistic identities by which we are basically known and by which we basically know ourselves. Counseling is less a kit of professional tools or a collection of skills than it is a way of life, and there may be considerable virtue in acknowledging this possibility and examining the operations of the therapist as merely a special case of the operations of a man struggling to achieve and to maintain personal integrity under difficult conditions. This conception puts some limits on what we can expect of science; it may open a wider window on the help-giving enterprise if we are willing to forego some of the trappings of science in our efforts at a greater understanding. (p. 200)

Both of the foregoing positions seem compatible with the psychobehavioral frame of reference, the former with its emphasis on technical eclecticism, the latter with its emphasis on the professional person (which will be elaborated upon in Chapter 6), and both with their emphasis on pragmatism.

It should be noted that eclecticism seems to be essential to all forms of counseling-therapy. In supporting eclecticism, Slavson (1970) states:

Eclecticism is more crucial to group therapy than to individual treatment. Because of the multiplicity of psychic factors in an assembly of persons, a unitary approach cannot but fail with a significant number of its participants. (p. 11)

Slavson does, however, caution against the too-willing acceptance of various techniques:

Group psychotherapy, especially, being still a new practice, must be guarded against the infiltration of unproven, doctrinal pronouncements unsupported by validated results. (p. 13)

While it might be questioned whether any one form of therapeutic intervention is more reliant on eclecticism than another, as Slavson would seem to support, it does appear that no form of therapeutic intervention can totally deny the benefits of eclecticism.

The eclectic nature of psychobehavioral counseling and therapy is compatible with the views of Frederick C. Thorne in many ways. Thorne (1969a) draws a supportive analogy for eclecticism from medical education:

The American system of medical education requires every student eclectically to master the broad field of medical knowledge *first*, acquiring minimal knowledge and competence in every specialty *before* being allowed to specialize. This eclectic requirement of a well-rounded education requires every student to acquire at least a minimal understanding of general medical practice before even trying to decide what to specialize in. The fact that many clinicians elect to specialize on post-graduate levels does not negate the value of a broad knowledge of the nature, indications and contraindications of all methods. (p. 464)

Thorne (1969a) finds further support for the eclectic position in the fact that accumulating research studies continue to reveal the invalidity of clinical judgment of even the best professionals and that this derives from the invalidity of therapy based on single theoretical systems; he feels the eclectic approach holds great promise in comparison to the demonstrably invalid single system approach. Further, Thorne offers two defining statements that seem applicable to what the psychobehavioral position would encompass:

*Eclectic-therapies* hypothesize a wide spectrum of etiologic factors potentially causing disorder, and therefore postulate that it is necessary to have a wide therapeutic armamentarium of methods suited to specific indications and contraindications. (Thorne, 1967, p. 322)

And on the strategic logic underlying an eclectic approach, he states:

The basic strategy of eclectic therapy is to differentiate all the possible etiologic causes of disorder and then to select appropriate methods specifically indicated to modify specific etiologic factors. This is not an hodge-podge approach, experimenting with shot-gun methods on a hit-or-miss basis (which sometimes has spectacular results). It is a rational method based on knowledge of valid indications and contraindications with reference to any specific etiologic equation. (Thorne, 1967, p. 322)

As may be inferred from Thorne's comments, the counselor-therapist must be capable of making assessments that are truly diagnostic. In other words, he must be able to make inferences as to the cause of a particular problem, describe, possibly in both psychodynamic and behavioral terms, the client's current functioning, and set forth prognoses for different treatment approaches. From the psychobehavioral diagnosis, the final—yet tentative, flexible, and always open for amendment—counseling-therapeutic format, in technical terms, is chosen. Psychobehavioral diagnosis is discussed in more detail in Chapter 3.

Allegiance to one theoretical position, the antithesis of eclecticism, can potentially have negative effects. One of the most apparent negative sources is the influence on professional judgments of the values intrinsic to a theoretical position. Thorne (1969b) states:

Particularly suspect are professionals who identify with limited viewpoints such as the various schools and systems of psychology, religionist psychologists, and all the orientations whose labels imply special interests or commitments which can influence clinical judgment. Only the thoroughgoing eclectic has a chance of being uninfluenced by potentially distorting irrelevant value considerations. (p. 231)

These distortions crop up in both diagnostic and treatment activities. In regard to diagnostics, Pasamanick, Dinitz, and Lefton (1959) analyzed the final psychiatric diagnoses given to first-admission female psychotics (in-patients), and summarized their conclusions as follows:

These findings provide concrete statistical affirmation for the view that despite protestations that their point of reference is always the individual patient, clinicians in fact may be so committed to a particular psychiatric school of thought, that the patient's diagnosis and treatment is largely predetermined. Clinicians, as indicated by these data, may be selectively perceiving and emphasizing only those characteristics and attributes of their patients which are relevant to their own preconceived system of thought. As a consequence, they may be overlooking other patient characteristics which would be considered crucial by colleagues who are otherwise committed. (p. 131)

Of particular interest to counselors and psychotherapists (because of the kinds of clients they serve) are the differences in diagnosis that occurred primarily in those cases where there were no clearly traceable organic causes (i.e., schizophrenia, psychoneurosis, and character disorders):

It was discerned that the greater the commitment to an analytic orientation, the less the inclination toward diagnosing patients as schizophrenics. (p. 131)

Regarding treatment, one of the crucial areas is determination of goals. In a comparison of the opinions of clients and counselors, Thompson and Zimmerman (1969) concluded it was not safe to assume goals from either the diagnosis made by the counselor or the diagnosis made by the client, because the counselor and client did not agree on what the goals were at a particular time, and the perceived goals of both varied over time. These results indicate that in diagnosis, care should be exercised to assure optimal awareness of what the client's needs and proclivities are (the term "diagnosis" typically includes the aspect of prescribing a treatment approach). It is unlikely that alliance with a sole theoretical approach would facilitate this awareness (and the treatment planning) as readily as would an eclectic posture.

Not only is technical integration logical, it is also theoretically sound. It should be noted that opposing theorists are typically willing to allow that other theories have an element of value. For example, Freeman (1968) states:

Psychoanalysts do not criticize behaviour therapy on therapeutic grounds. They recognize that all psychological treatments have their share of successes and failures. They do find fault with its theoretical base, which tends to present an over-simplified version of human mental function. (p. 58)

According to this statement, psychoanalysts believe that behavior therapy is over-simplified, but not necessarily totally invalid. This leads to a second point on the compatibility among the theories. Mowrer (1964, 1966) has clearly indicated theoretical commonalities, even in terms of etiologies, between such seemingly divergent theories as psychoanalysis, client-centered therapy, and behavior therapy; and Marks and Gelder (1966) identify a considerable amount of "common ground" between dynamic psychotherapy and behavior therapy, their conclusions being essentially that the two positions are not theoretically independent, that they reciprocally influence each other, and that the suitability of a given technique depends upon the disorder of the particular client. Murray and Jacobson (in press) made an extensive review of the learning theory implications for traditional psychotherapy and for behavior therapy, and evidence was found that demonstrated that learning theory, behavior therapy, and psychotherapy are moving closer together because they focus on many of the same problems and use many of the same parameters. They conclude that the current state of theory for psychotherapy and behavior therapy is inadequate, mainly because psychotherapy fails to consider properly the social learning and social influence processes in its personal growth and personality reorganization aspects, and because behavior therapy fails to accord proper consideration to cognitive and emotional response systems. They therefore urge the development of an integrative theoretical system. The foregoing views support the contention that certain problems can best be treated with insight-oriented counseling-psychotherapy, that others can best be treated with pure conditioning-based behavior therapy, and that still others can best be treated by a combination of insight and behavioral techniques. Some delineation of which technique is the most appropriate for a given problem or type of client may be deduced from the examples set forth in published research, and guidelines for technique selection are offered in Chapter 3. Unfortunately, there is as yet little clearly differentiating material on this matter.

Behavior therapists are becoming increasingly aware of the reciprocal value counseling-psychotherapy and behavior therapy can share. It is also interesting to note that the clinical research and service of one of the most prominent behavior therapists, Arnold A. Lazarus, has progressively shifted toward eclecticism, and specifically toward considering the importance of interpersonal factors within the behavior therapy context. Regarding eclecticism, he states:

To attempt a theoretical *rapprochement* is as futile as seriously trying to picture the edge of the universe. But to read through the vast mass of

literature on psychotherapy, *in search of techniques,* can be clinically en-
riching and therapeutically rewarding. (Lazarus, 1967, p. 416)

And he continues:

However, this should not presuppose a random melange of techniques taken
eclectically out of the air. While the basic point of this paper is a plea for
psychotherapists to try several effective techniques (even those not necessarily prompted by the logic of their own theories), it is nevertheless assumed that any selected maneuver will at least have the benefit of empirical
support. Complete unity between a systematic theory of personality and an
effective method of treatment derived therefrom remains a cherished ideal.
Meanwhile it is well for the practicing psychotherapist to be content in
the role of a technician rather than that of a scientist and to observe that
those who impugn technical proficiency are often able to explain every-
thing but to accomplish almost nothing. (Lazarus, 1967, p. 416)

From this eclectic position, he has become critical of the professed behavioral purists, and has observed that, in particular, systematic desensitization is often misapplied, namely as a sole technique that fails
to give proper consideration to other needs of the client; to give
proper consideration necessitates what he calls a "broad-spectrum
behavior therapy approach" (Lazarus and Serber, 1968). Lazarus'
subsequent writings give even more importance to placing behavior
therapy in a psychotherapeutic context, accepting that conditioning
is too limited to describe the "cognitive restructuring" that actually
occurs, and realizing that clinical eclecticism is necessary (Lazarus,
1968, 1969a, 1969b). This approach moves directly toward the psychobehavioral frame of reference.

### Critical Principles

There are two basic sets of principles underlying the technical
eclecticism of psychobehavioral counseling and therapy. The first set
includes the so-called traditional relationship factors found in insight-
oriented counseling and psychotherapy, and the second set encompasses learning-theory principles, particularly reinforcement.

Because the relationship factors of counseling and psychotherapy have been discussed previously and have received extensive
attention elsewhere (e.g., Carkhuff, 1969a, 1969b; Carkhuff and

Berenson, 1967; Ford and Urban, 1963; Patterson, 1969; Truax and
Carkhuff, 1967, to name but a few), the discussion of them herein
will be restricted to their relevancy to behaviorally oriented treatment.

Behavior therapists are progressively giving more consideration to the role of the therapeutic relationship (despite the fact that
it is still not attributed distinct value in the behavior-therapy outcome
studies). Wolpe (1969b) now acknowledges that the psychotherapeutic relationship "produces some variable effects on at least some
patients" (p. 47), but he explains these effects in behavioral terms:

A possible explanation of the similar beneficial effects of a plentitude of
therapeutic approaches is that a therapist may arouse in some of his patients
emotional responses that inhibit anxieties evoked by verbal means during
interviews and thus weaken the anxiety habit. (p. 47)

In other words, Wolpe believes that "reciprocal inhibition is inad-
vertently and unsystematically at work" (p. 47). This belief is in
accord with the comments made earlier in this chapter on desensitization in counseling and psychotherapy. On the other hand, Lazarus
(1969b) has enlarged his view from the original conditioning posture:

It is not that I have modified my views as much as the fact that I now see
how important it is to emphasize aspects that I may have mentioned *en
passant*. For instance . . . I underscored the fact that behavior therapy
takes place (or should take place) 'within the broad context of a warm,
sympathetic, and non-moralistic therapeutic relationship' and added a
footnote pointing out that behavior therapists err by ignoring interpersonal
factors. . . . The biggest change is the fact that I no longer embrace a
peripheral learning model, but lean very heavily on a 'cognitive restructuring' paradigm. I think that a term like 'conditioning' should be limited to
the laboratory and is a gross over-simplification of the kind of learning
which occurs in clinical situations. (personal communication)

Although perhaps somewhat tardily, the therapeutic relationship
seems to have entered into the thinking of some behaviorists.

It is important to note that the effects of the therapeutic relationship are not restricted to just insight-oriented facilitating conditions. Parloff (1961) found from an analysis of group psychotherapy
that the data supported the interpretation that "the better the patient-

psychotherapist relationship, the greater the symptomatic relief experienced by the patient" (p. 35), and that "patients who established better relationships with their therapist tended to show greater improvement than those whose relationship with the same therapist were not as good" (p. 37). Thus, the therapeutic relationship seems to be relevant to even the behavior-therapy criterion of symptom relief.

In the insightists' camp, there is increased recognition of the possibility of a complementary existence for insight and behavior therapies via consideration of the relationship dimension. For example, Patterson (1968) states:

All counseling and psychotherapy involves both a relationship and conditioning. The difference between relationship therapy and behavior therapy is essentially one of emphasis. The behavior therapist emphasizes conditioning techniques which he applies systematically, and is not systematic in his development of a relationship. The relationship therapist systematically develops a relationship, but is not so consciously systematic in applying conditioning techniques. (p. 230)

This view moves nicely toward psychobehaviorism. Psychobehavioral counseling and therapy would, of course, emphasize both; that is, the psychobehavioral counselor-therapist would strive for systematizing relationship and conditioning factors.

To summarize the concept of the therapeutic relationship, the dimensions identified by different investigators appear, despite some differences in terminology, to be relatively congruent; and the documentation shows that the relationship does, if used properly, facilitate the helping processes intrinsic to counseling and psychotherapy. Because the psychobehavioral frame of reference calls for techniques to be delineated on the basis of the needs of each individual client and, moreover, because these techniques should be subject to constant assessment and reassessment for suitability (with alterations being made whenever clinically deemed necessary), it is mandatory that the psychobehavioral counselor-therapist strive for the optimum quality in his relationships with his clients. Even if a behavioral technique, which does not rely on relationship factors per se, is the primary treatment modality, a facilitating relationship has to be established and be present throughout the treatment to allow the counselor-therapist the potential for the technical flexibility that is needed.

Reinforcement principles underlie behaviorally-oriented counseling and therapy. In both behavioral counseling and psychobehavioral counseling-therapy, the counselor-therapist serves as the source of reinforcement. In nonbehavioral counseling-therapy this is often unplanned, but in behaviorally-oriented counseling-therapy it is as controlled and planned at all times as the counselor-therapist's expertise will allow.

Reinforcement means simply that a performance is followed by a stimulus. The stimulus serves as a reinforcer, but whether such a bonding procedure has a noticeable influence on subsequent performance, that is, whether it increases the frequency of the same type of performance later, depends upon the collateral conditions. In behavioral counseling and therapy, a reinforcement contingency becomes the basis for the intervention; this means that the relationship between the reinforcer and the exact properties of the performance are used to define what is to be cultivated by the counselor-therapist. In practical terms, if the desired performance is a certain class of verbal responses from a client, e.g., information-seeking responses in vocational counseling, the properties include such elements as references in the counseling session to the seeking of such information. The reinforcer is defined as a verbal or nonverbal response from the counselor-therapist, and the reinforcement contingency is the counselor-therapist's responding to information-seeking responses from his client in counseling as a means of reinforcing the occurrence of this type of verbal responses. Reinforcement is usually presented according to a schedule. This is an established way of providing the reinforcing stimulus, and typically includes one of the following formats of responding: on a fixed-ratio, at a fixed-interval, at a variable-interval, or on a variable-ratio.

There are two principal types of conditioning: classical and operant. Classical conditioning, such as is exemplified by Pavlov, involves associating a stimulus with an unconditioned response. In this form, the subject, be it counseling-therapy client or dog, is relatively passive in the process of pairing the reinforcer with a stimulus. A formal definition of classical or Pavlovian conditioning is offered by Ferster and Perrott ( 1968):

The term *Pavlovian conditioning* is synonymous with reflex or respondent conditioning. It refers to pairing a neutral stimulus with an unconditioned stimulus. Eventually the neutral stimulus (now called a conditioned stimulus) comes to elicit a response as a result of the previous pairings. (p. 529)

Operant conditioning, which is the predominant form of conditioning employed in behaviorally-oriented counseling and therapy, provides that the reinforcement depends upon the response. The subject is more involved because it is his behavior that determines whether the response operates on the environment to produce a certain result. The definition of operant behavior by Ferster and Perrott (1968) is as follows:

*Operant behavior* refers to those performances which are increased in frequency by operant reinforcers. Operant performances are to be contrasted with reflexes, when the environment elicits a change within the organism. In general, an operant refers to a class of behaviors rather than a single performance. Thus, an operant performance might designate a specific instance of a performance while an operant designates a class of performances maintained by a common reinforcer. (p. 528)

Both of these conditioning forms are found in behaviorally oriented counseling and therapy.

A reinforcement contingency is either positive or negative. A positive contingency denotes that a rewarding stimulus follows the performance. These rewards may be objects or tokens that have a prescribed value or can be redeemed for prizes (e.g., money, candy, privileges), or social recognition (i.e., acceptance from a significant other, peer, or authority figure), or verbal praise (e.g., a counselor-therapist saying "good," or "that's a fine idea," or "I would certainly agree with that plan"). All of these positive stimuli have been used in behavioral modification, but in behavioral counseling the most frequently used reinforcer is verbal praise, that is, positive responses, from the counselor-therapist. Negative reinforcement refers to the procedure of eliminating an unpleasant situation by acting. That is, an unpleasant condition is created when an unacceptable behavior occurs, and when the behavior is altered to be acceptable the unpleasant condition (e.g., mild electric shock) is removed. Negative reinforcement is said to have occurred when the performance (i.e., behavior) that eliminates an aversive (i.e., unpleasant) stimulus increases in frequency. Incidentally, punishment should not be confused with negative reinforcement. Punishment follows a performance, whereas in negative reinforcement the aversive stimulus precedes the performance.[1]

### Guidelines for Technical Integration

Just as there seems to be theoretical compatibility for integrating insight and behavioral concepts, there is also evidence that the corresponding techniques may be integrated, and that therapeutic efficacy can be obtained through such a melding process. Lazarus (1961) found that several clients who had received interpretive therapy tended to recover more quickly when they subsequently received behavior therapy, i.e., desensitization, than those clients who received only behavior therapy. Katahn, Strenger, and Cherry (1966) successfully combined group counseling and behavior therapy to lower test-anxiety for college students. Leventhal (1968) used suggestion, relaxation, and desensitization, all behavioral techniques, while still maintaining the psychotherapeutic parameters (at least in part); in regard to the latter, the therapist-client relationship allowed the client to overcome reservations and enter into certain behavioral procedures that would have been previously "taboo" (e.g., using sexual words to overcome sexual anxiety). Wilson and Smith (1968) report on the use of free association with muscle relaxation. Other clinical examples of how various behavioral techniques can be integrated into traditional insight-oriented counseling and psychotherapy have been published by Chan, Chiu, and Mueller (1970), Clark (1963), Naar (1970), Sipprelle (1967), and Woody (1968a, 1969a).

The points at which a change in counseling-therapeutic techniques should be made rests on the ability of the counselor-therapist to assess the behavioral functioning at any particular point. Therefore, there is no feasible restriction on when a behavioral technique

[1]Understanding the learning theory principles that provide the theoretical basis for behavioral counseling and behavior therapy can be a complex task. The contents herein give but a skeletal overview. If the reader lacks knowledge of learning principles, some supplementary reading is advisable. Although there are several excellent texts, four that seem especially appropriate are those by Bugelski (1956), Ferster and Perrott (1968), Hilgard (1956), and Whaley and Malott (1969). Further, the transition from theory to practice might be aided by reference to the following texts: Bandura (1969), Franks (1969), Kanfer and Phillips (1970), and Ulrich, Stachnik, and Mabry (1966, 1970).

could be activated in counseling or psychotherapy. Research and clinical experience show, however, that the following three situations can justly serve as guidelines for psychobehavioral integration:

*Facilitation and acceleration of therapy.* This guideline assumes that there are points in the counseling-therapy when unnecessary barriers are deterring progress. The word unnecessary should be noted, because it is acknowledged that there are times when a "barrier" serves a constructive purpose; the client may not be psychically ready to proceed, perhaps because affect or anxiety would be greater than the individual could tolerate—thus delaying or defensive behavior may be justified. There are, however, times when blockage may be therapeutically unnecessary, when a particular "hang-up" is simply that; the barrier may at some time have to be resolved or further explored, but at a particular point it may be only delaying progress and could, via a behavioral technique, be eliminated, alleviated, or set aside for further work at another time. The counselor-therapist will have to assume the responsibility of judging when the processes merit behavioral acceleration or reorganization, and further, he must be able then to act competently upon his judgment by implementing a behavioral technique. This kind of assessment depends, quite obviously, on clinical judgment. It would seem that the ability to make such astute judgments is fostered via the study of personality theory as well as learning theory; or as Klein, Dittmann, Parloff, and Gill (1969) state: ". . . it is clear that many clinical decisions in the [behavior therapy] treatment are based on an understanding of some functional organization of behavior, and an appreciation of the power of the relationship" (p. 265)—this definitely has implications for training and supports a psychobehavioral posture. Examples of using behavioral techniques to facilitate and accelerate counseling and/or psychotherapy may be found in several published sources: Woody (1968a) integrated behavioral rehearsal, reciprocal inhibition including induced relaxation, systematic desensitization, and verbal reinforcement; Sipprelle (1964) added clinical hypnosis; and Woody, Krathwohl, Kagan, and Farquhar (1965) used hypnotic stimulated recall via video tape recordings.

*Elimination of uncomfortable symptoms.* This guideline is based on the premise that there are instances when it is clinically advisable to help a client involved in insight-oriented counseling and/or psychotherapy eliminate the irritation, discomfort, inconvenience, and restrictions produced by certain symptoms, which, if allowed to continue, might be an imposition on the insight processes. Examples in which this has proven to be clinically appropriate include: certain psychosomatic problems, resistances to therapy, and crises in the client's daily life (e.g., acute depression, sexual anxiety). It is assumed that treating the problem behaviors may not, at least not in all cases, serve to cure the neurotic components, and that insight-oriented treatment is also necessary. One stipulation that can then be made, especially if the counselor-therapist believes in the concept of underlying neurotic conflict, is that the client must relinquish the voluntary nature of the treatment to the counselor-therapist until such time as the counselor-therapist returns it. In other words, the counselor-therapist could specify the following: that he will treat the overt behavior problem, but does so believing that the behavioral-based treatment will not fully eliminate the cause for its occurrence; that the client must be willing to agree to enter into or remain in treatment, even though he may be outwardly free from the behavior problem that led him to seek help; and that this agreement would remain in force until such time as the counselor-therapist assesses that the client has achieved adequate resolution for his conflicts and returns the power to terminate to him. It is only logical that when this sort of agreement is made, the counselor-therapist should provide the client with a layman's rationale; this might mean, of course, supporting that there is a dynamic basis for his problem and that symptom removal might not be the total therapeutic goal—but this would depend upon the counselor-therapist's espoused theoretical position. Clinical experience has revealed that clients do not generally abuse this sort of stipulation, since they are willing to fulfill their end of the bargain and since successful treatment of the problems with a behavioral technique early in the relationship serves to instill confidence and foster motivation on the part of the client (and the counselor-therapist?).

*Treatment of therapeutically unresponsive clients.* Every counselor-therapist occasionally encounters a client who will not or cannot respond to verbal counseling-psychotherapy. There are many reasons as to why this happens. Research has suggested that some of these cases may be due to socio-cultural factors; for example, clients from a low social-economic background might not respond to certain forms of counseling-psychotherapy as well as clients from a higher, more enriched background. And often these cases will be extremely frustrating to both the counselor-therapist and the client because of a seemingly good therapeutic relationship. If this kind of unresponsiveness occurs and the client continues to be plagued with problems that might be amenable to behavioral techniques, psychobehavioral integration would seem justified. Clinical experience suggests that this guideline is especially apropos for culturally deprived and mentally retarded clients, but likewise there are other types of clients who might feasibly benefit from treatment in this manner; to generalize, they might be characterized as clients who lack the verbal skills, logical reasoning, and introspective abilities that are necessary for insight-oriented counseling-psychotherapy.

These three guidelines, which have been discussed and exemplified in more detail elsewhere (Woody, 1968a, 1968c, 1969a, 1969b), are in no way viewed as all-inclusive of possible points at which to integrate behavioral techniques into counseling and psychotherapy. The final criterion represents the combined needs of the client and the professional-personal skills and characteristics of the counselor-therapist.

### Termination

Attention must be given to the termination of psychobehavioral counseling and therapy. Behavior therapists view the relationship between the client and the counselor-therapist as being of no therapeutic consequence, and thus ignore the possibility of termination anxiety when the treatment is concluded. Insightists, particularly those of a psychoanalytic orientation, view termination as one of the most critical phases of treatment. Despite a lack of theoretical endorsement from behaviorism, clinical observations and research with clients of several behavior therapists support that near the close of their behavioral treatment the clients experience, just like their counterparts in insight counseling and psychotherapy, a sense of unresolved frustration about ending what has been a significant relationship. Therefore, the psychobehavioral frame of reference would maintain that termination anxiety should be dealt with via counseling-therapy, and that dealing with it in this manner may have a beneficial effect on the client's functioning. Even when the treatment has been predominantly behavioral, there may well be the aftereffects of transference phenomena that should be dealt with prior to termination if the treatment is to have optimal success.

### Follow-up

Behavior therapists and insight counselors and psychotherapists alike place an importance on following up on their clients. Follow-up lets the client sense a continuing connection with the counselor-therapist and provides the counselor-therapist with knowledge about the effects of his service. The latter is important since it furnishes the counselor-therapist with information about how the therapeutic intervention influenced the client being studied and how the effects might be applicable to other clients.

The use of behavioral techniques produces a special need for follow-up. When a client makes rapid changes in attitude and overt behavior, as typically happens when behavioral techniques are used, there is a sudden shift in emotional pressures within the client's life space. Obviously, then, when the client makes these changes, their effects will impinge upon those persons with whom he interacts, such as his parents, his spouse, and his children. It is, therefore, of paramount importance that regular follow-ups include the gaining of information as to how these significant others in the client's life are behaving or reacting subsequent to his treatment. Clinical experience reveals that many problem-creating reactions from family members could have been avoided if the counselor-therapist had helped the family to adjust progressively to the marked changes in the client. This helping-attention should be given both during the regular psychobehavioral treatment and during the follow-up period.

## THEORETICAL RECIPROCITY

Because of the focus of this book, the preceding contents of this chapter may create the impression that the insight-oriented counselor-therapists are the ones who stand to gain from the addition of behavioral techniques. It should therefore be emphasized that behavior therapists can improve the quality of their therapy by consistently incorporating insight-oriented techniques and principles into their conditioning practices. In order to shift the spotlight over to how behavior therapy can benefit from insight counseling and psychotherapy, let us consider the matter of failures in behavior therapy.

### Failures in Behavior Therapy

Analysis of the issue of failures yields four possibilities, the first three of which are well within the bounds of behavior therapy and the fourth unquestionably aligned with insight-oriented counseling-psychotherapy.

*Opposition to Treatment.* It is possible that some clients will be very much opposed to receiving behavior therapy or, in fact, any form of treatment. This type of client may be one referred by a criminal court or seen in a prison setting, or one pressured to come for treatment by a significant other, e.g., parent or spouse. In other words, the client is not resistant to behavior therapy per se, but is resistant to the possibility of losing his symptoms. As one of my clients, a man with a sexual fetish, forced by his wife to receive aversive (mild electric shock) behavior therapy, stated: "Let's face it, if I can make it through three weeks of treatment at the great —— Hospital and end up keeping both my fetish and my wife, then I'll be happy." It is surprising that this sort of client, including, incidentally, the man who made the foregoing statement, does, generally speaking, lose his problem behaviors via conditioning. But there are also clients in this category who are able to counteract adequately the conditioning process and do "fail" the therapeutic program.

*Resistance to Behavior Therapy.* In this category, the resistant client reacts specifically to the components of behavior therapy. One frequently encountered example is a reluctance to relinquish symptoms in a short time. Behavior therapy does promote changes in a relatively short time period, whereas traditional counseling-psychotherapy typically progresses over a period long enough to allow the client to adjust gradually to his new, symptom-free behaviors. Resistance may be manifested in the client's debunking behavior therapy, e.g., labeling the techniques "too magical" or "kind of hocus-pocus." This reaction seems to arise fairly often among defensive clients when relaxation training is part of the treatment; comments like "I don't believe in hypnosis" might be cast at the behavior therapist. Obviously, such a situation underscores the need for a psychobehavioral format; that is, the resistances to the behavior therapy should be interpreted and analyzed in a counseling-psychotherapeutic manner.

*Misdiagnosis.* Any diagnosis involves the task of prescribing a treatment approach, and, in so doing, prognosticating what the results will be from the various technical possibilities. Making behavior therapy operational requires that a behavioral analysis be made and that the behavioral technique be fitted accordingly. In other words, the behavior therapist must explore the reinforcement properties of the client's life space, describe the components in behavioral terms and objectives, and select a technical format that will accommodate the requisite reinforcers. Successful behavioral diagnosis is paramount to the desired treatment outcome. Perhaps because of limited expertise and the nebulous, hard-to-delineate nature of behavioral analysis, a misdiagnosis may result. Since behavior therapy is almost totally predicated on the initial behavioral analysis, as compared with the evolving diagnosis and subsequent technical alterations in insight approaches, it would seem that behavior therapy is more vulnerable to the effects of misdiagnosis than counseling-psychotherapy. Hopefully, the counselor-therapist using behavioral techniques will be continually reassessing the reinforcement contingencies and will become aware of his less-than-ideal prescription at an early point in the treatment, and will be able to remediate the situation promptly. There are, however, times when one's technical preferences, whether it be in counseling-psychotherapy or behavior therapy, can result in a constricted view as to what is the best treatment approach. A systematic behavioral analysis, employing objective criteria and definitive guidelines, serves to minimize this selection bias. The behavioral analysis receives further elaboration in Chapter 3.

*Transference in Behavior Therapy.* Transference is viewed by many counselors and psychotherapists as the "Beloved Infidel" that plagues, yet is cherished. Learning to deal effectively with transference may well be the key criterion for reaching professional stature as a counselor-psychotherapist. Thus it would be a blessing by some if a form of treatment, such as behavior therapy, could be freed from this baffling phenomenon.

Behavior therapists would probably maintain that psychoanalytic transference, just like unconscious motivation, is unnecessary and totally irrelevant to behavioral modification. For example, Wolpe and Lazarus (1966) state that psychoanalytic training may even be a "positive hindrance" to the behavior therapist. This does not seem to be true, however. Behavior therapy can have indisputable elements of transference, and if the counselor-therapist is unable to deal adequately with the transference, it can be the basis for therapeutic failure. There always appears to be a relationship between the behavior therapist and his clients, and where there is a relationship, it is difficult to doubt that there would be transference.

The following brief case study illustrates how transference phenomena can adversely influence behavior therapy: A 47-year-old, unmarried female client sought psychiatric treatment for excessive anxiety, much of which was transformed into clearly identifiable phobias. A psychological evaluation yielded a diagnosis of "anxiety state with a schizoid character." According to the psychobehavioral principle of using behavior therapy to treat unpleasant symptoms to allow the client to enter psychotherapy with a minimum of discomfort (which also serves as a motivator for therapy), the treatment approach involved the client's receiving psychoanalytically oriented psychotherapy from one therapist and behavior therapy for the phobias from another therapist (both of whom were members of the same clinic staff). After six psychotherapy sessions, the behavior therapy started. In the first four behavior therapy sessions, attempts were made to have the client develop hierarchies for systematic desensitization, but she forgot to "do the homework," which resulted in the hierarchies' having to be constructed in total during the therapy hour and thereby slowing the process; relaxation training was given, but the client could not close her eyes, was easily disturbed by noises outside the room, and forgot to practice regularly at home; despite her being a creative person (demonstrated in her daily vocational activities), she was unable to create visual images, and she could not conjure up either images or sensations even with detailed efforts via clinical-suggestion techniques from the therapist; and she made comments that indicated that she strongly doubted that the behavior therapy could be successful. In the fifth behavior-therapy session, the format was changed to counseling-psychotherapy, and emphasis was given to why the behavior therapy was failing. The client stated that the behavioral activities were strikingly similar to the instructional atmosphere she associated with her employment (a source of anxiety), i.e., she felt her efforts were being "graded by others," and, more important, she revealed that she associated both the behavior therapist and the psychotherapist with sexualized males (a major conflict area for her in her psychotherapy) and that the behavior therapist reminded her of "all those younger men at the office who always get ahead of me." And she said, "even though I want it [the behavior therapy] to work, I know it won't because it gets jumbled up in the 'relationships with men' jazz." It is interesting to note that while there was essentially no sign of success in the behavior therapy sessions, the client revealed in the fifth session that she had been experiencing marked success at overcoming previously experienced fears in the context of her day-to-day activities. The client's responsive nature to the psychotherapeutic format seemed to indicate that the behavior therapy should be terminated, presumably to start again when she was better able to deal with her transference.

### Values of Incorporating Insight Techniques Into Behavior Therapy

Opposition to treatment, resistance to behavior therapy, misdiagnosis, and transference constitute the primary potential sources of failure for therapists using behavioral techniques. However, these pitfalls can be circumvented by the use of insight techniques and principles. Obviously, such factors as academic expertise, clinical sensitivity, and technical flexibility are important, but the issue of avoiding behavior-therapy failures also underscores the contention that *it is preferable to integrate behavior therapy into counseling-psychotherapy, i.e., the psychobehavioral approach.*

A format that includes initial or concurrent counseling-psychotherapy readily accommodates dealing with each of the four failure sources. Clients with opposition to treatment should respond to the warm, empathic, congruent supportive elements of a counseling-psychotherapeutic relationship. Clients who are skeptical of or resistant to behavior therapy per se can achieve a resolution that will foster therapeutic change by examining thoroughly their motives for skepticism and resistance. In the case of misdiagnosis, the more complete psychodynamic case materials obtained via psychodynamic procedures should facilitate an optimal behavioral analysis for the application of behavioral techniques. Positive and negative transference phenomena, dealt with via counseling-psychotherapy, could result in much stronger reinforcement properties than if they went unattended; the interpretation and resolution of negative feelings (i.e., transference) toward the behavior therapist might well keep clients from dropping out of treatment thus increasing the chances for success of behavior therapy.

## REFERENCES

Auld, F. Vicissitudes of communication in psychotherapy. In J. M. Shlien (Ed.), *Research in psychotherapy, volume III*. Washington, D. C.: American Psychological Association, 1968, 169–178.

Bandura, A. *Principles of behavior modification.* New York: Holt, Rinehart and Winston, 1969.

Beech, H. R. Some theoretical and technical difficulties in the application of behaviour therapy. *Bulletin of the British Psychological Society,* 1963, *16,* 25–33.

Brammer, L. M. Eclecticism revisited. *Personnel and Guidance Journal,* 1969, *48,* 192–197.

Brammer, L. M., and Shostrom, E. L. *Therapeutic psychology* (2nd ed.). Englewood Cliffs, N. J.: Prentice-Hall, 1968.

Breger, L., and McGaugh, J. L. A critique and reformulation of "learning theory" approaches to psychotherapy and neurosis. *Psychological Bulletin,* 1965, *63,* 335–358.

Bugelski, B. R. *The psychology of learning.* New York: Henry Holt, 1956.

Carkhuff, R. R. Differential functioning of lay and professional helpers. *Journal of Counseling Psychology,* 1968, *15,* 117–126.

Carkhuff, R. R. *Helping and human relations: A primer for lay and professional helpers. Volume I. Selection and training.* New York: Holt, Rinehart and Winston, 1969. (a)

Carkhuff, R. R. *Helping and human relations: A primer for lay and professional helpers. Volume II. Practice and research.* New York: Holt, Rinehart and Winston, 1969. (b)

Carkhuff, R. R., and Berenson, B. G. *Beyond counseling and therapy.* New York: Holt, Rinehart and Winston, 1967.

Cautela, J. Hypnosis and behaviour therapy. *Behaviour Research and Therapy,* 1966, *4,* 219–244.

Chan, A., Chiu, Ada, and Mueller, D. J. An integrated approach to the modification of classroom failure and disruption: A case study. *Journal of School Psychology,* 1970, *8,* 114–121.

Clark, D. F. The treatment of hysterical spasm and agoraphobia by behaviour therapy. *Behaviour Research and Therapy,* 1963, *1,* 245–250.

Cole, S. N., and Sipprelle, C. N. Extinction of a classically conditioned G.S.R. as a function of awareness. *Behaviour Research and Therapy,* 1967, *5,* 331–337.

Cooper, J. E. A study of behaviour therapy in thirty psychiatric patients. *Lancet,* 1963, *1,* 411–415.

Dollard, J., and Miller, N. E. *Personality and psychotherapy: An analysis in terms of learning, thinking, and culture.* New York: McGraw-Hill, 1950.

Eysenck, H. J. The effects of psychotherapy: An evaluation. *Journal of Consulting Psychology,* 1952, *16,* 319–324.

Eysenck, H. J. The effects of psychotherapy. *International Journal of Psychiatry,* 1965, *1,* 99–142.

Eysenck, H. J., and Rachman, S. *The causes and cures of neurosis.* San Diego: R. R. Knapp, 1965.

Ferster, C. B., and Perrott, Mary Carol. *Behavior principles*. New York: Appleton-Century-Crofts, 1968.

Ford, D. H., and Urban, H. B. *Systems of psychotherapy: A comparative study*. New York: John Wiley, 1963.

Franks C. M. (Ed.). *Behavior therapy: Appraisal and status*. New York: McGraw-Hill, 1969.

Freeman, T. A psychoanalytic critique of behaviour therapy. *British Journal of Medical Psychology*, 1968, *41*, 53–59.

Geer, J. H. Phobia treated by reciprocal inhibition. *Journal of Abnormal and Social Psychology*, 1964, *69*, 642–645.

Geer, J. H., and Katkin, E. S. Treatment of insomnia using a variant of systematic desensitization: A case report. *Journal of Abnormal Psychology*, 1966, *71*, 161–164.

Gelder, M. G. Assessment of behaviour therapy. *Proceedings of the Royal Society of Medicine*, 1965, *58*, 525–529.

Gladstein, G. A. Is empathy important in counseling? *Personnel and Guidance Journal*, 1970, *48*, 823–827.

Heap, R. F., and Sipprelle, C. N. Extinction as a function of insight. *Psychotherapy: Theory, Research and Practice*, 1966, *3*, 81–84.

Hilgard, E. R. *Theories of learning* (2nd ed.). New York: Appleton-Century-Crofts, 1956.

Hussain, A. Behavior therapy using hypnosis. In J. Wolpe, A. Salter, and L. J. Reyna (Eds.), *The conditioning therapies*. New York: Holt, Rinehart and Winston, 1964, 54–61.

Kamil, L. J. Psychodynamic changes through systematic desensitization. *Journal of Abnormal Psychology*, 1970, *76*, 199–205.

Kanfer, F. H. Implications of conditioning techniques for interview therapy. *Journal of Counseling Psychology*, 1966, *13*, 171–177.

Kanfer, F. H., and Phillips, Jeanne S. *Learning foundations of behavior therapy*. New York: John Wiley and Sons, 1970.

Katahn, M., Strenger, S., and Cherry, Nancy. Group counseling and behavior therapy with test-anxious college students. *Journal of Consulting Psychology*, 1966, *30*, 544–549.

Kiesler, D. J. Some myths of psychotherapy research and the search for a paradigm. *Psychological Bulletin*, 1966, *65*, 110–136.

Klein, Marjorie H., Dittmann, A. T., Parloff, M. B., and Gill, M. M. Behavior therapy: Observations and reflections. *Journal of Consulting and Clinical Psychology*, 1969, *33*, 259–266.

Kraft, T. Behaviour therapy and target symptoms. *Journal of Clinical Psychology*, 1969, *25*, 105–109.

Krumboltz, J. D. Behavioral counseling: Rationale and research. *Personnel and Guidance Journal*, 1965, *44*, 383–387.

Lazarus, A. A. Group therapy of phobic disorders by systematic desensitization. *Journal of Abnormal and Social Psychology*, 1961, *63*, 504–510.

Lazarus, A. A. The results of behaviour therapy in 126 cases of severe neurosis. *Behaviour Research and Therapy*, 1963, *1*, 69–79.

Lazarus, A. A. Behaviour therapy with identical twins. *Behaviour Research and Therapy*, 1964, *1*, 313–319.

Lazarus, A. A. In support of technical eclecticism. *Psychological Reports*, 1967, *21*, 415–416.

Lazarus, A. A. Variations in desensitization therapy. *Psychotherapy: Theory, Research and Practice*, 1968, *5*, 50–52.

Lazarus, A. A. Broad-spectrum behavior therapy. *Newsletter of the Association for Advancement of Behavior Therapy*, 1969, *4*, 5–6. (a)

Lazarus, A. A. Personal communication, April 30, 1969. (b)

Lazarus, A. A., and Serber, M. Is systematic desensitization being misapplied? *Psychological Reports*, 1968, *23*, 215–218.

Leventhal, A. M. Use of a behavioral approach within a traditional psychotherapeutic context: A case study. *Journal of Abnormal Psychology*, 1968, *73*, 178–182.

London, P. *The modes and morals of psychotherapy*. New York: Holt, Rinehart and Winston, 1964.

Marks, I. M., and Gelder, M. G. Common ground between behaviour therapy and psychodynamic methods. *British Journal of Medical Psychology*, 1966, *39*, 11-23.

Marks, J., Sonoda, Beverly, and Schalock, R. Reinforcement versus relationship therapy for schizophrenics. *Journal of Abnormal Psychology*, 1968, *73*, 397–402.

Mowrer, O. H. Freudianism, behaviour therapy and "self-disclosure." *Behaviour Research and Therapy*, 1964, *1*, 321–337.

Mowrer, O. H. The behavior therapies with special reference to modeling and imitation. *American Journal of Psychotherapy*, 1966, *20*, 439–461.

Murray, E. J. A content-analysis method for studying psychotherapy. *Psychological Monographs*, 1956, *70* (13, Whole No. 420).

Murray, E. J., and Jacobson, L. I. The nature of learning in traditional and behavioral psychotherapy. In A. E. Bergin and S. L. Garfield (Eds.), *Handbook of psychotherapy and behavior change*. New York: John Wiley, in press.

Naar, R. Client-centered and behavior therapies: Their peaceful coexistence: A case study. *Journal of Abnormal Psychology*, 1970, *76*, 155–160.

Parloff, M. B. Therapist-patient relationships and outcome of psychotherapy. *Journal of Consulting Psychology*, 1961, *25*, 29–38.

Pasamanick, B., Dinitz, S., and Lefton, M. Psychiatric orientation and its relation to diagnosis and treatment in a mental hospital. *American Journal of Psychiatry*, 1959, *116*, 127–132.

Patterson, C. H. Relationship therapy and/or behavior therapy. *Psychotherapy: Theory, Research and Practice*, 1968, *5*, 226–233.

Patterson, C. H. What is counseling psychology? *Journal of Counseling Psychology*, 1969, *16*, 23–29.

Roberts, R. R., Jr., and Renzaglia, G. A. The influence of tape recording on counseling. *Journal of Counseling Psychology*, 1965, *12*, 10–16.

Rogers, C. R. *On becoming a person.* Boston: Houghton Mifflin, 1961.

Schmidt, L. D. Some ethical, professional, and legal considerations for school counselors. *Personnel and Guidance Journal*, 1965, *44*, 376–382.

Shoben, E. J., Jr. Stray thoughts on revisited eclecticism. *Personnel and Guidance Journal*, 1969, *48*, 198–200.

Sipprelle, C. N. Non-hypnotizability as resistance. *Psychotherapy: Theory, Research and Practice*, 1964, *1*, 75–79.

Sipprelle, C. N. Induced anxiety. *Psychotherapy: Theory, Research and Practice*, 1967, *4*, 36–40.

Slavson, S. R. Eclecticism versus sectarianism in group psychotherapy. *International Journal of Group Psychotherapy*, 1970, *20*, 3–13.

Thompson, A., and Zimmerman, R. Goals of counseling: Whose? When? *Journal of Counseling Psychology*, 1969, *16*, 121–125.

Thorne, F. C. *Integrative psychology: A systematic clinical viewpoint.* Brandon, Vt.: Clinical Psychology, 1967.

Thorne, F. C. Editorial opinion: Towards a better understanding of the eclectic method. *Journal of Clinical Psychology*, 1969, *25*, 463–464. (a)

Thorne, F. C. Editorial opinion: Value factors in clinical judgment. *Journal of Clinical Psychology*, 1969, *25*, 231. (b)

Truax, C. B. Reinforcement and nonreinforcement in Rogerian psychotherapy. *Journal of Abnormal Psychology*, 1966, *71*, 1–9. (a)

Truax, C. B. Some implications of behavior therapy for psychotherapy. *Journal of Counseling Psychology*, 1966, *13*, 160–170. (b)

Truax, C. B. Therapist interpersonal reinforcement of client self-exploration and therapeutic outcome in group psychotherapy. *Journal of Counseling Psychology*, 1968, *15*, 225–231.

Truax, C. B., and Carkhuff, R. R. *Toward effective counseling and psychotherapy: Training and practice.* Chicago: Aldine, 1967.

Ulrich, R., Stachnik, T., and Mabry, J. (Eds.). *Control of human behavior.* Glenview, Ill.: Scott, Foresman, 1966.

Ulrich, R., Stachnik, T., and Mabry, J. (Eds.). *Control of human behavior: From cure to prevention. Volume two.* Glenview, Ill.: Scott, Foresman, 1970.

Whaley, D. L., and Malott, R. W. *Elementary principles of behavior* (3rd ed.). Kalamazoo, Mich.: Behaviordelia, 1969.

Wilson, A., and Smith, F. J. Counterconditioning therapy using free association: A pilot study. *Journal of Abnormal Psychology*, 1968, *73*, 474–478.

Wilson, G. T., Hannon, Alma E., and Evans, W. I. M. Behavior therapy and the therapist-patient relationship. *Journal of Consulting and Clinical Psychology*, 1968, *32*, 103–109.

Wolpe, J. The comparative clinical status of conditioning therapies and psychoanalysis. In J. Wolpe, A. Salter, and L. J. Reyna (Eds.), *The conditioning therapies*. New York: Holt, Rinehart and Winston, 1964, 5–20.

Wolpe, J. *The practice of behavior therapy*. New York: Pergamon, 1969. (a)

Wolpe, J. Therapist and technique variable in behavior therapy of neurosis. *Comprehensive Psychiatry*, 1969, *10*, 44–49. (b)

Wolpe, J., and Lazarus, A. A. *Behavior therapy techniques*. New York: Pergamon, 1966.

Woody, R. H. Integrating behavior therapy and psychotherapy. *British Journal of Medical Psychology*, 1968, *41*, 261–266. (a)

Woody, R. H. Reinforcement in school counseling. *School Counselor*, 1968, *15*, 253–258. (b)

Woody, R. H. Toward a rationale for psychobehavioral therapy. *Archives of General Psychiatry*, 1968, *19*, 197–204. (c)

Woody, R. H. *Behavioral problem children in the schools: Recognition, diagnosis, and behavioral modification*. New York: Appleton-Century-Crofts, 1969. (a)

Woody, R. H. Psychobehavioral therapy in the schools: Implications for counselor education. *Counselor Education and Supervision*, 1969, *8*, 258–264. (b)

Woody, R. H., Krathwohl, D. R., Kagan, N., and Farquhar, W. W. Stimulated recall in psychotherapy using hypnosis and video tape. *American Journal of Clinical Hypnosis*, 1965, *7*, 234–241.

# 2

# Behavioral Modification Techniques

Beyond the theoretical rationale and the necessary step of assessing behaviors lies the challenge of applying technical skills to modify behaviors beneficially. Behavioral methodology, although being relatively clear-cut and easy to understand, is of little value unless it is supported by a counselor-therapist who is comprehensively trained. While there is evidence that lay persons can serve as behavior reinforcers, this practice is appropriate for only the application of techniques. The determination of what techniques should be used, the continual assessing of the effects, and the amendments to the ongoing technical format necessitate that a professional be directly involved. Thus lay persons or lower-level professionals might apply certain behavioral techniques, but only when supervised by a highly-skilled professional counselor-therapist. The implications for training will receive further attention in Chapters 4, 5, and 6. At this point it should be adequate to state that the use of behavioral modification procedures in no way lowers the amount of relevant academic knowledge a counselor or therapist must have—if anything, it increases the requirements to encompass a greater understanding of learning theory, scientific methodology, and a body of behaviorally-oriented research that counselors and therapists might heretofore have neglected.

This chapter emphasizes the components of different behavioral modification techniques. It is designed to provide an orientation to the techniques, not to fully prepare the reader to apply them. It is possible, depending upon the reader's training, that some of the techniques will be understood adequately from this presentation to accommodate immediate implementation, but in most instances, additional reading and study will be necessary before technical knowledge will be adequate; references for relevant materials are selectively included. Further, it is requisite for any clinical procedure that the user have had supervised clinical experience. Therefore, the materials herein will provide only the academic foundation for technical usage, and practical experience under competent supervision cannot be too strongly recommended.

Despite what may seem like cut-and-dried technical characteristics, the selection of a technique constitutes a major challenge for counselors and therapists. Lazarus (1966b) indicates that it is comparatively easy to prepare trainees in the administration of behavioral techniques, but there is a major difficulty in communicating "(a) when to apply a specific technique or preselected combination of techniques, and (b) how to ferret out and identify the relevant dimensions along which therapy should proceed" (p. 97); he concludes that there is no substitute for appropriate clinical experience. Caution is therefore recommended to would-be users of behavioral modification techniques: the prognosis for treatment and, moreover, professional ethics demand that special attention be given to developing precise and expert skills for judging the suitability of behavioral techniques for the problem being treated.[1]

The behavioral modification techniques presented in this chapter vary in complexity and difficulty. Some require more professional capability than others, and some can even be used on different levels —that is, a technique might be used for some problems by a relatively lower-level professional (or paraprofessional), whereas the same technique would be applicable to more severe disorders when in the hands of a more highly trained professional. Moreover, the techniques are not equal in importance (meaning, in this case, suitability for the types of problems encountered by counselor-therapists and the frequency with which the technique is used by counselors and therapists).

The techniques will be presented in a sequence that seems to reflect their suitability for counselors and therapists.[2] Arrangement

[1]Numerous behavioral modification techniques can be facilitated by laboratory apparatus, specifically electromechanical devices. Schwitzgebel (1968) provides a survey of electromechanical devices than can be employed for behavioral modification. Subsequently, Schwitzgebel (1970) describes the many possible adaptations of behavioral instrumentation. Also, the *American Psychologist* (1969, Volume 24, Number 3) devoted an entire issue to instrumentation in psychology; several of the articles included have direct bearing on clinical behavioral modification.

[2]This sequence is designed to start at the "counseling" segment and progress to the "therapy" segment of the counseling-psychotherapy continuum.

in this sequnce does not mean that all of these techniques *are* being used by counselors or that they *should* be used by *all* counselors. Rather, the order and selection connote that these techniques have been investigated on the degree to which they merit consideration, that they are potentially appropriate for certain types of problems that counselors and therapists encounter, and that with adequate training a counselor-therapist could use them within the confines of the psychobehavioral frame of reference. The techniques to be considered include: verbal conditioning, object and social recognition rewards, systematic desensitization, modeling, clinical suggestion and hypnosis, stimulated recall, covert sensitization, implosive therapy, aversive conditioning, and negative practice.

The presentation sequence for the ten categories of techniques should also be looked at from a theoretical vantage point. One theoretical classification scheme would be to dichotomize the techniques into *maladaptive avoidance responses* and *maladaptive approach responses*. Maladaptive avoidance responses are those problem behaviors that lead a client to attempt to avoid particular anxiety-eliciting or fear-provoking objects, situations, or circumstances; phobias represent the most common type of problem in this group. The techniques used for maladaptive avoidance responses come from the categories of verbal conditioning, object and social recognition rewards, modeling, systematic desensitization, stimulated recall, and implosive therapy. Maladaptive approach responses are those problems behaviors that witness the client's undue attraction to an object, situation, or set of circumstances; these include obsessions and compulsions, homosexuality, alcoholism, and psychological (as opposed to physiological) addiction to drugs. The techniques used for maladaptive approach responses include covert sensitization, aversive conditioning, and negative practice. Clinical suggestion and hypnosis could feasibly contribute to the treatment of both types of maladaptive responses. It should also be noted that, while verbal conditioning, object and social recognition rewards, and modeling could probably best be described as "conditioning" (because they increase the probability of a new behavior's occurring), systematic desensitization, covert sensitization, aversive conditioning, and negative practice might be termed "counter-conditioning" (because they decrease the probability of an old behavior's occurring). Clinical suggestion and hypnosis, and stimulated recall might be characterized as having potential for both "conditioning" and "counter-conditioning." In a broad sense, however, all are "conditioning" techniques.

Chapter 1 included definitions of numerous aspects of conditioning. Of particular importance for understanding the following techniques are the definitions of positive reinforcement, negative reinforcement, schedule of reinforcement, and punishment. In approaching the behavioral modification techniques, one should emphasize that each technique can potentially be used alone or in conjunction with another behavioral procedure, as well as be integrated with insight-oriented counseling and psychotherapy. As will be noted in some of the research cited, except for the investigations of the properties of a particular technique, clinical services more often than not include a combination of techniques. Therefore, while studying each respective technique, and when the inevitable (and desirable) mental applications are made, the reader should also consider whether the effects of a technique could be enhanced by combining more than one behavioral technique into the treatment format; this process would, of course, also mean combining the behavioral procedures with the dimensions of the facilitating relationship and counseling-psychotherapeutic processes.

## VERBAL CONDITIONING

Verbal conditioning appears to merit primary attention from all counselors and psychotherapists, because there seems to be reason to believe that it is present in some form in essentially all counseling and psychotherapy (albeit unplanned and unacknowledged in many instances). For example, there are probably reinforcing elements in such supposedly nonbehavioral activities as the counselor-therapist's offering information or helping the client evaluate different alternatives: he may consciously or unconsciously reinforce by his approval and special attention the alternative that seems most logical to him. Even pushing for introspection or dream content could be a reinforcement procedure. This assertion is supported by the research as was presented in Chapter 1 indicating the presence of reinforcers in counselor-therapist responses (e.g., Murray, 1956; Truax, 1966a, 1966b, 1968; Woody, 1968).

Verbal conditioning typically occurs within the operant conditioning paradigm. The reinforcer is usually some sort of social approval mediated by another person. To exemplify this in counseling-therapy terms: the client makes a verbal response that fits into a class or type previously selected by the counselor-therapist as being critical; the counselor-therapist "rewards" the client's verbal response by being socially responsive, i.e., giving verbal praise or a nonverbal sign of approval or acceptance; that class of client-response then has the reinforced basis to occur more frequently than those classes of responses that receive no reinforcement. This form of verbal conditioning has had diverse applications in both laboratory and clinical settings. Of importance to counselor-therapists, the research evidence supports the view that verbal conditioning does, in fact, influence the probability of certain classes of client responses' occurring in counseling and psychotherapy. Williams (1964) offers a review of studies of conditioning of verbalization, and notes that such studies are most relevant to applied counseling and psychotherapy. Hosford (1969) has provided a review of behavioral counseling research and gives emphasis to verbal conditioning.

There were several early laboratory or quasi-therapy experiments, namely those conducted by Greenspoon (1951, 1955) and Verplanck (1955), that attracted the attention of clinicians. What these and subsequent studies essentially found was that stimuli can be used to reinforce classes of verbal responses; obviously it was only a short step from these laboratory studies to the counseling and therapy offices. Following up on the classes of responses that could be reinforced, investigators began to study the types of reinforcers that could be used and the variables that influenced the reinforcement processes (Krasner, 1965). It has been repeatedly documented that such factors as the characteristics of the experimenter and the relationship that is formed between the experimenter and the subject, even in the laboratory, can influence the findings (Binder, McConnell, and Sjoholm, 1957; Hildum and Brown, 1956; Sapolsky, 1960). Similarly, the expectancy of the experimenter has been shown to have an effect on the outcomes of various types of psychological experiments; this definitely includes verbal conditioning and probably most behavior studies, where the intention is frequently clear, if disguised at all. For example, Rosenthal (1967) points out how covert communication can exert an influence; such effects as might be provoked by the sex of the examiner or the subject can easily be recognized (e.g., female subjects evoke more smiling from their experimenters than males do from theirs, and female subjects tend to elicit more protective treatment). But there are also more subtle influences that can be covertly communicated in an uncontrolled fashion. In other words, even seemingly well-planned psychological research does not present uncontaminated findings; reinforcement may come from much less obvious sources than the verbal or overt behavioral responses, e.g., the philosophy of the agency in which the service occurs, the environmental tone of the treatment setting, and stereotyped characteristics of the personnel.

In addition to conditioning the occurrence of specified classes of verbal responses, the concept of verbal conditioning can be extended to certain aspects of directing or structuring an interview. When a counselor-therapist directs or structures, he is acting on the premise that there are certain types of materials that should be accorded more attention than others. This would, logically, lead the client to infer that these are the preferred verbal behaviors; and when he wishes to continue to receive the rewards from the relationship, i.e., the social approval of the counselor-therapist, the client probably automatically gives these selected topics or preferences priority. Thus, verbal conditioning could be extended beyond classes of words in an experimental sense and could be applicable to the directive characteristics within counseling and psychotherapy.

This directive-type counselor-therapist behavior, if diagnostically correct (that is, if the counselor-therapist has been accurate in judging what should be considered), could have beneficial behavioral outcomes. To offer but one example, there is reason to believe that merely encouraging the client to verbalize is desirable. Shore and Massimo (1967) investigated the effects on adolescent delinquent boys of a therapist's helping them to become aware of the consequences of their hostile behaviors, offering directive suggestions to them as to how to achieve more socialized modes for the expression of manifested frustration and rage, and affording them with opportunities for mastery of the hostile behaviors. With these guidelines for the therapists' responses, over a ten-month period it was found that the treated delinquents increased their verbalizations, the untreated delinquents decreased theirs, and the nondelinquent control boys showed no change in amount of verbalization. These findings were interpreted as showing that overreacting verbally might serve to insure that there is no breakthrough of frustration and rage into overt hostile behavior. This sort of control is similar to that of the child who verbalizes his prohibitions, e.g., "Mommy said not to touch," as a means of gaining a regulation over behavior.

The main interest in this section is, however, the reinforcing of classes of client responses, and specifically, what contribution to counseling-therapy the occurrence of the types of verbal responses might make. Before research studies on numerous response classes and behavioral counseling-therapy are cited, the distinction between behaviorally-oriented counseling-therapy and other theoretical approaches to counseling-therapy must be clear. Table 1 provides three hypothetical responses from a 12th-grade boy seeking vocational-educational counseling. Following each of the possible responses is a response that might be made by a psychoanalytically-oriented counselor-therapist, a client-centered counselor-therapist, and a behavioral counselor-therapist. As is evident, the psychoanalytically-oriented counselor-therapist bases most of his responses on interpretation, the client-centered counselor-therapist bases most of his responses on reflection (both of the counselor-therapists strive for insight), and the behavioral counselor-therapist bases his responses on assessing and promoting selected behavioral functioning and, in the process, facilitates insight.

To provide additional clarity as to what might take place in behavioral or psychobehavioral counseling-therapy interviews, the following is a hypothetical excerpt from a behaviorally-oriented initial session. The client is a young married man in his twenties who has sought treatment from a community mental health clinic.

*Client:* My goal is to make more friends. I'm pretty lonely, and just don't know how to go about doing anything about it.

*Counselor:* Based on this, one thing we should probably strive for is to consider ways you can establish meaningful relationships. Of course, this would mean we would need to understand how you have entered into relationships in the past, what you got from relationships, what you gave to them in return, and what you expected and will expect from others. (Note: The counselor accepts the client's initial goal, and defines some of the avenues by which the interview can progress.)

*Client:* Yes, that would help. (Long pause)

*Counselor:* Well, how would you describe your past relationships?

| Client Response | Psychoanalytically Oriented Counselor-Therapist |
|---|---|
| The real reason I came to see you was because I can't seem to decide on what I should major in next fall at college. One minute I would like to study drama and the next minute I think I think I should be in engineering. | There seems to be a conflict between what you "would like to do" and what you "think you should do." "Like" and "should" represent quite divergent bases for selecting a major. |
| Underneath it all, no doubt, is the fact that drama is my idea, but my Mom and Dad have always wanted me to become an engineer like Dad. I must admit that I would probably do better in engineering in the long run. | If you went into engineering, you would, in part, be identifying with you. father. I gather this would provoke some special feelings. |
| Engineering represents work to me, real work—you know, monotonous day-in-and-day-out, doing the same thing, even if it is pretty challenging in terms of having to know a lot and discovering new things. Drama is, well, just fun. I guess I think about how much I enjoyed practicing for the junior play last year. | Engineering would mean entering a confining world; perhaps you mean entering a *real adult world* and you would like to avoid moving into that way of life. It would be easier to maintain your current role than to have to assume a role that is more demanding. |

| Client-Centered Counselor-Therapist | Behavioral Counselor-Therapist |
| --- | --- |
| t's very difficult to make decision. | What sort of basis do you have for making your decision? For example, have you had any vocational interest tests or have you investigated the requirements and the pros and cons of both drama and engineering? |
| Imm. You would hate to give p drama since it was your lea, kind of a part of you; et you believe you would lo better" in engineering. Silence) Perhaps your ords "do better" contain le key to just how much itisfaction could be gained om either area. | Assuming that you understand the objectives of studying drama and engineering, as you seem to do, the issue would appear to be: What are your criteria or requirements for a profession? What do you want or need from your studies and eventually your work? Perhaps if we can identify these factors, we can consider some means to help you make a decision. |
| ou would like to have a iallenging career, but iis would restrict you in ame ways. | It sounds as though the "meat" of your thinking is with engi- neering. In other words, although it might be possible for some people, you don't view drama in a very academic manner; it's as though drama was a way of avoiding assuming responsibility. If any of this is true, I wonder how it would fit into your long-range aspirations. |

(Note: The counselor senses the client has difficulty in proceeding, and takes the initiative of prompting him.)

*Client:* Oh, I don't know. (Pause) I've never had many friends, at least not close friends—there was one fellow in high school I used to run around with, but he went into the Army right after we graduated and I haven't seen or heard from him since.

*Counselor:* How would you compare different types of relationships? For example, have there been differences between relationships you formed or tried to form in high school, in college, at work, among your neighbors, or within your family? (Note: The counselor assumes the responsibility for structuring and for attempting to accelerate the interview.)

*Client:* In my family, I feel close, you know—except maybe when it comes to my father. He used to be a policeman. He's retired now, but he used to be right on the four-corners of town most of the time. He's pretty fed up with the police force now though. He wasn't going to retire for a couple of more years, but his chief started giving him a rough time. And he . . . (counselor interrupts).

*Counselor:* It seems we're getting a little off the question of possible differences between types of relationships. (Note: The counselor firmly brings the client back to a point relevant to the counseling goal. This is gentle negative reinforcement.)

*Client:* Yeah (laughs), you're right. But Dad and I have our difficulties.

*Counselor:* Mmm. (Note: The counselor is accepting of this transitional response, and subtly reinforces the client toward the idea of relationships.)

*Client:* In general, I suppose I get along with my family as well as anybody could, even with Dad.

*Counselor:* So with family members you're able to get involved, to relate, to accept and be accepted. (Note: The counselor accepts the client's opinion about family relationships and brings closure, thereby connoting that the client can proceed to another type of relationship.)

*Client:* Yes, I think so. As for high school, well, I was working part-time and didn't really want to do much at school. In my free time I usually just stayed around home. I read a lot of car magazines then, and, well, I might have played baseball or something with my brothers or some of the guys in the neighborhood.

*Counselor:* The guys in the neighborhood accepted you. (Note: The counselor ignores irrelevant factors, such as cars and baseball per se, and selectively reinforces the aspect of peer relationships within the client's response.)

*Client:* Oh sure. We used to have a ball team that was really good. We played some other teams, like from Oakmont and Carpton. I played short-stop, and even pitched occasionally.

*Counselor:* (No response) (Note: The counselor avoids reinforcing content material that is not aligned with the counseling goal; this is done by withholding all verbal and nonverbal reactions.)

*Client:* Pitching wasn't for me though, so I stuck to the infield.

*Counselor:* (No response) (Note: The counselor continues to withhold cues and to avoid reinforcement of verbal behaviors not in accord with the specified goal.)

*Client:* I sure did enjoy that, now that I think of of. It's too bad you can't stay carefree all of your life.

*Counselor:* Apparently your relationships with the guys on the team were satisfying. I wonder if there were some specific ways. (Note: The counselor accepts the return to relevant material and encourages consideration of a specific aspect.)

*Client:* You mean ways that were satisfying?

*Counselor:* Yes.

*Client:* I guess the main thing was they accepted me.

*Counselor:* Why would they accept you while persons in other relationships haven't? (Note: By responding at this time and in this manner, the counselor reinforces introspection.)

*Client:* Mainly because I was a good hitter.

*Counselor:* So you contributed something to their goals. In other words, you performed well and it helped them be on a winning team. Could this be transferred to your current job? (Note: The counselor used a content response to make an interpretation relevant to the counseling goal, and then structures.)

*Client:* It might. It would be nice, because I sure don't feel very accepted there. Boy, I don't even have a desk as good as the others. A few months ago I asked for a new desk, and the boss said "It's a poor workman who blames his tools," and just walked away.

*Counselor:* The factors of performing well and contributing to the others' goals, as you did on the baseball team, must not hold true at the office. (Note: The counselor ignores, i.e., avoids reinforcing, the irrelevancies about the desk, but encourages further consideration of work relations.)

*Client:* No, I suppose they don't. See I pushed for this job in the Purchasing department that I don't know much about; in fact, I must admit that I'm always screwing things up.

*Counselor:* But you wanted the job. (Note: The counselor selectively reinforces introspection about motives.)

*Client:* Not really. I pushed for it because it paid more and I thought it might be a step toward Personnel.

*Counselor:* To use our baseball analogy, apparently you aren't hitting so well. Maybe you even forced your way into the line-up. (Note: The counselor uses the client's language and leads him toward making a summary statement.)

*Client:* And it was a bit heavy handed, when you stop to think of how I swung the change. See, my wife's brother is in Personnel and he kind of arranged it so I got it over some guys who were already in Purchasing and hoped to move into this job I got. It's no wonder the guys in the department treat me like I don't speak their language—yea, I am a foreigner.

*Counselor:* You seem to be saying a couple of things. First, you realize you kind of stepped on some men who were in line for the job by getting your brother-in-law to earn, in a sense, the position for you, and second, you aren't performing well, in terms of being able to do the work adequately. As you indicated, these two factors could undoubtedly influence your relationships with your co-workers. (Note: The counselor reinforces via restatement and implied accuracy.)

This hypothetical example shows how the atmosphere for subsequent counseling sessions becomes patterned during the initial session. The counselor responds when the client's comments are aligned with the client-stated goal, but he does not respond, unless possibly with negative reinforcement properties, when comments are not within the selected boundaries for verbal behavior. Parenthetically, some counselor-therapists view accepting the client's initially stated goal as being unwise (granted there would typically be more diagnostic interviewing than was present in this excerpt to determine what were probably the primary goals), because what the client states early in the counseling-therapy as his problems may camouflage some more deeply-seated difficulties that he is not sure he can trust himself or the counselor-therapist to handle. But the behaviorist would say that these initial goals should be accepted, after they have been explored to ascertain that they probably are in order of preferability for treatment; if these early goals are treated successfully, the behaviorist would believe that the more significant problems would emerge readily and would be presented to the counselor-therapist because he had proven his ability to accept the client and to help him deal effectively with his difficulties, even though they may have been cover-ups for others.

There is an impressive amount of research on the reinforcement of specific verbal response classes. Table 2 lists representative studies especially applicable to counseling and psychotherapy. Although there were differences in the designs and methodology, one may generalize that these studies all found that the designated classes of verbal responses could be reinforced to occur significantly more frequently than nonreinforced verbal behaviors, and the verbal conditioning was typically accomplished by the experimenter's (i.e., the counselor-therapist) giving either verbal comments, e.g., "good," or "yes," or "that's a good idea," or physical gestures, e.g., a smile, a nod of the head, leaning toward the client, to connote acceptance or approval.

Examination of the classes of verbal responses that were successfully reinforced reveals the applicability of verbal conditioning to counseling and psychotherapy in any setting. A few examples will suffice: certainly a client entering counseling to achieve additional career-vocational or educational planning could benefit from having a major portion of his responses be information-seeking (especially because the research has found that these clients tend to engage in more actual information-seeking behaviors outside of the interview if these responses were reinforced by the counselor); a client with a self-concept problem, i.e., feelings of inadequacy, could probably benefit from making positive self-references; and almost any client, especially those seeking insight into emotional conflicts, could benefit from dealing with the appropriateness of behaviors, self-exploration, deliberation, and positive affect responses. What bears repeated emphasis is that the use of many behavioral modification techniques, and particularly verbal conditioning, can serve to enhance insight-oriented counseling and psychotherapy, and, therefore, provides not only superficial behavioral manipulation, but also facilitates attaining insight and understanding in the best counseling-psychotherapy tradition.

The list of studies in Table 2 also attests to the comprehensive efficacy of verbal conditioning. In a counseling-psychotherapy format, reinforcement from the counselor-therapist has significantly modi-

TABLE 2: Selected Behavioral Counseling-Therapy Studies

| Investigation | Classes of Responses | Type of Subjects |
|---|---|---|
| Bryan and Kapche, 1967 | First-person pronoun responses | Male psychopaths |
| Dicken and Fordham, 1967 | Positive self-reference and positive affect responses | Female college students |
| Doubros, 1967 | Human-reference and animal-reference responses | Male and female mentally retarded adolescents |
| Drennen, Gallman, and Sausser, 1969 | Plural noun responses | Male and female hospitalized psychiatric patients |
| Hansen, Niland, and Zani, 1969 | Social acceptance | Male and female elementary school children |
| Ince, 1968 | Positive self-reference responses | Female college students |
| Johnson, 1964 | Verbal participation | Male and female elementary school children |
| Kramer, 1968 | Questioning appropriateness of past and present behaviors, responsibility, and positive responses | Male and female college students |
| Krumboltz and Schroeder, 1965 | Information-seeking responses | Male and female high school students |
| Krumboltz and Thoresen, 1964 | Information-seeking responses | Male and female high school students |
| Krumboltz, Varenhorst, and Thoresen, 1967 | Information-seeking responses | Female high school students |
| Lanyon, 1967 | Relevant-to-parents responses | Female college students |

| Meyer, Strowig, and Hosford, 1970 | Information-seeking responses | Male and female high school students |
| Myrick, 1969 | Self-reference responses | Male junior high school students |
| Ryan and Krumboltz, 1964 | Deliberation and decision responses | Male college students |
| Rogers, 1960 | Positive and negative self-reference responses | Male college students |
| Thoresen and Krumboltz, 1967 | Information-seeking responses | Male and female high school students |
| Thoresen and Krumboltz, 1968 | Information-seeking responses | Male high school students |
| Thoresen, Krumboltz, and Varenhorst, 1967 | Information-seeking responses | Male and female high school students |
| Truax, 1968 | Self-exploration responses | Mental (schizophrenic) patients |
| Williams and Blanton, 1968 | Feeling responses | Male (non-psychotic) psycho-therapy in-patients |

fied the verbal behaviors of elementary school, high school, and college students, and mentally retarded and mentally disturbed persons —both male and female.

One of the most frequently asked questions from counselor-therapists just beginning to use verbal conditioning is: Does it matter whether the client knows he is being conditioned? In other words: Will the reinforcement processes be influenced by the client's knowledge of the verbal conditioning format? One of the important variables in this matter is the expertise of the counselor-therapist. In a study of verbal conditioning, Denner (1970) found that "crafty" therapists, i.e., those who could condition their clients without their being aware of the conditioning process, were more effective conditioners and that their verbal style was rated less clear and less certain. But if the craftiness of the counselor-therapist is set aside, it appears that those clients who are informed about the conditioning procedure end up being conditioned better than those clients who are left uninformed (Denner, 1970). In the latter situation, however, one must wonder, as is true with so many other behavioral techniques, if the difference in outcome could be attributed, at least in part, to the effects of clinical suggestion, persuasion, and a set toward change. It seems that the basic question of whether the knowledge of the verbal conditioning format is critical cannot be answered in a definitive way.

The research on verbal conditioning is impressive, and the results have a readily-apparent practical value. Ince (1968) states:

By using behavioral principles, such as those employed in this study, the counselor or psychotherapist will be able to quantifiably measure the behavior of the client or patient when the client first comes for assistance, measure his own responses to this, and finally to note the effects of his behavior upon the client. By refusing reinforcement, in specified amounts and at specified times, the counselor will be able to precisely determine which of his behaviors produced the desired effect upon the client's behavior. And, by measuring the behavior of the client prior to, during, and following the reinforcement procedure, the counselor will be able to state the degree and direction of change in the client's behavior. (p. 144)

In view of the often uncontrolled reinforcement intrinsic to counseling and psychotherapy, and because verbal conditioning can be planned and controlled in accord with the needs and goals of the client (for both greater insight and important outside-of-counseling behaviors), there is no question that counselors and therapists should include verbal conditioning in their technical repertoire.

## OBJECT AND SOCIAL RECOGNITION REWARDS

Both objects and social recognition can be used as positive reinforcement. When an undesirable behavior occurs, the counselor-therapist carefully avoids giving any cues that would be rewarding, but when appropriate behavior occurs, he gives some sort of reward. Objects that either have definite value or can be redeemed for something of value or social recognition from the counselor-therapist can be used. Planned use of object and social recognition rewards can, therefore, increase the frequency of occurrence of preferred behaviors, while those behaviors that are unacceptable, since they receive no reinforcement, will tend to occur less and less.

This procedure has been used successfully with a number of problem behaviors. A few studies will exemplify the types of problems that can be dealt with in this way. Hudson and DeMyer (1968) used food as a primary reinforcer to improve skills in the arts and crafts activities of autistic children. Miller (1964) used food to condition a teenage girl's study habits. Patterson, Jones, Whittier, and Wright (1965) rigged up a buzzer system as a signal to a hyperactive brain-injured boy so he would know when his behavior in class had been controlled adequately and when he was to receive a reward of candy and pennies; the boy was conditioned to control unacceptable behaviors thought to stem from his neurological condition. McKerracher (1967) used the object reward of candy to reinforce reading improvement for a boy with low educational achievement. McInnis and Ullman (1967) found that short-term schizophrenics were more responsive to both positive (object rewards redeemable for money) and negative (taking away object rewards) reinforcement than were long-term schizophrenics; similarly, it was found that short-term schizophrenics were more responsive to positive than to negative reinforcement, but the reverse was true with the long-term schizophrenics. Wolf, Giles, and Hall (1968) used tokens to reinforce mastery of instructional materials (homework and remedial work completed) for low-achieving fifth- and sixth-grade children who were enrolled in a remedial education program in an urban poverty area; the analysis revealed that the reinforcement-based training had significant effects on subsequent academic achievement and report card grades, as compared to controls who had no remedial program. Similar reinforcement procedures have improved the learning of mentally retarded children (Birnbrauer, Wolf, Kidder, and Tague, 1965), and improved the toilet training of severely mentally retarded persons (Hundziak, Maurer, and Watson, 1965). Social recognition as a reward, i.e., not responding to unacceptable behaviors but responding to and praising acceptable ones, led emotionally disturbed children to control their behaviors and to be more productive in the classroom (Zimmerman and Zimmerman, 1962), nursery school children to control aggressive responses (Brown and Elliott, 1965), and elementary school children to control disruptive behavior (Goodlet, Goodlet, and Dredge, 1970) and to improve verbal and nonverbal communication (Brison, 1966) and attitudes (Barclay, 1967).

Several studies have combined object rewards with social-recognition rewards, and in some cases have used these positive stimuli in conjunction with other behavior therapy or insight counseling-therapy procedures or both of these. Schwitzgebel and Kolb (1964) induced delinquents to talk into a tape recorder; their participation was reinforced by money, bonuses (sharing an orange with the experimenter), and praise. Special rewards were made when the subject discussed his feelings and experiences in detail and with affect; obviously this kind of verbal behavior could assume the properties of counseling-psychotherapy. Following up on the subjects after three years, the investigators found that there was a significant reduction in arrests and amount of time in jail, as compared with the control counterparts (who received no intervention). In a subsequent study along the same lines, Schwitzgebel (1967) gave both positive and negative responses to adolescent male delinquents for four classes of operants: hostile statements (receiving a mild negative response, i.e., disagreement or inattention), positive statements, prompt arrivals at work, and general employability (all receiving a positive response, i.e., verbal praise or a small gift). The subjects' responses in both laboratory and natural settings indicated that a significant increase was achieved in the three positively reinforced classes, but that hostile statements were apparently not influenced significantly by the negative responses. Browning (1967) combined token rewards, social reinforcers, and relaxation to modify stuttering in a schizophrenic boy. Patterson (1965) used object rewards, social recognition, and doll-play activities to treat school phobia. In a similar combination, Grieger (1970) used social, object, and token reward techniques for a format in which teachers modified the behavior of total classes of students; the behavioral acts altered included hitting, spraying noises, name calling, and calling out in a disruptive fashion.

From the foregoing research it is plainly evident that diverse behaviors—overt acting-out, attitudes, verbal ability, and learning skills—can be modified by systematic use of valued objects and social recognition from others. The key lies in avoiding any uncontrolled reward when an unacceptable behavior occurs. For example, according to this system, when an unacceptable behavior occurs, the teacher or counselor or therapist would not respond, because to respond —whether positively or negatively—leads to reinforcement; the classic example is the child who misbehaves in order to get his mother to nag at him, for if he cannot get her to express affection to him, he would rather have a negative reaction than no reaction at all. Of course, a systematic use of negative reinforcement could be combined with systematic positive reinforcement. Parenthetically, this is why it is essential that parents delineate for their children how positive reactions can be earned, in other words, what behaviors will get them (the parents) to react warmly to the children. In family counseling, it is frequently found that the children have never been able to determine how to earn a consistent, positive response from their parents. In such cases, it seems that because of the parents' personal problems, the children end up resorting to problem behaviors. In summary, object and social recognition rewards can be used in a reinforcing format and can effectively modify numerous problem behaviors. If the counselor-therapist is well acquainted with these techniques, he can either use them within the counseling-therapy sessions to reinforce specific in-session behaviors, or serve as a consultant to another person in the client's life, such as a teacher, parent, or attendant, who can program rewards for behaviors outside of the counseling-therapy setting, but which would complement the treatment goals.

## SYSTEMATIC DESENSITIZATION

Systematic desensitization encompasses several techniques, all of which progressively prepare the client to deal with anxiety-provoking situations or stimuli by actually or vicariously experiencing them, so that when the anxiety begins, it is eliminated in favor of a nonanxious situation or stimulus. This approach is based on the reciprocal inhibition principle; Wolpe (1964) defines the principle:

*if a response inhibitory of anxiety can be made to occur in the presence of anxiety-evoking stimuli it will weaken the bond between these stimuli and the anxiety.* (p. 10)

In other words, anxiety-evoking stimuli or situations are ordered in terms of how much anxiety each is capable of provoking. The client is then exposed to the stimulus or situation that provokes the lowest degree of anxiety, and when the anxiety begins, he is directed to forget it and dwell on something that produces no anxiety, such as a pleasant scene. Therefore, the reciprocal inihibition principle operates: the nonanxious stimulus occurs when an anxiety-evoking one does, and the bond between the stimulus and the anxiety is weakened. The client can eventually, after experiencing the lowest level of the hierarchy until the anxiety-evoking power has been eliminated, progress on up the hierarchy, so that he is gradually desensitized to each respective level of anxiety-provoking stimuli.

Wolpe (1958, 1964, 1969) provides a description of a wide range of anxiety-inhibiting responses. The most widely used are assertion, relaxation, and sexual responses. That is, when the client is counteracting the experiencing of anxiety by putting it aside for a stimulus that produces no anxiety, the latter stimulus usually has assertive, relaxation, or sexual properties.

An example of assertion would be the client who, when he experiences anxiety at picturing himself in front of a church congregation (i.e., he fears being in front of groups), counteracts this by picturing himself in a leadership role with persons who would not provoke fear or anxiety; assertion is also the basis for behavioral rehearsal, which will receive attention at a later point in this section.

Relaxation seems to lower anxiety psychologically and physiologically (Jacobson, 1938). The techniques for inducing relaxation generally require that the client concentrate on feeling relaxed and focus his attention on various parts of his body until he feels totally relaxed. It should be noted that the techniques for inducing relaxation for systematic desensitization are striking similar to those used to induce the so-called hypnotic state. Wolpe and Lazarus (1966) provide verbatim and descriptive accounts of relaxation induction.

There is controversy over the actual need for relaxation training in systematic desensitization. McReynolds (1969) questions whether pure relaxation treatment is a real treatment analogue; he states: "Without the knowledge of the goal and expected result of treatment, the experience of relaxation cannot be expected to have more relevance to Ss' 'symptomatic' behavior than any other pleasant experience" (p. 562). Rachman (1968) maintains that muscular relaxation facilitates systematic desensitization, but is not a "necessary element" for this form of behavorial treatment. To the contrary, Laxer, Quarter, Kooman, and Walker (1969) found that relaxation training seemed more effective than systematic desensitization for reducing general anxiety. In a study of high school students with test-taking anxiety, Laxer and Walker (1970) compared a variety of combinations of behavioral procedures (systematic desensitization, relaxation alone, simulation alone, relaxation simulation, attention control, and no treatment control), and found that there was a reduction in test-taking anxiety for only those students who received a method employing relaxation training; this led them to state: "At least part of the effectiveness of systematic desensitization must be attributed to the effects of relaxation training" (p. 431).

Lomont and Edwards (1967) present evidence that the efficacy of systematic desensitization is dependent on the contiguity of muscular relaxation with the experiencing of the anxiety stimulus. Rachman (1968), however, maintains that muscular relaxation facilitates systematic desensitization, but is not a "necessary element" for this form of behavorial treatment. The role of relaxation in systematic desensitization will be clarified when selected research studies are cited.

Sexual responses are employed to help persons overcome habituated reactions to sexual situations. Sexual situations are manipulated so as to help the client become progressively more comfortable with the feelings, such as anxiety, that occur when various sexual situations or activities take place. Impotence, frigidity, and premature ejaculation have been quickly and effectively relieved with this procedure (Wolpe and Lazarus, 1966).

Eysenck and Rachman (1965), in an analysis of research, conclude that there are basically three forms of inhibitory responses that can be used with desensitization techniques; they are affection, feeding, and social reassurance. According to the Eysenck-Rachman view, the best way to counteract anxiety or fear is to provide some form of affection, feeding, or social reassurance in a planned manner; that is, to provide these inhibitory sources when the anxiety occurs in order to activate the reciprocal inhibition principle.

The procedure for conducting systematic desensitization is as follows. The client is interviewed and particular emphasis is placed on situations or things, i.e., stimuli, that have provoked fear or anxiety. From this social case history, the counselor-therapist questions the client as to what types of circumstances related to the problems that brought the client to treatment would provoke anxiety, and to what degree. From this inquiry, the counselor-therapist and the client draw up a tentative hierarchy of anxiety-evoking situations, subject to revision at any point when either the client or the counselor-therapist senses that a new stage should be added, or that the order should be changed.

While the clinical assumption that a well-ordered hierarchy is essential is usually made, there is a lack of research on this issue. Krapfl and Nawas (1970) divided fifty snake-phobic females into five groups (increasing aversiveness, decreasing aversiveness, randomized degrees of aversiveness, pseudodesensitization, and no treatment); it was found that all three desensitization groups (the first three cited) made significantly greater improvements than either of the control groups (the latter two cited), that there was no difference between the increasingly aversive and the decreasingly aversive procedures, and that the random order procedure tended to be less effective than the former two procedures. Krapfl and Nawas (1970) conclude: "An ascending aversive order of stimulus presentations is not an essential and integral part of successful desensitization" (p. 333). A more prudent position would seem to be, as stated in the discussion of their results by Krapfl and Nawas (1970): "It seems clear that the processes underlying systematic desensitization are still far from understood" (p. 337).

Regardless of varying opinions, the construction of the hierarchy is crucial to the overall success of the desensitization. Therefore, special and continued care should be given to the development of the hierarchy of anxiety-provoking situations. The hierarchy, in most cases, should be tailored to the psychological needs of each client. The words "in most cases" are used because there is evidence to show that clients can be grouped together for treatment, and that an individualized hierarchy may not be superior to a standardized one (Emery and Krumboltz, 1967); however, if a standardized hierarchy is used, it is necessary that a clinical judgment be made as to whether it is suitable for the given client. In general, and especially for beginning attempts at systematic desensitization, it seems advisable to construct individually all hierarchies for clinical use (exceptions, at this point in time, should be limited to experimental use).

Progressing through the stages of the desensitization hierarchy may be done in either or both of two ways. *In vivo* desensitization means that the client actually experiences the situations or actually encounters samples of feared stimuli. Vicarious desensitization means that the client simulates the stimuli by imagining scenes or objects or by viewing pictures, films, or some other medium for stimulating the existence of anxiety-provoking conditions.

To clarify the procedures, let us consider a hypothetical case of test-anxiety. Presume that Chuck, a freshman in college, comes to the counseling center because he becomes very anxious as examination time approaches. In the initial interview it becomes evident that, while he had the same type of anxiety in high school, there appear to be no severe pathological factors. Chuck expresses several concerns about education, such as why he is really in college and what he hopes to do in the future; therefore, the counselor and Chuck agree that they will continue to meet together to work through some of Chuck's concerns, but in order to help him handle the anxiety regarding examinations and to survive the semester academically so they can continue to meet, systematic desensitization will be used to treat his test-taking anxiety. The counselor and Chuck spend a session or two developing a hierarchy of testing situations that would typically produce anxiety; and Chuck might be asked to take the hierarchy home between sessions to mull over the appropriateness at the stages and their order. The following hierarchy (from highest to lowest levels) evolves:

*Stage 1:* Sitting in the front of the classroom, taking the examination with a professor watching him.

*Stage 2:* Sitting in the front of the classroom, taking the examination with a student-proctor observing.

*Stage 3:* Sitting in the back of the classroom, taking the examination with a professor at the front of the room.

*Stage 4:* Sitting in the back of the classroom, taking the examination with a student-proctor at the front of the room.

*Stage 5:* Approaching the classroom on the day an examination is to occur.

*Stage 6:* Studying in his dormitory room the night before an examination.

*Stage 7:* Studying in his dormitory room any time.

*Stage 8:* Studying in the library.

*Stage 9:* Seeing one of his professors on campus.

*Stage 10:* Thinking about the possibility of being tested.

As Chuck progresses up the hierarchy of situations, he experiences increasing anxiety; in other words, Stage 10 may make him feel a bit uneasy, Stage 9 more so, and so on until at Stage 1 he might even experience near-panic. Note that this hierarchy is kept simple for demonstration purposes; in an actual case it would more than likely involve a greater number of stages (some behavior therapists believe that twenty stages is an average number for a hierarchy). And, of course, this hierarchy could be changed at any time. Once the hierarchy is established, or perhaps concurrent with its development, the counselor begins to train Chuck to relax quickly and effectively. When the desensitization is actually started, the counselor instructs Chuck to relax (Chuck would signal, perhaps by raising a finger, when he had accomplished this); he is then told to think about the possibility of being tested and to signal when or if he begins to experience anxiety; if he experiences anxiety, upon the signal the counselor instructs him to forget the possibility of being tested and to picture himself in a pleasant situation (the pleasant situations are usually agreed upon before hand) and to signal when he has a clear image (note: this leads to the counteracting of the anxiety, i.e., the reciprocal inhibition principle). After a period of relaxation in the pleasant, nonanxious imagined situation, the counselor again has Chuck think of being tested. The cycle is repeated until such time as thinking about being tested fails to provoke any anxiety (and often it requires surprisingly few trials) so that they could then move on to imagining Stage 9; and the cycle would be repeated at that stage as many times as would be necessary to eliminate its anxiety-provoking powers. After Chuck has mastered the scenes in his imagination, he is asked to begin actually experiencing them. That is, he is told to spend a couple of sessions each day thinking about taking examinations, logically reasoning about the need for anxiety, and if anxiety erupted to quickly put the thought out of his mind, relax and think on something pleasant. When thinking about an examination fails to elicit anxiety, Chuck is told to station himself on the campus quadrangle and watch for his professors. Eventually, and probably in a relatively short time, he will have overcome, i.e., have been desensitized to, the test-anxiety. With Chuck now able to meet his examinations free from undue anxiety, he and the counselor proceed to an insight-type counseling-psychotherapeutic relationship and work through some of his personal conflicts.

The research on systematic desensitization is extensive and impressive. Table 3 presents a list of selected studies on systematic desensitization, indicating the types of clients served. Each of these studies found that systematic desensitization was a successful mode of treatment. The types of problems here are but a few that could be treated via systematic desensitization; theoretically, its application is suitable to essentially any problem behavior involving anxiety or fear, and its application is limited only by the ingenuity and skills of the counselor-therapist and the accessibility of the client. It should be noted that systematic desensitization is effective with adults and children, males and females, mentally healthy (except for the habit being treated) and mentally ill persons, and may be used individually or in groups.

There is also evidence that systematic desensitization can be programmed and placed on video tape so that it may be used in groups, that the quality of the vicarious stimuli can be controlled, and that the therapist's involvement can be minimal (Woody and Schauble, 1969a, 1969b). There are similar findings for the use of audio-taped desensitization (Dubner, 1969; Migler and Wolpe, 1967).

## TABLE 3: Selected Systematic Desensitization Studies

| Investigation | Problem and Subjects |
| --- | --- |
| Cooper, Gelder, and Marks, 1965 | Varied neurotic disorders with psychiatric patients |
| Cotler and Garlington, 1969 | College students with fear of snakes |
| Davison, 1968 | Male with sadistic sexual fantasies |
| Emery and Krumboltz, 1967 | Test-anxious college students |
| Folkins, Lawson, Opton, and Lazarus, 1968 | Adults with anxiety over industrial accidents |
| Garlington and Cotler, 1968 | Test-anxious college students |
| Katahn, Strenger, and Cherry, 1966 | Test-anxious college students |
| Krapfl and Nawas, 1969 | Snake phobic females |
| Lanyon, Manosevitz, and Imber, 1968 | College students with fear of spiders |
| Lazarus, 1961 | Phobic (mixed) adults |
| Lazarus, 1963 | Varied neurotic adults |
| Lazarus and Abramovitz, 1962 | Fearful children |
| Lazarus, Davison, and Polefka, 1965 | School phobic children |
| Leitenberg, Agras, Barlow, and Oliveau, 1969 | Snake phobic female college students |
| Marcia, Rubin, and Efran, 1969 | Snake and spider phobic college students |
| McFall and Marston, 1970 | Nonassertive college students |
| Migler and Wolpe, 1967 | Male with fear of public speaking |
| Obler and Terwilliger, 1970 | Phobic neurologically impaired children |
| Paul, 1966 | College students with public speaking-anxiety |
| Paul, 1967 | College students with public speaking-anxiety |
| Paul, 1968 | College students with public speaking-anxiety |
| Paul and Shannon, 1966 | College students with public speaking-anxiety |
| Ritter, 1968 | Children with fear of snakes |
| Shrauger and Katkin, 1970 | Adults with marital and interpersonal fears |
| Suinn, 1968 | Test-anxious college students |
| Woody and Schauble, 1969a, 1969b | College students with fear of snakes |
| Zeissett, 1968 | Male neurotic and psychotic in-patients with anxiety |

Not only can therapist contact-time be kept to a minimum by auto-mated methodologies, but Kahn and Baker (1968) report a unique do-it-yourself form of systematic desensitization. Phobic patients were divided into two groups: one group received regular individual systematic desensitization sessions; each member of the other group received one interview for the construction of a hierarchy, a do-it-yourself desensitization manual, and a progress-check telephone call once a week. After six weeks of treatment, both approaches to systematic desensitization were successful, but more important, it appeared that the members of the second group made as much im-provement as those who had received one-to-one regular behavior-therapy sessions. While the Kahn and Baker (1968) study found support for self-administered desensitization, it should be noted that one follow-up study indicates self-administered desensitization has less long range effects than therapist-administered desensitization (Nolan, Mattis, and Holliday, 1970).

Systematic desensitization can also involve techniques designed to develop assertive behavior for the client. Much on the order of a desensitization hierarchy, assertive behaviors are cultivated by grad-ually learning progressively more assertive behaviors.

While being trained in assertive behavior, patients are told to keep careful notes of all their significant interpersonal encounters and to discuss them in detail with the therapist. It is necessary to know the circumstances of the encounter, the patient's feelings at the time, the manner in which he reacted, how he felt immediately after, and his subsequent appraisal of the situation. (Wolpe and Lazarus, 1966, p. 46)

On the basis of a knowledge of clinical ramifications, the counselor-therapist helps the client begin to learn new behaviors that will en-able him to cope more adequately with situations that in the past proved to be alarming, anxiety provoking, and constricting. After he has learned how to rid himself of anxiety, e.g., by becoming con-ditioned to some calm-restoring stimulus, such as the word "relax," or by using some diversionary action like flexing muscles or yawning, the client may proceed through an imaginary hierarchy of assertive behaviors. That is, he pictures himself being assertive, imagines or feels what it is like to behave that way, discusses it with the coun-selor-therapist, achieves insight into the dynamics of the situation, and tries it again, possibly with a modification in his coping be-

haviors—all in his imagination. After conquering the imaginary anxiety-evoking situation, he would start to act it out, each day trying
out his derived coping behaviors in real life situations. His counseling-
therapy sessions would then consist of discussing what he had experienced, deciding if he might have dealt with it better, and planning his next week's activities.

Assertive training is comparable to the technique called behavior rehearsal. Wolpe and Lazarus (1966) describe this technique
as follows:

Play-acting, or prescribed behavior, known as *behavior rehearsal,* is often
helpful. Where the patient's reaction pattern is considered deficient or inappropriate, he is required to re-enact the incident while the therapist
plays the role of the other person(s). The therapist may then switch roles
and act the part of the patient, sometimes presenting a deliberately over-
dramatized picture of assertion, thus affording the patient an opportunity
for learning adaptive responses by imitation. (p. 46)

Assertive training, especially that involving role-playing or behavior
rehearsal, is closely related to psychodrama. In fact, Sturm (1965)
calls it "behavioristic psychodrama." Despite the similarities, behaviorists claim the results of behavior rehearsal and assertive training are based strictly on conditioning, whereas psychodrama is viewed
by most counselors and psychotherapists as being a mode of facilitating insight. A psychobehavioral counselor-therapist would say that
the techniques involve both conditioning and insight, and would
accept them for their technical value, which appears to be great
(Lazarus, 1966a).

Closely related to assertive training and behavior rehearsal is the
idea that clients should progressively exercise more initiative in in-
stigating behaviors that will reduce their problems. Typically, there
is a point where any assertive behavior is beyond the volition of
the client; otherwise he probably would not have sought professional
treatment. For achieving self-assertive behaviors, it is helpful to use
a reinforcer. An experiment by Rehm and Marston (1968) provides
a suitable example of this process: members of a group of male college students with anxiety in social situations with females were
helped to increase the rate and accuracy of positive self-reinforcement via pursuit of assignments according to a hierarchy of related
situations. Another comparable group received nondirective therapy

(reflections and clarifications of feelings, but no suggestions), and a third (comparable) group received no therapy, but thought through their problems and reported weekly. The self-reinforcement group made the greatest improvement in terms of changes in anxiety, overt behavior, verbal output in a simulated social interactive situation, and test scores for anxiety and personality. This procedure reflects, of course, a form of self-desensitization. In practical terms, clients who are practicing assertive behaviors in their day-to-day activities can enhance their probabilities for success by making a self-imposed and self-enforced restriction that unless they accomplish the planned assertive behavior, they will not allow themselves some rewarding experience.

Systematic desensitization, with its related techniques, has been, for the most part, confined to behavior therapy. It seems, however, that, given adequate professional and personal preparation, counselors and psychotherapists should be able to use this treatment approach. Certainly the clients of counselors and psychotherapists present behaviors that are potentially modifiable by systematic desensitization.

## MODELING

Models have two primary roles in psychobehavioral counseling-therapy. Clients can be presented with a sample or "ideal" counseling-therapy interview in order to influence their behaviors when they begin treatment with a counselor-therapist. The second role is to use models to shape behaviors; just as the client might adopt the "ideal" client's behaviors, clients exposed to models performing a variety of out-of-treatment behaviors tend to modify their behaviors to conform to that of the models because of the consequences the models experienced. Although the modeling could be accomplished by having the clients actually observe others, it is usually done by presenting filmed or audio- or video-taped situations.

### Model Counseling-Therapy

Several of the behavioral counseling studies cited earlier in this chapter (see Table 2) employed a modeling technique in conjunction with the verbal conditioning. An audio-taped, video-taped, or filmed counseling-therapy session is presented to new clients for purposes of orienting them to what goes on in counseling-therapy; it exposes them to presumably typical behaviors of both the counselor-therapist and the client, and thereby gives them a frame of reference or a prefacing set that will influence their own behaviors when they actually start counseling-therapy. Most of the research supports the generalization that an appropriate social model, that is an "ideal" client, can be an effective means for beneficially influencing clients' behaviors once they enter counseling-therapy; this is applicable to both men and women (e.g., Hansen, Niland, and Zani, 1969; Krumboltz and Thoresen, 1964; Krumboltz, Varenhorst, and Thoresen, 1967; Myrick, 1969; Thoresen and Krumboltz, 1968). To cite but one example, Myrick (1969) conducted a study of junior high school boys and girls and found that those exposed to either an audio-tape or a video-tape recording of a model using a large number of self-reference responses made significantly greater numbers of self-reference responses in their own counseling sessions than did the control group who did not hear or view a tape recording; there was no significant difference between the video and audio groups, nor between the boys and the girls.

The personal characteristics of the model are important to the behavioral effects, whether it be cultivating ideal in-treatment behavior or shaping the behavior of children. Thoresen and Krumboltz (1968) found that the success level of peer social models was related to the degree of influence on information-seeking behaviors of eleventh-grade boys, that a high-success athletic-model was most effective, and that different levels of academic-models did not produce differences. Hansen, Niland, and Zani (1969) found that low-sociometric elementary school children who shared a group counseling experience with high-sociometric children made significantly greater gains in social acceptance than low-sociometric children sharing the same type of experience with a group of other low-sociometric children. It is interesting to note that, in accord with the psychobehavioral approach, the experimental counseling groups were reinforced by their counselors for ideas and insights, that suggestions relevant to acceptable social behaviors were given, and that these students made significantly greater therapeutic gains (i.e., increased social acceptance) than did students participating in a control-activities group. Further discussion on the characteristics of models can be found in Woody (1969). In general it seems that a model-reinforcement technique is most effective when the characteristics of the model provide the observer-client with a direct or vicarious benefit, e.g., associating with a high-status peer, and when the model's characteristics are fairly compatible with those of the observer-client, e.g., age and sex should be the same.

## Shaping Behaviors via Social Models

There seems little doubt that persons are influenced by what they learn from observing the behaviors of others. This kind of behavior shaping can be transferred to therapy by exposing the client to a hierarchic progression of models. In some ways, the process is similar to systematic desensitization. To shape a client's behavior, the counselor-therapist would expose him to a modeled behavior that is relatively close to his current behavior, with the difference in the direction of the desired therapeutic outcome. By viewing behavior that is slightly different from his own, and seeing the model rewarded for this behavior (whereas the model is not rewarded for behavior exactly like the client's current behavior), the client adopts the model's behavior. Next, he is exposed to another set of modeled behaviors, again slightly different from his own, and again in the desired direction of change. He adopts this behavior, and so on. The client's behavior progressively changes, having been shaped by modeled behaviors.[3] The modeling could be done live or could be recorded or filmed situations involving others with characteristics similar to those of the client. Some of the most notable research on

[3] It must be acknowledged that there is debate over the theoretical issue of whether imitation requires reinforcement. Some maintain that the seeds of imitation are sown if the observer simply views a model's behavior, i.e., that reinforcement is not necessary (Bandura and Walters, 1963); others believe that the observer must receive some form of direct or vicarious reinforcement if he is to imitate a model's behavior (Miller and Dollard, 1941), and there is evidence that when reinforcement for the observer-imitator is made contingent upon his imitating the model, the reward increases the imitative behavior (Flanders, 1968). For the clinical purposes of counseling-therapy, it would appear that the theoretical controversy can remain unresolved, and that practical applications should include planned reinforcers to both the models and the clients.

behavior shaping has been provided by Bandura and his colleagues (Bandura, 1965; Bandura and Walters, 1963). Flanders (1968) provides a review of relevant research.

As an example to clarify the procedure, children could be exposed to a film of children the same age playing in an activities room. One group of children might see a film in which the children (the models) splattered paint all over the activities room and were punished for it by the teacher. A second group of children might see a film in which the children (the models) also splattered paint but got no reaction from the teacher. Research would suggest that if each group of children were placed in a comparable activity room with paints, the first group would not splatter paint because their identification with the peer-models in the film would have shaped their behavior (they would have learned what the negative consequences would be), but the second group would probably identify with the peer-models in such a manner that they would splatter paint, knowing that their models had not been punished for such behavior. If children viewed a film of models' being rewarded for an alternative use of paints, it would be predicted that they perform the preferred painting act because of an expectation of receiving a reward as their models did. Walters and Parke (1964) conducted a study similar to this example in which just such results were found.

Modeling is a technique that could be used in isolation or in conjunction with other psychobehavioral procedures. It seems to accelerate other therapeutic processes, such as conventional insight counseling-psychotherapy, and seems especially appropriate for use with children. The main task is for the counselor-therapist to develop a hierarchy of experiences that will shape the client's behavior to gradually better or more acceptable forms.

## CLINICAL SUGGESTION AND HYPNOSIS

Extensive clinical and experimental research has amply documented that people can be influenced by suggestion; more specifically, clients can be beneficially influenced by clinical suggestions and hypnosis. No attempt will be made to teach these techniques, because they require much more rigorous attention than could be accommodated, but this section will provide an orientation to some of the most controversial, difficult to measure, yet clinically useful, techniques available to counselors and psychotherapists.

Aside from behavioral techniques, it has long been recognized that the role (and inherent status) of the counselor-therapist has effects in the therapeutic processes. For example, Frank (1961) emphasized that psychotherapists, essentially regardless of theoretical orientation, have ascendancy or power as a significant part of their therapeutic process. Other terms used to describe this phenomenon are "clinical persuasion" and "clinical suggestion," neither of which is "hypnotic" in the "induced trance" sense of the word. Truax, Fine, Moravec, and Millis (1968) found that clients seemed to make greater improvement if their therapists were high in persuasive potency. And it appeared that this persuasive quality operated somewhat independently of the other personal qualities of the therapist (e.g., accurate empathy and nonpossessive warmth). This sort of quality is one that is frequently not accounted for in research findings, and seldom gets direct cultivation in professional training programs. It is certainly more subtle than specific techniques, such as clinical suggestions, hypnosis, and relaxation training.

Persuasibility seems to operate within counseling-therapy, regardless of the theoretical position maintained by the counselor-therapist. Bednar (1970) has reviewed recent empirical and theoretical developments relevant to the persuasibility of clients in counseling and psychotherapy. After considering the research evidence on the concepts of susceptibility to persuasion, expectancies, and placebo reactivity, he concludes:

The client's heightened expectations for improvement, and his belief that he will improve, provide him with additional security and self-confidence and allow him to deal with his life situation more effectively. In brief, the client's resources for self-help are fully activated by a placebo reaction. The literature reviewed has indicated that (a) heightened client expectations for improvement are associated with client improvement; (b) client placebo reactivity is associated with client improvement; (c) some people are highly susceptible to persuasion; and (d) some improved clients become more like their counselors in the counseling process. (p. 651)

These findings would accommodate, according to Bednar, the fact that all of the divergent approaches to counseling, i.e., the different theoretical modalities, accurately report successful counseling cases. This point does not reflect on the validity of the counseling-therapy modality as much as on the persuasibility of the clients. It would, therefore, be important to the outcome efficacy for the counselor-therapist purposefully to instill in the client an expectation that he will improve as the result of the treatment. As will be noted shortly, behavior therapists do capitalize on the persuasibility of their clients, and this may well be the determining factor for the superior "cure" rates reported by behavior therapists as compared to those reported by psychotherapists.

As was mentioned in Chapter 1, there is reason to believe that suggestion may be present in the research and practice of behavior therapy. For example, when Klein, Dittmann, Parloff, and Gill (1969) observed the clinical behavior therapy practices of Wolpe and Lazarus, they noted:

Perhaps the most striking impression we came away with was of how much use behavior therapists make of suggestion and of how much the patient's expectations and attitudes are manipulated. Behavior therapists are not at all silent on this point in their descriptions of technique, but the literature did not prepare us for the unabashed suggestions that therapists directed toward their patients. The major arena for suggestion is in the orientation period of treatment. Here the therapist tells the patient at length about the power of the treatment method, pointing out that it has been successful with comparable patients and all but promising similar results for him, too. The patient is provided with a detailed learning-theory formulation of the etiology of his problems and is given a straightforward rationale for the way in which the specific treatment procedures will "remove" his symptoms. That patient's motives and values may also be considered so as to "correct misconceptions" which block desirable courses of action or restrict the effect of treatment. Indeed it seemed to us that treatment plans and goals were laid out in such a detail that the patient was taught precisely how things would proceed and what responses and changes were expected of him all along the way. (p. 262)

And they further state:

Although Wolpe and other behavior therapists are reluctant to ascribe therapeutic effectiveness to these features of the relationship it is difficult for us to believe that they do not constitute an important part of the treatment. Certainly the explicit, positive, and authoritative manner with which the therapist approaches the patients seems destined if not designed to establish the therapist as a powerful figure and turn the patient's hopes for success into concrete expectations. The introductory education in learning theory, in addition, must function to make the treatment more plausible and provide a simple and coherent frame of reference for the patient's understanding of his difficulty. Further, the focus of the treatment philosophy on the role of external psychonoxious environmental factors in the formation of the patient's problems must be quite reassuring for many patients. At the very least the therapist's evident willingness to assume major responsibility for correcting the patient's problems may be especially important in helping him overcome inertia and start on the path to change. (pp. 262–263)

These observations are totally compatible with ones made by this author, and add clinical evidence to the assertion made in Chapter 1 that the effects attributed to conditioning principles in behavior therapy research probably represent the effects of other unmeasured factors, such as suggestion. However, it should be emphasized that there does not seem to be any logical reason why a counselor-therapist should not capitalize on suggestion or persuasion or any proven therapeutic procedure or condition that can potentially contribute benefits to the client. But the point is that these kinds of factors are often incorporated into the effects attributed to insight counseling-psychotherapy and behavior therapy alike, and thus it is erroneous to claim validity for a particular technique or greater efficacy for one form of treatment over another when in actuality there is primarily contaminated evidence on which to base one's views.

Because induced relaxation is often used in conjunction with behavioral procedures, particularly systematic desensitization, training in behavior therapy necessitates development of skills for applying hypnotic techniques (Wolpe and Lazarus, 1966). Analysis of what occurs suggests that there is a continuum ranging from self-induced relaxation to the therapist-induced deep relaxation that is conducive to the so-called hypnotic phenomena. The hypnotic state can commence with any degree of relaxation, from very light to very deep. When it begins, the client relinquishes certain ego-oriented planning functions to the counselor-therapist, apparently being unable to be self-regulating at the moment (which is not necessarily true), and his attention is selected, redistributed, and refocused from its normal state; the client is more suggestible, will more easily adopt a role, may have amnesia for the events that occur during the hypnosis, usually has stronger visual memories and an improved ability for the production of fantasy, and may have limited reality-testing (Hilgard, 1965). These changes clearly illustrate why hypnotic conditions used by a skilled clinician might facilitate either behavior therapy or counseling-psychotherapy.

As is true with so many professional terms, there is some disagreement about what hypnosis actually is:

Hypnosis is above all subjective and is one of the many varieties of altered states of consciousness. It is both a state and a dynamic, multi-level relationship. It is a state to which multi-dimensional processes have contributed, as well as a dynamic relationship in which the subject is always aware of and in contact with the operator. More specifically, hypnosis can be characterized as being a change in reality-testing, which includes the "conviction" that the world as structured ("suggested") by the operator is "subjectively real rather than a pseudo-perception." (Conn, 1966, p. 10)

Erickson (1970), one of the pioneers in professional hypnosis in the United States, offers the following definition:

But what is hypnosis as we understand it scientifically today? It is certainly not physiological sleep, even though it may seem to resemble it, and may even be used to produce physiological sleep. It is not some special power or magic, nor is it some barbaric force arising from evil sources. It is, in simple terms, nothing more than a special state of conscious awareness in which certain chosen behavior of everyday life is manifested in a direct manner, usually with the aid of another person. But it is possible to be self-induced. Hypnosis is a special, but normal type of behavior, encountered when attention and the thinking processes are directed to the body of experiential learnings acquired from or achieved in the experiences of living. (p. 72)

And part of a definition by Kroger (1967) states:

No demarcation exists between suggestion and hypnosis; responses in the latter result from *selective attention to relevant signals with concomitant selective inattention to irrelevant ones.* (p. 15)

These three definitions indicate, for the purposes of this section, the key elements.

No discussion of definitions of hypnosis would be complete without consideration being given to the experimental research of Theodore X. Barber. He has been very prolific, yet has maintained a high scientific quality in an area that has often been treated with a degree of magical thinking; his extensive research is summarized elsewhere (Barber 1969a, 1969b, 1970). Basically, Barber has found that simply asking subjects to simulate so-called hypnotic phenomena (e.g., analgesia, hallucinations, age-regression, etc.) can produce results comparable to the more traditional approach of inducing a presumed "hypnotic trance." Further, he believes that the term "trance" is misleading, being erroneously burdened with a centuries-old accumulation of mythology, and that many of the effects attributed to hypnosis do not, in fact, exist. Although his position is disputed by many clinicians (such as those who assert that what is produced in the laboratory is not the same as what occurs in the clinical treatment room), Barber has built a seemingly strong empirical formulation for hypnosis.

While at first blush it might appear that there is a major clinical-versus-empirical schism that would negate a justifiable stance on the issue of hypnosis, close analysis of the diverse publications and conversations with professionals in the supposedly "opposing camps" readily reveal that there is still much more commonality than disagreement. The primary dispute is over the so-called "trance state."

After consideration of the research and clinical circumstances, it seems appropriate to state: Hypnosis refers to the state in which the client has achieved a degree of relaxation and confidence to allow him to relegate a limited command-of-ego functioning to the counselor-therapist, who alters his habituated behaviors, whether attitudinal or acting-out, by offering suggestions designed to benefit the client and derived from the counselor-therapist's clinical appraisal of the client's functioning and needs.

Clinical suggestion is a specific technique that is separate from, but related to, hypnosis. It is not hypnosis in and of itself; in other words, when a counselor-therapist makes a suggestion based on clinical evidence to his client, he is not practicing "hypnosis." Therefore, a counselor-therapist could make subtle, planned, clinically-derived suggestions, following the conditioning principles, as a means of modifying his client's behavior without fearing that he is practicing "black magic" or without opening himself to the misconceptions about highly-trained professionals who use hypnosis clinically. There is reason to believe that if these suggestions are offered to the client when he is relaxed, the effects might be enhanced. Thus, induced relaxation and clinical suggestions can be combined, and, if they are carried to a certain point on the continuum (which is different to each client), the procedure evolves into hypnosis. To work with a client at this depth, the counselor-therapist must be highly trained. The two primary professional societies that deal with hypnosis, the American Society of Clinical Hypnosis and the Society for Clinical and Experimental Hypnosis, require that their members hold a doctorate and have specialized training in hypnosis from an approved source. Likewise, some states have legal restrictions on the practice of "hypnotic techniques"; essentially they conform with the requirements of the societies.[4]

Clinical suggestions and hypnosis may be applied in several formats. One of the most common is to give the client direct suggestions while he is in an induced state of relaxation and presumably in a heightened state of suggestibility. There seems to be real therapist-phenomena attached to this approach. There are some therapists who are highly successful while others are not; it is likely that the characteristics of the therapist, such as his persuasibility, and the characteristics of the client contribute to the outcome. Another treatment approach is hypnoanalysis, in which psychoanalytic principles are applied within a psychotherapeutic relationship while the client is in a state of induced relaxation. A third format is one requiring the client to visualize clinically relevant scenes to facilitate insight, e.g., the client might be asked to visualize himself as a child, to re-experience what is believed to be a clinically significant situation, to discuss and interpret it, and to resolve its neurotic properties. What might be deemed a fourth approach is the use of a behavioral modification technique and the use of relaxation or suggestion or both to complement it. For example, while conducting systematic desensitization, the client, in a state of induced relaxation, would be asked to visualize an anxiety-provoking encounter; after experiencing the encounter, he would be calmed and told that the next time he visualized the scene he *would* be able to control his anxiety.

The value of suggestion as a supplement to behavior therapy should not be underestimated. Woody and Schauble (1969a, 1969b) videotaped a hierarchy of situations involving a fear-provoking stimulus (a harmless boa constrictor), and treated two experimental groups

[4]In 1969, the American Psychological Association inaugurated the Division of Psychological Hypnosis to deal with just such interests and problems.

by having them watch the video tape: Group I received induced (nonhypnotic) relaxation and clinical suggestions to facilitate desensitization (the suggestions were: you can relax more; you are becoming less anxious with each trial; you take pride in your ability to relax and lower anxiety; the next time you view the clip your anxiety will be significantly lower; your logical mind tells you that anxiety is unnecessary when snakes are known to be harmless; when encountering the snake again you will be able to walk right up to it with no anxiety); Group II received conventional desensitization, i.e., induced (nonhypnotic) relaxation, no suggestions, and pictured a pleasant scene after each anxiety-provoking viewing. These groups and a control group were exposed to the snake before and after the treatments; the control subjects did not, of course, receive any treatment. The results revealed that, while all three groups had significantly less anxiety on the post trial, the two experimental groups (Groups I and II) had a significantly greater decrease in their anxiety than the control group. Moreover, Group I, which had received clinical suggestions, had significantly greater change than Group II, which had only traditional desensitization. This study aptly demonstrates the value of clinical suggestions for enhancing behavioral procedures.

It should be reiterated that clinical hypnosis is endorsed only for the doctoral level, specially trained clinician. But there is no reason why relaxation (which is known to have definite value in lowering physiological elements of anxiety in and of itself) and clinical suggestions cannot be used by a professional counselor or therapist as part of his psychobehavioral armament. Wolpe and Lazarus (1966) discuss in greater detail the induction of relaxation, and Hartland (1967) presents the general principles of suggestion. It should be added that these techniques are not alien to insight-oriented counseling and psychotherapy; Woody and Herr (1965) found that clinical hypnosis was used by psychologists who ascribed to essentially every major theoretical approach to counseling and psychotherapy.

## STIMULATED RECALL

There are several techniques—both behavioral and insight in orientation—that involve stimulated recall. The objective of a stimulated recall technique is to prompt the client to remember, recall vividly, reexperience, or relive clinically significant events and feelings. Most approaches to counseling and psychotherapy view recall as being of critical importance to the quest for understanding of or insight into the psychological conflicts underlying the problems that lead a client into treatment.

Historically, the antecedent technique was catharsis, a psychoanalytic procedure for having the analysand, the client, think back over his life experiences and verbalize them. Hypnosis was soon added to facilitate catharsis; more specifically, suggestions were given to relaxed clients that they could recall events or situations that had been relegated to the unconscious. Hypnotic revivification, the imaginary reliving of actual events experienced by the client, and age regression, the role-playing of previous events in the context of the present, were both used by insight-oriented psychotherapists.

With the advent of technological changes, it was logical to adapt these principles to contemporary communication media. Stimulated recall has been accomplished by using films and audio- and video-tape recordings. Nielsen (1962) describes an early therapeutic use of filmed stimulated recall: he filmed stress-provoking situations involving his clients, and together the therapist and client viewed them and had "self-confrontations."

Audio- and video-tape recordings, which allow immediate playback, provide the basis for an improved approach. The Interpersonal Process Recall technique, developed by Professor Norman Kagan and his colleagues at Michigan State University, has evolved into a sound procedure for use in counseling and psychotherapy. The procedure is as follows: a regular counseling session, lasting perhaps for thirty minutes, is recorded on audio or video tape. Immediately following the counseling session, another counselor, called an "interrogator," replaces the first counselor, and he and the client replay the recording of the initial session. During the "interrogation" session, the second counselor and the client stop at any point in the tape that either thinks may be relevant (although the interrogator typically takes the initiative, the client usually becomes progressively more active) and they explore the possible meaning, covert or overt, of verbal comments, facial expressions, body movements, or gestures; in other words, the client analyzes what was happening both within himself and between him and the counselor. The procedure or methodology is described in greater detail elsewhere (Kagan, Krathwohl, and Miller, 1963; Kagan, Krathwohl, and Farquhar, 1965; Kagan and Krathwohl, 1967; Kagan, Schauble, Resnikoff, Danish, and Krathwohl, 1969; Woody, Krathwohl, Kagan, and Farquhar, 1965). Although there are many nuances to this extensive research project, the important point is that the Interpersonal Process Recall (IPR) technique has served to facilitate the training of counselors (the counselor trainees receive an IPR "interrogation" as a mode of supervision) and to accelerate counseling and psychotherapeutic processes with clients. Clients have been drawn from diverse samples, such as rehabilitation cases (Schauble, 1968), prisoners (Schauble, Kagan, and Resnikoff, 1968), high school and college students (Kagan, Krathwohl, and Farquhar, 1965; Kagan and Krathwohl, 1967; Woody, Krathwohl, Kagan, and Farquhar, 1965), and psychotic patients (Resnikoff, Kagan, and Schauble, 1970). Comparable techniques have focused on learning problems (Alger, 1969a) and marital conflicts (Alger and Hogan, 1967; Alger and Hogan, 1969).

Two supplemental procedures that have been developed are the use of confrontive vignettes and interrogations involving the counselor-therapist, client, and interrogator together. In regard to the first, professional actors have been filmed presenting scenes designed to stimulate intense degrees of feelings, e.g., hostility, affection, fear of hostility, and fear of affection; the objective is to confront the client with the sort of affect he needs to deal with, but which might not arise in regular counseling or psychotherapy for innumerable sessions. Exploratory research shows that this may be even more effective than the regular IPR procedure (Schauble, 1968; Kagan and Schauble, 1969). Interrogation involving the counselor-therapist, the client, and the interrogator, termed "mutual recall," appears to be more effective in some instances than the form of interrogation in which the counselor-therapist leaves the room. In mutual recall, the counselor (or therapist) remains, but is seated behind the interrogator, and the client as the two of them replay and analyze the recording; however, the interrogator gradually draws the counselor into the analysis, and eventually he moves to the rear, leaving the counselor and client with the primary responsibility for the interrogation (i.e., the analysis). The conclusions of the exploratory research on mutual recall are:

The Interpersonal Process Recall procedure provides the client with insights into his interpersonal behavior, but it is necessary that the counselor be able to integrate these insights into his ongoing relationship with the client if growth is to be accelerated. It would appear that the more competent counselors gain new understanding from studying the session between interrogator and his client, and gain less from taking part in the interrogation. The less competent therapists, on the other hand, may either not understand the dynamics uncovered in recall or may not be able to implement them, thus frustrating the client's new understandings—perhaps even retarding client growth. The less competent counselor becomes more effective with his client by participating directly with the client and an interrogator in the mutual recall session. (Schauble, Kagan, and Resnikoff, 1968, p. 14)

It seems that stimulated recall via audio- and video-tapes is a technique that, although needing further experimental refinement, is ready for calculated practical counseling-therapy service.

The Interpersonal Process Recall series of studies has been complemented by numerous related investigations. Alger (1969b) has described his approach to the therapeutic use of video-tape playback, and Berger (1970) has discussed the integration of video recordings into private psychiatric practice. From the published accounts, it seems that there are definitely more similarities than differences and that the basic IPR format is representative of the primary parameters of stimulated recall via audio- and video-tape recordings.

The consensus among professionals who have used recorded methods for stimulated recall appears to be that it is a "powerful" set of techniques and that carefully developed expertise is necessary for maximum effectiveness. Danet (1969) cautions against the effects of playbacks of audio- and video-tape recordings; specifically, in a group psychotherapy context, he found that such playbacks tended to have a "disrupting influence" and that the group members viewing playbacks of their sessions were "hampered in establishing itself as a productive, cohesive unit" (p. 632), as contrasted to a control (no playback) group. This kind of negative reaction seems, however, to be indicative of something other than the video-tape recording method per se; negative effects could most likely be attributed to an ill-advised decision to use the procedure with a given clinical type of client or at a point in the evolution of treatment (particularly in the group psychotherapy setting) that was premature because of psychodynamic processes (i.e., the client might not have been properly oriented to the procedure and might be focused on other psycho-dynamic issues, thereby resisting the video-tape playback), or a therapist who was not trained adequately in the use of recorded methods for stimulated recall could produce negative reactions (as would be true for almost any therapeutic technique that a poorly prepared therapist tried to use). What should be underscored is that techniques for stimulated recall via audio- and video-tape recordings are effective and must, therefore, be used by a professional who has been systematically prepared for the idiosyncratic aspects of this form of intervention.

Related to stimulated recall methods, media therapy has received an increasing amount of experimental and clinical attention. Media therapy involves the counselor-therapist serving as a facilitator or consultant, video recordings of brief social interactions, playbacks of the interactions for analysis, and practice of more effective coping behaviors. Clients are allowed to practice any behavioral skill until they have effectively mastered it. Obviously, this approach to treatment is quite similar to the IPR techniques, and it is essentially the same as microteaching or microcounseling; for example, see the description of the use of microcounseling as an approach to prepracticum counselor training (Ivey, Normington, Miller, Morrill, and Haase, 1968). Media therapy may be used as a sole treatment approach or as an adjunct to traditional counseling and psychotherapy. Higgins, Ivey, and Uhlemann (1970) compared media therapy as a sole treatment approach, the use of a programmed text and video models for target behaviors only, and reading materials only. They found that direct mutual communication was most improved by media therapy, with the programmed group being second in efficacy.

It should be noted that there might be some question as to whether stimulated recall techniques via audio- and video-recordings are behavioristic, since they unquestionably aim to facilitate insight. The IPR project defines the procedure as being insight-oriented, i.e., nonbehavioristic, but in the IPR procedure the interrogator has the prerogative of stopping the tape recording at points he believes are important, and he trains (conditions?) the clients to assume joint responsibility for stopping the tape. If reinforcement principles are applicable (and there is no reason to think they are not), the client wants to continue to receive the reinforcement from the interrogator, and so he quickly learns to pick up the kind of cues the interrogator prefers. The interrogator assumes responsibility for the processes; in a sense he prescribes what the counseling-therapy will consist of. The use of counselor-selected scenes to provoke affects prescribed as being important is definitely behavioristic; there is an element of programmed techniques. Certainly there is no objection to these activities, but they do illustrate how stimulated recall, even though its primary goal is to accelerate counseling-psychotherapy and facilitate insight, has properties of behaviorism. Obviously, the technique is quite compatible with the psychobehavioral frame of reference.

## COVERT SENSITIZATION

Covert sensitization, initially described by Cautela (1967), is designed to treat maladaptive approach responses; this includes obsessions, compulsions, homosexuality, alcoholism, and stealing, among others. Covert sensitization is explained as follows:

It is called "covert" because neither the undesirable stimulus nor the aversive stimulus is actually presented. These stimuli are presented in imagination only. The word "sensitization" is used because the purpose of the procedure is to build up an avoidance response to the undesirable stimulus. (Cautela, 1967, p. 459)

The client is trained to relax in essentially the same manner as when systematic desensitization, clinical suggestion, and hypnosis are used; he is then taught a signal system for nonverbally denoting when he experiences anxiety or other feelings and when he has clear images; a scene is then verbalized for him by the therapist. In the imagined scene, the therapist describes the client as beginning to engage in the behavioral act being treated, verbally leads him through precipitating activities, has him begin the undesirable act in his imagination, and then turns his verbal account into a description of how the client becomes disgusted, nauseated, and miserable as he is performing the imagined act; the therapist then allows calm and pleasant feelings to be restored, still in the imagination, but only when the client pictures himself escaping from and rejecting the undesirable act. Presumably, the relaxation and consequential heightened suggestibility of the client foster vivid images and keen sensing of the conjured sensations.

To take a practical example and paraphrase Cautela (1967): an alcoholic, after his relaxation training and induction, would be told to picture himself entering a tavern, approaching the bar, ordering a glass of beer, having the bartender place it in front of him, starting to pick it up, having it touch his lips, and then having a feeling of his stomach turning, the need to vomit, and finally puke coming up and out and all over himself, the bartender, and the man next to him. He is embarrassed, humiliated, and sick, so he flees from the bar, and as he leaves the clean air starts to make him feel better. The therapist uses numerous verbal skills to enhance the process; he tries to make the scene as vivid and realistic as possible, and also tries to make the undesirable act and its consequences as negative and the recovered feeling as positive as possible. It should be noted that there is strong reliance upon clinical suggestion, and it seems quite likely that hypnotic phenomena contribute to the effects.

Cautela (1967) reports successful use of covert sensitization for treating alcoholism, obesity, and homosexuality, and for counter-acting socially-offensive behaviors with juveniles. Ashem and Don-ner (1968), in a study of alcoholics, found that covert sensitization proved to be significantly better than no treatment for matched con-trols over a six months follow-up period, and termed it an effective short-term treatment for the modification of drinking behavior; 40 percent of those clients treated with covert sensitization were not drinking after six months, whereas all of the nontreated controls were still drinking. This is rather impressive in that clinicians cite alcoholics as among the most difficult clients to treat.

Although this technique has had only limited experimentation and clinical usage, its theoretical rationale and its therapeutic suc-cesses thus far make it a potentially valuable technique. Psychobe-havioral counselor-therapists would probably not want to use it as a sole treatment approach, but it could be incorporated into the psy-chobehavioral frame of reference like any of the other behavioral modification techniques. Further research is needed, however, be-fore its value can be estimated.

## IMPLOSIVE THERAPY

Implosive therapy is credited to Stampfl, but its first published description was made by London (1964). After a few years of relative dormancy, it has begun to receive considerable experimental interest and clinical usage.

Implosive therapy, because it incorporates formulations from psychodynamic systems into a learning-theory approach to treatment, is compatible with the rationale for psychobehavioral counseling and therapy. As with the psychobehavioral posture, implosive therapy theory maintains that the dynamically-oriented clinician can use conditioning techniques without relinquishing his fundamental psychodynamic conceptions of behavior and personality. The premise is that the human organism can be conditioned into responding to a previously neutral stimulus by pairing it with a noxious stimulus; this is a description of how an anxiety or fearful state develops, or, as Stampfl and Levis (1967a) state:

The fear or anxiety state functions as a motivator of behavior, and the reduction or elimination of the fear state serves as a reinforcer of behavior. If the tone is conditioned to produce fear, then any action taken which terminates the tone will be strengthened automatically. A danger signal paired with another neutral stimulus will transfer some of its fear-eliciting properties to the new neutral stimulus (higher-order conditioning). It is important, however, to note that the stimulus preceding noxious stimulation whether applied to subhuman or human fear conditioning ordinarily involves multiple-stimulus patterns sequentially organized in time. (p. 497)

The goal of implosive therapy is to promote extinction of anxiety-evoking conditioned stimuli (cues); these are the factors that provide motivation and reinforcement for the perpetuation of the client's behavioral problems or symptoms (avoidance responses).

The technical procedure is as follows. The counselor-therapist conducts two or three diagnostic interviews for the purpose of making a dynamic analysis of the problems, and from this information formulates hypotheses about what sorts of situations or stimuli provoke the anxiety relevant to the problem behaviors. It should be noted that additional information may be sought via interviewing at any time, and the hypotheses can be discarded or modified at any point that significant contradictory evidence becomes available. Following the derivation of hypotheses regarding anxiety-provoking cues, the counselor-therapist instructs the client in the implosive procedure: the client is asked to act out various scenes, which the therapist describes vividly to him, that involve the anxiety-inducing cues; in other words, the client is asked to portray feelings and emotions and, moreover, to experience them. The therapist typically becomes involved and dramatic, especially when describing or directing the scenes, and will most likely be assuming a role or part to complement the client's efforts. Stampfl and Levis (1967a) describe the therapeutic action as follows:

At each stage of the process an attempt is made by the therapist to attain a maximal level of anxiety evocation from the patient. When a high level of anxiety is achieved, the patient is held on this level until some sign of spontaneous reduction in the anxiety-inducing value of the cues appears (extinction). The process is repeated, and again, at the first sign of spontaneous reduction of fear, new variations are introduced to elicit an intense anxiety response. This procedure is continued until a significant diminution in anxiety has resulted. After a few repetitions of a particular scene, the patient is given an opportunity to act out the scene by himself. He is encouraged to verbalize his own role-playing behavior. Between sessions the patient is instructed to re-enact in his imagination the scenes which were presented during the treatment sessions. This homework provides additional extinction trials. As therapy progresses he is given more instructions on how to handle fearful situations through use of the implosive process. (p. 500)

It should be apparent that the counselor-therapist's activities, such as offering encouragement and instructions on how to cope with anxiety, could easily foster a therapeutic relationship, and this, as Stampfl acknowledges, aligns the implosive approach with psychotherapy. Parenthetically, Stampfl and Levis (1968) maintain that overall implosive therapy is primarily a behavior-therapy approach; the basis for this conclusion is the fact that it adheres to learning or conditioning models of symptom origin and modification.

The foregoing is admittedly a brief account of the theoretical rationale and techniques of implosive therapy. More extensive discussion is available elsewhere (Hogan, 1966, 1968; Levis, 1967; London, 1964; Stampfl, 1967; Stampfl and Levis, 1967a, 1967b, in press).

Evidence of the efficacy of implosive therapy still leaves many questions, but the compilation of data thus far provides the basis for encouragement. In a comparative study, Hogan and Kirchner (1968) assigned female college students with a fear of snakes to one of three treatments: implosive therapy, eclectic-verbal therapy, and bibliotherapy. There was a significant difference in success of implosive therapy over bibliotherapy, but there was no significant difference between implosive therapy and the eclectic-verbal therapy. Barrett (1969) found a comparable degree of efficacy for implosive therapy and systematic desensitization for the reduction of snake-phobic behavior; implosive therapy did, however, require less treatment time than systematic desensitization. Implosive therapy has been successfully used with psychoses (Hogan, 1966), learned fears (Hogan and Kirchner, 1967), and phobias (Stampfl and Levis, 1967b). To quote Stampfl and Levis (1967a):

It appears to be highly effective over a wide range of psychoneurotic disorders including anxiety, phobic, obsessive-compulsive, and depressive reactions and has been applied successfully to psychotic disorders including affective, schizophrenic, and paranoid reactions. It shows promise in the treatment of personality disorders including homosexuality, alcoholism, and speech disturbances. (p. 502)

To the prudent and judicious researcher, such all-encompassing claims may seem premature, but the initial evidence is certainly supportive. Further, Levis and Carrera (1967) found that short-term implosive therapy with out-patients led to a distinct shift from psychopathology, and that their progress was greater than that of controls, even those controls who were in or had been in psychotherapy, regardless of duration. Stampfl and Levis (1967a) state that the total treatment time for successful implosive therapy rarely exceeds 30 hours, and that marked changes are frequently found after from 1 to 15 one-hour sessions.

## AVERSIVE THERAPY

Aversive therapy employs unpleasant stimuli as both negative reinforcement and punishment. When the client performs the undesirable act, the aversive stimulus is administered and continues until the client stops doing the undesirable act. Thus, the reward comes when the aversive stimulus is stopped, i.e., when the problem behavior (the undesirable act) has stopped, and has been replaced by other, acceptable acts. The client is also conditioned to expect punishment when an unacceptable situation arises. The aversive stimulus is usually a mild electric shock, an unpleasant noise, or an emetic. (Note that the electric shock is very mild, and is not electroconvulsive therapy.)

To illustrate the technique, let us assume a young man is being treated for homosexuality. He is told what the procedure will be, and is then placed in a therapy room with a slide projector containing sexually stimulating pictures of nude or seminude men and women. Electrodes are attached to his wrist, and a picture is projected on the screen. If it is female, nothing happens, but if it is male, a mild electric shock would begin and would continue until he pressed a button to change the picture to that of a female. The electric shock would then be stopped, restoring calm and giving relief from the aversive stimulus. This example illustrates the differences between negative reinforcement and punishment. If a shock occurred each time a picture of a sexually seductive male was flashed on, regardless of how the client reacted, it would be punishing. If, on the other hand, the electric shock could only be eliminated by the client's taking action in the desired direction (substituting a picture of a sexually seductive female for the sexual male), negative reinforcement would be occurring. Note that punishment would condition the client to have a negative reaction whenever a picture of a seductive male was shown, while negative reinforcement would condition a redirection of his sexual response from men to women. Further, apparatus is available to measure psychophysically whether a picture is sexually stimulating; therefore, another approach could be to give the electric shock only when sexual arousal was measured for the target pictures (i.e., seductive males).

Aversive conditioning has been successful with a wide variety of behavioral disorders in both adults and children. Lovaas, Schaeffer, and Simmons (1965) used painful electric shock to modify behaviors of schizophrenic children, increasing the children's socialization with adults. The most successful use of aversive therapy has been in the treatment of sexual deviations. Aversion therapy seems effective with problems that prove difficult for other treatment approaches, most notably drug addiction and alcoholism (Vogler, Lunde, Johnson, and Martin, 1970; Wolpe, 1969). Marks (1968) summarizes the research in this area, and describes the methodology for using electric aversion for treating transvestites and fetishists. Rachman and Teasdale (1969) provide an authoritative text on aversion therapy.

Aversive stimuli have been used in conjunction with counseling and psychotherapy. Heckel, Wiggins, and Salzberg (1962) used unpleasant noise to eliminate the occurrence of extensive silence in group psychotherapy, Drennan and Wiggins (1964) increased verbal interaction in schizophrenic patients in group psychotherapy by having the therapist make negative (i.e., grossly hypercritical) comments. Both of these studies, and related ones, are described in more detail in Chapter 3 (see the "Group Counseling and Therapy" section). Woody (1969) reports a case in which unpleasant noise was used as part of the treatment: a teenage boy who would not respond to psychiatrists even to allow diagnostic evaluations, not to mention counseling or psychotherapy, was conditioned by aversive noise to respond verbally.

That aversive conditioning is effective for modifying behavior cannot be questioned, but what can be questioned is whether there are not better treatment modes. Perhaps the same behavioral changes could be achieved just as easily and adequately by a procedure that does not cause the client discomfort. This view is most applicable to those studies that use painful electric shock or emetic drugs. It would seem that the use of unpleasant but not painful stimuli, like noise, would be less susceptible to criticism on this basis. Although aversive techniques are adaptable to counseling and psychotherapy and to the problems that counseling-psychotherapy clients present, there are philosophical issues to confront before implementing them. Hypnosis and aversive therapy seem to be two behavioral techniques that will definitely require the professional user, regardless of competence, to make a special effort to gain philosophical accord between the techniques and the setting before making applications (Woody, 1966, 1969; Woody and Herr, 1966).

## NEGATIVE PRACTICE

Negative practice is based on the principle that continued repetition of an undesirable response will satiate the need for its occurrence and will thus extinguish it. Obviously, this position contradicts the general reinforcement position. When negative practice is used, the client, under the control of the counselor-therapist, repeats the unacceptable behavioral act over and over until he is bored, fatigued, and no longer getting any satisfaction from the act. Finally, the act takes on negative properties, and is extinguished from his repertoire of preferred behaviors.

Dunlap (1932) offered the initial description of the negative practice technique and recommended that it be used for stammering, tics, thumb-sucking, nail-biting, masturbation, and homosexuality. More recently, Lehner (1960) reviewed the research and described the application of negative practice. It should be noted that the act repeatedly practiced presumably does not have to be the exact problem behavior; it can be one that is similar or that is an approximation act. For example, one behavior therapist treated a girl who pulled out her hair by having her spend hours pulling strands from a ball of cotton with tweezers. In other words, generalization is supposed to occur. Negative practice has been successful with obsessive-compulsive disorders; in a review of the research, Woody (1969) cites successful treatment of writer's cramp, hysterical aphonia (loss of voice), tics, stuttering, learning difficulties, sexual deviations, and numerous other problem behaviors. In general, it seems that the client must be motivated to lose the problem, and that the behavior must be repeated until it is not satisfying—stopping before that point might reinforce it.

Related to negative practice, DiCaprio (1970) has described a technique termed "Verbal Satiation Therapy." The premise is that language symbols connote real objects and events and may produce emotional responses associated with the actual stimuli. Therefore, to eliminate adverse language symbols which could presumably trigger unpleasant feelings or unacceptable behavior, satiation procedures (e.g., verbal repetition, visual fixation, and auditory exposure) are used. Purportedly, this technique results in critical language symbols' being reduced to a neutral influence and in unwanted negative and positive emotions' being altered.

The published research for these techniques is meagre and scarcely constitutes an irrefutable basis for their use. And there have been therapeutic failures (which, of course, do not get published). Therefore, it would seem that psychobehavioral counselors and therapists should be aware of the negative practice technique and what it might be used for, but should keep it in an experimental framework. That is, negative practice should be viewed as a technique that might work with some clients for some problems, but which needs further research before it can unquestionably receive clinical acceptance.

## RELEVANT ISSUES

In considering the use of behavioral modification techniques, there are several issues that merit attention, namely: symptom substitution, treatment generalization to other problems, the use of nonprofessionals as reinforcers, and professional ethics and philosophy.

### Symptom Substitution

Counselors and psychotherapists who are opposed to behavior therapy claim that it is a superficial technique in that it modifies overt behaviors but does not eliminate the neurotic conflicts, and that the remaining conflicts will cause a new problem or symptom to appear. These critics believe that eliminating one symptom but not its causative factors will result in *symptom substitution*. Obviously this criticism reflects the disparate position regarding etiology, the learned maladaptive habit versus the underlying neurotic conflict.

Behaviorists reply that the objection is greatly exaggerated (Rachman, 1963; Lazarus, 1965). Their position is that if a maladaptive behavior is counterconditioned or unlearned, it will not appear again, nor will there be any substitution. When the behavior does appear again, or when a new problem behavior or symptom appears that might seem, by psychodynamic standards, to be related to the original behavior eliminated by behavior therapy, it is due to relearning. In other words, the same or a new problem could develop because the person had reentered the same kind of situations that had led him to adopt the initial problem behavior. He has, therefore, been reconditioned into the problem behavior; it is not that the behavior therapy was ineffective.

This explanation exemplifies why counseling and/or psychotherapy should accompany behavioral-modification techniques. Counseling-psychotherapy is the best means to help the person realize those elements of his life that reinforce undesirable behaviors and to help him evolve coping (counteracting) behaviors.

Symptom substitution seems to be less a real problem than a manifestation of theoretical differences. In fact, Grossberg (1964), in an extensive review of behavior therapy research, states:

The overwhelming evidence of the present review is that therapy directed at elimination of maladaptive behavior ("symptoms") is successful and long-lasting. (p. 83)

Grossberg goes on to criticize the insight approaches to treatment:

Unfortunately, psychotherapists seem to have stressed the hypothetical dangers of only curing the symptoms, while ignoring the very real dangers of the harm that is done by not curing them. (p. 83)

The research seems to confirm that some problem behaviors can be permanently eliminated by behavioral-modification techniques. The psychobehavioral position, however, would maintain that it is possible that some conditions are simply maladaptive habits but others may have a neurotic conflict as part of their etiology, and thus treatment for all clients should be extensive enough to allow the counselor-therapist to make a clinical judgment, via psychodynamic and behavioral-diagnostic techniques, on whether a behavioral approach is adequate as a primary treatment source or whether a continuation of insight counseling-psychotherapy is advisable.

### Treatment Generalization to Other Problems

The seemingly ill-founded concept of symptom substitution is closely related to the question: If a person receives behavior therapy for a specific problem behavior, is it possible that it would generalize to other problems? In other words, could other problems with related characteristics be modified without direct treatment? Basic learning theory affirms that such generalization is possible, at least to some degree. Conversations with both behavior therapists and psychotherapists frequently yield anecdotes of how a client's improvement in one behavior has resulted in improvement in another behavior, and how there might be a generalization effect. In most instances, the possibility of generalization is primarily conjecture, there being a lack of definitive connecting evidence.

The generalization issue has two sides. The negative side is exemplified by a female client who, when consulting about whether behavior therapy would be appropriate for her preoccupation with and sexual excitation from female breasts (which was interfering with her sexual relations with her husband and which was not accompanied by any overt lesbian behavior or tendencies), asked: "If I become desensitized to becoming sexually excited by female breasts, is it also possible I will become desensitized to becoming sexually excited by male genitals?" This kind of question is fair to ask (the client was a professional mental health worker and had read extensively on behavior therapy and psychotherapy). The answer, however, is that such deleterious generalization will not occur if the behavior therapist exercises proper clinical-technical expertise, but that faulty case handling might well result in negative side effects. Once more the need for professional competence is underscored, and is obviously predicated on a proper system of training. Parenthetically, the above client had her fears intensified because she had posed the question to an apparently inexperienced behavior therapist who was proposing to use aversive treatment; he neither answered her academically, nor counseled with her about her fears, but said simply "That's an irrelevant question." This ended the "therapeutic relationship" between them, and she sought treatment elsewhere. The important point in this situation is that part of the therapeutic process is dealing with the client's feelings about treatment, whether they be positive or negative, and this often involves both information-giving and counseling. In this brief anecdote, it is clearly illustrated that even in rather clearcut behavioral interventions, such as aversive conditioning (whether that was the most appropriate behavioral technique for the above case is open to debate), there is also a need for relationship and insight factors, i.e., psychobehaviorism.

The positive side to the generalization issue is whether a decrease in power for one anxiety-provoking stimulus will lead to a decrease in power for a related stimulus. Experimentation is beginning to support the conclusion that this may be true in actual clinical situations. The use of desensitization techniques for test-taking anxiety has led to significant decreases in general fears (Garlington and Cotler, 1968; Suinn, 1968), and desensitization of snake-anxiety led to significant reductions in behavioral and self-report responses to other anxiety-provoking stimuli (spiders) (Cotler and Garlington, 1969). Lanyon, Manosevitz, and Imber (1968) found that desensitization to fear of spiders led to a reduction in general fears; they also interpreted their results as providing evidence against the symptom-substitution issue.

## Nonprofessional Reinforcers

In this era of great demand for the services of professional mental health workers, it is important to note that certain behavioral modification techniques can be carried out by nonprofessionals. This does not mean that lay persons can practice behavior therapy; they cannot! But it does mean that a professional counselor-therapist can develop a treatment plan and can employ nonprofessionals, such as parents or teacher-aides, as technicians to provide reinforcement to the client. Object- and social-recognition rewards, and possibly some aspects of *in vivo* systematic desensitization, can be conducted by lay persons under proper professional supervision. Parents, undergraduate college students, and other lay persons have been successfully used as reinforcers for modifying the behaviors of problem children (Bernal, Duryee, Pruett, and Burns, 1968; Bijou, 1965; Davison, 1964; Russo, 1964; Straughan, 1964; Wahler and Erickson, 1969; Wahler, Winkel, Peterson, and Morrison, 1965; O'Leary, O'Leary, and Becker, 1967; Gardner, 1967). Peers and siblings can be powerful reinforcers too; for example, Harter and Zigler (1968) found that institutionalized retardates responded better to adult reinforcement than to peer reinforcement, but noninstitutionalized retardates reversed this result, with a peer being a more effective reinforcer than an adult. The main point is that the psychobehavioral counselor-therapist should try to make use of whoever can provide reinforcement for the behaviors being treated. If given proper supervision from the counselor-therapist, parents would be especially appropriate for helping reinforce the desired behaviors for their behavioral problem children; their involvement in the treatment should enhance the chances for therapeutic success and might even modify some of their own behaviors.

## Ethical and Philosophical Factors

In the early stages of behavior therapy, one of the primary concerns of professionals was: What are the ethical and philosophical factors unique to behavior therapy? The answer is simple: There are none. Counselor-therapists employing behavioral techniques are neither more nor less susceptible to unethical behavior than counselor-

therapists who use only insight procedures. All counselors and therapists are ethically obligated to be well-trained in whatever techniques
they may employ, and this obligation naturally means also having an
adequate theoretical background. Therefore, psychobehavioral counselors and therapists must have training sufficient to justify their using
the behavioral techniques; training will be elaborated upon in Chapters 4, 5, and 6.

Nonbehaviorists often point at the behaviorists and level a
charge of "violation of the value of individuality," "depriving man of
his right to be," "treating man like a machine that can be programmed."
These charges are totally false. Goldiamond (1965) asserts that much
of the alarm about behavioral modification is unjustified, and that it
results from a misunderstanding of advances in scientific knowledge
about behavioral control and the nature of behaviorism. If anything,
behaviorists are accused of the antithesis of what actually occurs. Behavioral techniques are used to help the client alleviate or eliminate
the exact problems for which he seeks treatment; the client is typically
fully informed as to what the treatment processes involve (can the
same be said for regular insight counseling-pschotherapy?); the so-
called "program" is always geared to the individual needs and feelings
of the given client; and the client's well-being supersedes all other factors. Morality, ethics, and values are of crucial importance to all mental health services (London, 1969). Certainly the psychobehavioral
counselor-therapist must maintain the strongest of ethical and moral
commitments at all times, and so should all of his counterparts who
practice within other theoretical-technical frameworks. Techniques
must serve the client and the counselor-therapist, not the opposite.
The innovative nature of behavioral techniques necessitates that considerable effort go into orienting both the lay and professional community to what the rationale, techniques, and objectives are; but there
is no reason to prescribe any degree of ethical or philosophical vulnerability to the use of such behavioral techniques by a properly quali-
fied professional.

## REFERENCES

Alger, I. Psychotherapeutic approaches to the problem learner: Audio-
visual feedback and therapeutic change. In *Professional School Psychology,
Volume III*. New York: Grune and Stratton, 1969, 302–317. (a)

Alger, I. Therapeutic use of videotape playback. *Journal of Nervous and Mental Disease*, 1969, *148*, 430–436. (b)

Alger, I., and Hogan, P. The use of videotape recordings in conjoint marital therapy. *American Journal of Psychiatry*, 1967, *123*, 1425–1430.

Alger, I., and Hogan, P. Enduring effects of videotape playback experience on family and marital relationships. *American Journal of Orthopsychiatry*, 1969, *39*, 86–93.

Ashem, Beatrice, and Donner, L. Covert sensitization with alcoholics: A controlled replication. *Behaviour Research and Therapy*, 1968, *6*, 7–12.

Bandura, A. Behavioral modification through modeling procedures. In L. Krasner and L. P. Ullmann (Eds.), *Research in behavior modification*. New York: Holt, Rinehart and Winston, 1965, 310–340.

Bandura, A., and Walters, R. H. *Social learning and personality development*. New York: Holt, Rinehart and Winston, 1963.

Barber, T. X. An empirically-based formulation of hypnotism. *American Journal of Clinical Hypnosis*, 1969, *12*, 100–130. (a)

Barber, T. X. *Hypnosis: A scientific approach*. New York: Van Nostrand Reinhold, 1969. (b)

Barber, T. X. *LSD, marihuana, yoga and hypnosis*. Chicago: Aldine, 1970.

Barclay, J. R. Effecting behavior change in the elementary classroom: An exploratory study. *Journal of Counseling Psychology*, 1967, *14*, 240–247.

Barrett, C. L. Systematic desensitization versus implosive therapy. *Journal of Abnormal Psychology*, 1969, *74*, 587–592.

Bednar, R. L. Persuasibility and the power of belief. *Personnel and Guidance Journal*, 1970, *48*, 647–652.

Berger, M. M. Integrating video into private psychiatric practice. *Voices: The Art and Science of Psychotherapy*, 1970, *5*, 78–85.

Bernal, Martha E., Duryee, J. S., Pruett, H. L., and Burns, Beverlee J. Behavior modification and the brat syndrome. *Journal of Consulting and Clinical Psychology*, 1968, *32*, 447–455.

Bijou, S. W. Experimental studies of child behavior, normal and deviant. In L. Krasner and L. P. Ullmann (Eds.), *Research in behavior modification*. New York: Holt, Rinehart and Winston, 1965, 56–81.

Binder, A., McConnell, D., and Sjoholm, Nancy A. Verbal conditioning as a function of experimenter characteristics. *Journal of Abnormal and Social Psychology*, 1957, *55*, 309–314.

Birnbrauer, J. S., Wolf, M. M., Kidder, J. D., and Tague, Cecilia E. Classroom behavior of retarded pupils with token reinforcement. *Journal of Experimental Child Psychology*, 1965, *2*, 219–235.

Brison, D. W. A non-talking child in kindergarten: An application of behavior therapy. *Journal of School Psychology*, 1966, *4*, 65–69.

Brown, P., and Elliott, R. Control of aggression in a nursery school class. *Journal of Experimental Child Psychology,* 1965, *2,* 103–107.

Browning, R. M. Behavior therapy for stuttering in a schizophrenic child. *Behaviour Research and Therapy,* 1967, *5,* 27–35.

Bryan, J. H., and Kapche, R. Psychopathy and verbal conditioning. *Journal of Abnormal Psychology,* 1967, *72,* 71–73.

Cautela, J. R. Covert sensitization. *Psychological Reports,* 1967, *20,* 459–468.

Conn, J. H. Wanted: Definitions of hypnosis! *Newsletter of the Society for Clinical and Experimental Hypnosis,* 1966, *8,* 10.

Cooper, J. E., Gelder, M. G., and Marks, I. M. Results of behaviour therapy in 77 psychiatric patients. *British Medical Journal,* 1965, *1,* 1222–1225.

Cotler, S. B., and Garlington, W. K. The generalization of anxiety reduction following systematic desensitization of snake anxiety. *Behaviour Research and Therapy,* 1969, *7,* 35–40.

Danet, B. N. Impact of audio-visual feedback on group psychotherapy. *Journal of Consulting and Clinical Psychology,* 1969, *33,* 632.

Davison, G. C. A social learning theory programme with an autistic child. *Behaviour Research and Therapy,* 1964, *2,* 149–159.

Davison, G. C. Systematic desensitization as a counterconditioning process. *Journal of Abnormal Psychology,* 1968, *73,* 91–99.

Denner, B. Etiquette of verbal conditioning. *Journal of Consulting and Clinical Psychology,* 1970, *34,* 80–85.

DiCaprio, N. S. Essentials of verbal satiation therapy: A learning-theory-based behavior therapy. *Journal of Counseling Psychology,* 1970, *17,* 419–424.

Dicken, C., and Fordham, M. Effects of reinforcement of self-references in quasi-therapeutic interviews. *Journal of Counseling Psychology,* 1967, *14,* 145–152.

Doubros, S. G. An invesigation of verbal conditioning in level II adolescent retardates. *American Journal of Mental Deficiency,* 1967, *71,* 806–810.

Drennen, W., Gallman, W. and Sausser, G. Verbal operant conditioning of hospitalized psychiatric patients. *Journal of Abnormal Psychology,* 1969, *74,* 454–458.

Drennen, W. T., and Wiggins, S. L. Manipulation of verbal behavior of chronic hospitalized schizophrenics in a group therapy situation. *International Journal of Group Psychotherapy,* 1964, *14,* 189–193.

Dubner, Mary Ann. The effects of audio-taped relaxation with suggestion on the reduction of test anxiety. Unpublished masters thesis, University of Maryland, 1969.

Dunlap, K. *Habits, their making and unmaking.* New York: Liveright, 1932.

Emery, J. R., and Krumboltz, J. D. Standard versus individualized hierarchies in desensitization to reduce test anxiety. *Journal of Counseling Psychology*, 1967, *14*, 204–209.

Erickson, M. H. Hypnosis: Its renascence as a treatment modality. *American Journal of Clinical Hypnosis*, 1970, *13*, 71–89.

Eysenck, H. J., and Rachman, S. *The causes and cures of neurosis*. San Diego: R. R. Knapp, 1965.

Flanders, J. P. A review of research on imitative behavior. *Psychological Bulletin*, 1968, *69*, 316–337.

Folkins, C. H., Lawson, Karen D., Opton, E. M., Jr., and Lazarus, R. S. Desensitization and the experimental reduction of threat. *Journal of Abnormal Psychology*, 1968, *73*, 100–113.

Frank, J. D. *Persuasion and healing*. Baltimore: Johns Hopkins Press, 1961.

Gardner, J. E. Behavior therapy treatment approach to a psychogenic seizure case. *Journal of Consulting Psychology*, 1967, *31*, 209–212.

Garlington, W. K., and Cotler, S. B. Systematic desensitization of test anxiety. *Behaviour Research and Therapy*, 1968, *6*, 247–256.

Goldiamond, I. Justified and unjustified alarm over behavioral control. In O. Milton (Ed.), *Behavior disorders: Perspectives and trends*. New York: Lippincott, 1965, 237–262.

Goodlet, G. R., Goodlet, Margaret M., and Dredge, Karen. Modification of disruptive behavior of two young children and follow-up one year later. *Journal of School Psychology*, 1970, *8*, 60–63.

Greenspoon, J. The effect of verbal and non-verbal stimuli on the frequency of members of two verbal response classes. Unpublished doctoral dissertation, Indiana University, 1951.

Greenspoon, J. The reinforcing effect of two spoken sounds on the frequency of two responses. *American Journal of Psychology*, 1955, *68*, 409–416.

Grieger, R. M., II. Behavior modification with a total class: A case report. *Journal of School Psychology*, 1970, *8*, 103–106.

Grossberg, J. M. Behavior therapy: A review. *Psychological Bulletin*, 1964, *62*, 73–88.

Hansen, J. C., Niland, T. M., and Zani, L. P. Model reinforcement in group counseling with elementary school children. *Personnel and Guidance Journal*, 1969, *47*, 741–744.

Harter, Susan, and Zigler, E. Effectiveness of adult and peer reinforcement on the performance of institutionalized and noninstitutionalized retardates. *Journal of Abnormal Psychology*, 1968, *73*, 144–149.

Hartland, J. The general principles of suggestion. *American Journal of Clinical Hypnosis*, 1967, *9*, 211–219.

Heckel, R. V., Wiggins, S. L., and Salzberg, H. C. Conditioning against silences in group therapy. *Journal of Clinical Psychology*, 1962, *28*, 216–217.

Higgins, W. H., Ivey, A. E., and Uhlemann, M. R. Media therapy: A programmed approach to teaching behavioral skills. *Journal of Counseling Psychology*, 1970, *17*, 20–26.

Hildum, D. C., and Brown, R. W. Verbal reinforcement and interviewer bias. *Journal of Abnormal and Social Psychology*, 1956, *53*, 108–111.

Hilgard, E. R. *Hypnotic susceptibility*. New York: Harcourt, Brace and World, 1965.

Hogan, R. A. Implosive therapy in the short term treatment of psychotics. *Psychotherapy: Theory, Research and Practice*, 1966, *3*, 25–32.

Hogan, R. A. The implosive technique. *Behaviour Research and Therapy*, 1968, *6*, 423–431.

Hogan, R. A., and Kirchner, J. H. Preliminary report of the extinction of learned fears via short-term implosive therapy. *Journal of Abnormal Psychology*, 1967, *72*, 106–109.

Hogan, R. A., and Kirchner, J. H. Implosive, eclectic verbal and bibliotherapy in the treatment of fears of snakes. *Behaviour Research and Therapy*, 1968, *6*, 167–171.

Hosford, R. E. Behavioral counseling—A contemporary overview. *Counseling Psychologist*, 1969, *1* (4), 1–33.

Hudson, Elizabeth, and DeMyer, Marian K. Food as a reinforcer in educational therapy of autistic children. *Behaviour Research and Therapy*, 1968, *6*, 37–43.

Hundziak, M., Maurer, Ruth A., and Watson, L. S., Jr. Operant conditioning in toilet training of severely mentally retarded boys. *American Journal of Mental Deficiency*, 1965, *70*, 120–124.

Ince, L. P. Effects of fixed-interval reinforcement on the frequency of a verbal response class in a quasi-counseling situation. *Journal of Counseling Psychology*, 1968, *15*, 140–146.

Ivey, A. E., Normington, Cheryl J., Miller, C. D., Morrill, W. H., and Haase, R. F. Microcounseling and attending behavior: An approach to prepracticum counselor training. *Journal of Counseling Psychology*, 1968, *15* (Pt. 2), 1–12.

Jacobson, E. *Progressive relaxation*. Chicago: University of Chicago Press, 1938.

Johnson, C. L., Jr. The transfer effect of treatment group composition on pupils' classroom participation. Unpublished doctoral dissertation, Stanford University, 1964.

Kagan, N., and Krathwohl, D. R. *Studies in human interaction: Interpersonal process recall stimulated by videotape*. East Lansing, Mich.: Educational Publication Services, Michigan State University, 1967.

Kagan, N., Krathwohl, D. R., and Farquhar, W. W. *IPR—Interpersonal process recall: Stimulated recall by videotape in exploratory studies of counseling and teaching-learning.* Educational Research Series, No. 24. East Lansing, Mich.: Michigan State University, 1965.

Kagan, N., Krathwohl, D. R., and Miller, R. Stimulated recall in therapy using video tape—A case study. *Journal of Counseling Psychology,* 1963, *10,* 237–243.

Kagan, N., and Schauble, P. G. Affect simulation in interpersonal process recall. *Journal of Counseling Psychology,* 1969, *16,* 309–313.

Kagan, N., Schauble, P., Resnikoff, A., Danish, S. J., and Krathwohl, D. R. Interpersonal process recall. *Journal of Nervous and Mental Disease,* 1969, *148,* 365–374.

Kahn, M., and Baker, B. Desensitization with minimal therapist contact. *Journal of Abnormal Psychology,* 1968, *73,* 198–200.

Katahn, M., Strenger, S., and Cherry, Nancy. Group counseling and behavior therapy with test-anxious college students. *Journal of Consulting Psychology,* 1966, *30,* 544–549.

Klein, Marjorie H., Dittmann, A. T., Parloff, M. B., and Gill, M. M. Behavior therapy: Observations and reflections. *Journal of Consulting and Clinical Psychology,* 1969, *33,* 259–266.

Kramer, H. C. Effects of conditioning several responses in a group setting. *Journal of Counseling Psychology,* 1968, *15,* 58–62.

Krapfl, J. E., and Nawas, M. M. Client-therapist relationship factor in systematic desensitization. *Journal of Consulting and Clinical Psychology,* 1969, *33,* 435–439.

Krapfl, J. E., and Nawas, M. M. Differential ordering of stimulus presentation in systematic desensitization. *Journal of Abnormal Psychology,* 1970, *75,* 333–337.

Krasner, L. Verbal conditioning and psychotherapy. In L. Krasner and L. P. Ullmann (Eds.), *Research in behavior modification.* New York: Holt, Rinehart and Winston, 1965, 211–228.

Kroger, W. S. Wanted: Definitions of hypnosis! *Newsletter of the Society for Clinical and Experimental Hypnosis,* 1967, *8,* 15.

Krumboltz, J. D., and Schroeder, W. W. Promoting career planning through reinforcement. *Personnel and Guidance Journal,* 1965, *44,* 19–26.

Krumboltz, J. D., and Thoresen, C. E. The effect of behavioral counseling in group and individual settings on information-seeking behavior. *Journal of Counseling Psychology,* 1964, *11,* 324–333.

Krumboltz, J. D., Varenhorst, Barbara B., and Thoresen, C. E. Nonverbal factors in the effectiveness of models in counseling. *Journal of Counseling Psychology,* 1967, *14,* 412–418.

Lanyon, R. I. Verbal conditioning: Transfer of training in a therapy-like situation. *Journal of Abnormal Psychology,* 1967, *72,* 30–34.

Lanyon, R. I., Manosevitz, M., and Imber, Ruth R. Systematic desensitization: Distribution of practice and symptom substitution. *Behaviour Research and Therapy*, 1968, *6*, 323–329.

Laxer, R. M., Quarter, J., Kooman, Ann, and Walker, K. Systematic desensitization and relaxation of high-test-anxious secondary school students. *Journal of Counseling Psychology*, 1969, *16*, 446–451.

Laxer, R. M., and Walker, K. Counterconditioning versus relaxation in the desensitization of test anxiety. *Journal of Counseling Psychology*, 1970, *17*, 431–436.

Lazarus, A. A. Group therapy of phobic disorders by systematic desensitization. *Journal of Abnormal and Social Psychology*, 1961, *63*, 504–510.

Lazarus, A. A. The results of behaviour therapy in 126 cases of severe neurosis. *Behaviour Research and Therapy*, 1963, *1*, 69–79.

Lazarus, A. A. Behavior therapy, incomplete treatment, and symptom substitution. *Journal of Nervous and Mental Disease*, 1965, *140*, 80–86.

Lazarus, A. A. Behaviour rehearsal vs. non-directive therapy vs. advice in effecting behaviour change. *Behaviour Research and Therapy*, 1966, *4*, 209–212. (a)

Lazarus, A. A. Broad-spectrum behaviour therapy and the treatment of agoraphobia. *Behaviour Research and Therapy*, 1966, *4*, 95–97. (b)

Lazarus, A. A., and Abramovitz, A. The use of "emotive imagery" in the treatment of children's phobias. *Journal of Mental Science*, 1962, *108*, 191–195.

Lazarus, A. A., Davison, G. C., and Polefka, D. A. Classical and operant factors in the treatment of a school phobia. *Journal of Abnormal Psychology*, 1965, *70*, 225–229.

Lehner, G. F. J. Negative practice as a psychotherapeutic technique. In H. J. Eysenck (Ed.), *Behaviour therapy and the neuroses*. New York: Pergamon, 1960, 194–206.

Leitenberg, H., Agras, W. S., Barlow, D. H., and Oliveau, D. C. Contribution of selective positive reinforcement and therapeutic instructions to systematic desensitization therapy. *Journal of Abnormal Psychology*, 1969, *74*, 113–118.

Levis, D. J. Implosive therapy: Part II. The subhuman analogue, the strategy, and the technique. In S. G. Armitage (Ed.), *Behavior modification techniques in the treatment of emotional disorders*. Battle Creek, Mich.: Veterans Administration Publication, 1967, 22–37.

Levis, D. J., and Carrera, R. Effects of ten hours of implosive therapy in the treatment of outpatients: A preliminary report. *Journal of Abnormal Psychology*, 1967, *72*, 504–508.

Lomont, J. F., and Edwards, J. E. The role of relaxation in systematic desensitization. *Behaviour Research and Therapy*, 1967, *5*, 11–25.

London, P. *The modes and morals of psychotherapy*. New York: Holt, Rinehart and Winston, 1964.

London, P. Morals and mental health. In S. C. Plog and R. B. Edgerton (Eds.), *Changing perspectives in mental illness.* New York: Holt, Rinehart and Winston, 1969, 32–48.

Lovaas, O. I., Schaeffer, B., and Simmons, J. Q. Building social behavior in autistic children by use of electric shock. *Journal of Experimental Research in Personality,* 1965, *1,* 99–109.

Marcia, J. E., Rubin, B. M., and Efran, J. S. Systematic desensitization: Expectancy change or counterconditioning? *Journal of Abnormal Psychology,* 1969, *74,* 382–387.

Marks, I. M. Aversion therapy. *British Journal of Medical Psychology,* 1968, *41,* 47–52.

McFall, R. M., and Marston, A. R. An experimental investigation of behavior rehearsal in assertive training. *Journal of Abnormal Psychology,* 1970, *76,* 295–303.

McInnis, T. L., and Ullmann, L. P. Positive and negative reinforcement with short- and long-term hospitalized schizophrenics in a probability learning situation. *Journal of Abnormal Psychology,* 1967, *72,* 157–162.

McKerracher, D. W. Alleviation of reading difficulties by a simple operant conditioning technique. *Journal of Child Psychology and Psychiatry,* 1967, *8,* 51–56.

McReynolds, W. T. A note on relaxation treatment groups in studies of systematic desensitization. *Journal of Abnormal Psychology,* 1969, *74,* 561–562.

Meyer, J. B., Strowig, W., and Hosford, R. E. Behavioral-reinforcement counseling with rural high school youth. *Journal of Counseling Psychology,* 1970, *17,* 127–132.

Migler, B., and Wolpe, J. Automated self-desensitization: A case report. *Behaviour Research and Therapy,* 1967, *5,* 133–135.

Miller, L. K. A note on the control of study behavior. *Journal of Experimental Child Psychology,* 1964, *1,* 108–110.

Miller, N. E., and Dollard, J. *Social learning and imitation.* New Haven: Yale University Press, 1941.

Murray, E. J. A content-analysis method for studying psychotherapy. *Psychological Monographs,* 1956, *70* (13, Whole No. 420).

Myrick, R. D. Effect of a model on verbal behavior in counseling. *Journal of Counseling Psychology,* 1969, *16,* 185–190.

Nielsen, G. *Studies in self confrontation.* Copenhagen, Denmark: Munksgaard, 1962.

Nolan, J. D., Mattis, P. R., and Holliday, W. C. Long-term effects of behavior therapy: A 12-month follow-up. *Journal of Abnormal Psychology,* 1970, *76,* 88–92.

Obler, M., and Terwilliger, R. F. Pilot study of the effectiveness of systematic desensitization with neurologically impaired children with phobic disorders. *Journal of Consulting and Clinical Psychology*, 1970, *34*, 314–318.

O'Leary, K. D., O'Leary, Susan, and Becker, W. C. Modification of a deviant sibling interaction pattern in the home. *Behaviour Research and Therapy*, 1967, *5*, 113–120.

Patterson, G. R. A learning theory approach to the treatment of the school phobic child. In L. P. Ullmann and L. Krasner (Eds.), *Case studies in behavior modification*. New York: Holt, Rinehart and Winston, 1965, 279–285.

Patterson, G. R., Jones, R., Whittier, J., and Wright, Mary A. A behaviour modification technique for the hyperactive child. *Behaviour Research and Therapy*, 1965, *2*, 217–226.

Paul, G. L. *Insight vs. desensitization in psychotherapy: An experiment in anxiety reduction*. Stanford, Calif.: Stanford University Press, 1966.

Paul, G. L. Insight versus desensitization in psychotherapy two years after termination. *Journal of Consulting Psychology*, 1967, *31*, 333–348.

Paul, G. L. Two-year follow-up of systematic desensitization in therapy groups. *Journal of Abnormal Psychology*, 1968, *73*, 119–130.

Paul, G. L., and Shannon, D. T. Treatment of anxiety through systematic desensitization in therapy groups. *Journal of Abnormal Psychology*, 1966, *71*, 124–135.

Rachman, S. Introduction to behaviour therapy. *Behaviour Research and Therapy*, 1963, *1*, 3–15.

Rachman, S. The role of muscular relaxation in desensitization therapy. *Behaviour Research and Therapy*, 1968, *6*, 159–166.

Rachman, S., and Teasdale, J. *Aversion therapy and behaviour disorders: An analysis*. Coral Gables, Fla.: University of Miami Press, 1969.

Rehm, Lynn P., and Marston, A. R. Reduction of social anxiety through modification of self-reinforcement: An instigation therapy technique. *Journal of Consulting and Clinical Psychology*, 1968, *32*, 565–574.

Resnikoff, A., Kagan, N., and Schauble, P. G. Innovative techniques in psychotherapy—Interpersonal process recall: A case study. *American Journal of Psychotherapy*, 1970, *24*, 102–111.

Ritter, Brunhilde. The group desensitization of children's snake phobias using vicarious and contact desensitization procedures. *Behaviour Research and Therapy*, 1968, *6*, 1–6.

Rogers, J. M. Operant conditioning in a quasi-therapy setting. *Journal of Abnormal and Social Psychology*, 1960, *60*, 247–252.

Rosenthal, R. Covert communication in the psychological experiment. *Psychological Bulletin*, 1967, *67*, 356–367.

Russo, S. Adaptations in behavioural therapy with children. *Behaviour Research and Therapy*, 1964, *2*, 43–47.

Ryan, T. Antoinette, and Krumboltz, J. D. Effect of planned reinforcement counseling on client decision-making behavior. *Journal of Counseling Psychology*, 1964, *11*, 315–323.

Sapolsky, A. Effect of interpersonal relationships upon verbal conditioning. *Journal of Abnormal and Social Psychology*, 1960, *60*, 241–246.

Schauble, P. G. Emotional simulation in personal counseling: An application of research innovations in counseling to accelerate client movement. Paper presented at the American Personnel and Guidance Association Convention, Detroit, 1968.

Schauble, P. G., Kagan, N., and Resnikoff, A. Stimulated recall in the acceleration of client growth. Unpublished manuscript, Michigan State University, 1968.

Schwitzgebel, R. L. Short-term operant conditioning of adolescent offenders on socially relevant variables. *Journal of Abnormal Psychology*, 1967, *72*, 134–142.

Schwitzgebel, R. L. A survey of electromechanical devices for behavior modification. *Psychological Bulletin*, 1968, *70*, 444–459.

Schwitzgebel, R. L. Behavior instrumentation and social technology. *American Psychologist*, 1970, *25*, 491–499.

Schwitzgebel, R., and Kolb, D. A. Inducing behaviour change in adolescent delinquents. *Behaviour Research and Therapy*, 1964, *1*, 297–304.

Shore, M. F., and Massimo, J. L. Verbalization, stimulus relevance, and personality change. *Journal of Consulting Psychology*, 1967, *31*, 423–424.

Shrauger, J. S., and Katkin, E. S. The use of nonspecific underlying motivational factors in the systematic desensitization of specific marital and interpersonal fears: A case study. *Journal of Abnormal Psychology*, 1970, *75*, 221–226.

Stampfl, T. G. Implosive therapy: The theory, the subhuman analogue, the strategy, and the technique. In S. G. Armitage (Ed.), *Behavior modification techniques in the treatment of emotional disorders*. Battle Creek, Mich.: Veterans Administration Publication, 1967, 12–21.

Stampfl, T. G., and Levis, D. J. Essentials of implosive therapy: A learning-theory based psychodynamic behavioral therapy. *Journal of Abnormal Psychology*, 1967, *72*, 496–503. (a)

Stampfl, T. G., and Levis, D. J. Phobic patients: Treatment with the learning theory approach of implosive therapy. *Voices: The Art and Science of Psychotherapy*, 1967, *3*, 23–27. (b)

Stampfl, T. G., and Levis, D. J. Implosive therapy—A behavioral therapy? *Behaviour Research and Therapy*, 1968, *6*, 31–36.

Stampfl, T. G., and Levis, D. J. Implosive therapy. In R. M. Jurjevich (Ed.), *Handbook of direct and behavior psychotherapies*, in press.

Straughan, J. H. Treatment with child and mother in the playroom. *Behaviour Research and Therapy*, 1964, *2*, 37–41.

Sturm, I. E. The behavioristic aspect of psychodrama. *Group Psychotherapy*, 1965, *18*, 50–64.

Suinn, R. M. The desensitization of test-anxiety by group and individual treatment. *Behaviour Research and Therapy*, 1968, *6*, 385–387.

Thoresen, C. E., and Krumboltz, J. D. Relationship of counselor reinforcement of selected responses to external behavior. *Journal of Counseling Psychology*, 1967, *14*, 140–144.

Thoresen, C. E., and Krumboltz, J. D. Similarity of social models and clients in behavioral counseling: Two experimental studies. *Journal of Counseling Psychology*, 1968, *15*, 393–401.

Thoresen, C. E., Krumboltz, J. D., and Varenhorst, Barbara. Sex of counselors and models: Effects on client career exploration. *Journal of Counseling Psychology*, 1967, *14*, 503–508.

Truax, C. B. Reinforcement and nonreinforcement in Rogerian psychotherapy. *Journal of Abnormal Psychology*, 1966, *71*, 1–9. (a)

Truax, C. B. Some implications of behavior therapy for psychotherapy. *Journal of Counseling Psychology*, 1966, *13*, 160–170. (b)

Truax, C. B. Therapist interpersonal reinforcement of client self-exploration and therapeutic outcome in group psychotherapy. *Journal of Counseling Psychology*, 1968, *15*, 225–231.

Truax, C. B., Fine, H., Moravec, J., and Millis, W. Effects of therapist persuasive potency in individual psychotherapy. *Journal of Clinical Psychology*, 1968, *24*, 359–362.

Verplanck, W. S. The control of the content of conversation: Reinforcement of statements of opinion. *Journal of Abnormal and Social Psychology*, 1955, *51*, 668–676.

Vogler, R. E., Lunde, S. E., Johnson, G. R., and Martin, P. L. Electrical aversion conditioning with chronic alcoholics. *Journal of Consulting and Clinical Psychology*, 1970, *34*, 302–307.

Wahler, R. G., and Erickson, Marie. Child behavior therapy: A community program in Appalachia. *Behaviour Research and Therapy*, 1969, *7*, 71–78.

Wahler, R. G., Winkel, G. H., Peterson, R. F., and Morrison, D. C. Mothers as behavior therapists for their own children. *Behaviour Research and Therapy*, 1965, *3*, 113–124.

Walters, R. H., and Parke, R. D. Influence of response consequence to a social model on resistance to deviation. *Journal of Experimental Child Psychology*, 1964, *1*, 269–280.

Williams, Juanita H. Conditioning of verbalization: A review. *Psychological Bulletin*, 1964, *62*, 383–393.

Williams, R. I., and Blanton, R. L. Verbal conditioning in a psychotherapeutic situation. *Behaviour Research and Therapy*, 1968, 6, 97–103.

Wolf, M. M., Giles, D. K., and Hall, R. V. Experiments with token reinforcement in a remedial classroom. *Behaviour Research and Therapy*, 1968, 6, 51–64.

Wolpe, J. *Psychotherapy by reciprocal inhibition*. Stanford, Calif.: Stanford University Press, 1958.

Wolpe, J. The comparative clinical status of conditioning therapies and psychoanalysis. In J. Wolpe, A. Salter, and L. J. Reyna (Eds.), *The conditioning therapies*. New York: Holt, Rinehart and Winston, 1964, 5–20.

Wolpe, J. *The practice of behavior therapy*. New York: Pergamon, 1969.

Wolpe, J., and Lazarus, A. A. *Behavior therapy techniques*. New York: Pergamon, 1966.

Woody, R. H. Behavior therapy and school psychology. *Journal of School Psychology*, 1966, 4, 1–14.

Woody, R. H. Reinforcement in school counseling. *School Counselor*, 1968, 15, 253–258.

Woody, R. H. *Behavioral problem children in the schools: Recognition, diagnosis, and behavioral modification*. New York: Appleton-Century-Crofts, 1969.

Woody, R. H., and Herr, E. L. Psychologists and hypnosis: Part I. Psychotherapeutic theories and practices. *American Journal of Clinical Hypnosis*, 1965, 8, 80–88.

Woody, R. H., and Herr, E. L. Psychologists and hypnosis. Part II. Use in educational settings. *American Journal of Clinical Hypnosis*, 1966, 8, 254–256.

Woody, R. H., Krathwohl, D. R., Kagan, N., and Farquhar, W. W. Stimulated recall in psychotherapy using hypnosis and video tape. *American Journal of Clinical Hypnosis*, 1965, 7, 234–241.

Woody, R. H., and Schauble, P. G. Desensitization of fear by video tapes. *Journal of Clinical Psychology*, 1969, 25, 102–103. (a)

Woody, R. H., and Schauble, P. G. Videotaped vicarious desensitization. *Journal of Nervous and Mental Disease*, 1969, 148, 281–286. (b)

Zeisset, R. M. Desensitization and relaxation in the modification of psychiatric patients' interview behavior. *Journal of Abnormal Psychology*, 1968, 73, 18–24.

Zimmerman, Elaine H., and Zimmerman, J. The alteration of behavior in a special classroom situation. *Journal of Experimental Analysis of Behavior*, 1962, 5, 59–60.

# 3

# Issues in Application

The foregoing chapters have described the theoretical and technical bases for psychobehavioral counseling and therapy. As is true with so many areas of science, there is a potential for difficulty when the theoretical and technical aspects are translated into applied services. Some of these potential sources of difficulty can be predicted and prepared for, but others cannot.

This chapter focuses on several of the key issues in the process of achieving effective application of the integrated insight-behavioral approach to counseling and therapy. Specifically, consideration will be given to: *psychobehavioral diagnosis,* that is, the process of making psychological assessments and behavioral analyses that are meaningful to a behaviorally-oriented form of counseling-psychotherapy; the *selection of behavioral techniques* that will fit into the psychobehavioral frame of reference and that will be optimally tailored to the specific problem and the client being dealt with; *personal-social counseling and therapy,* that is, applying the psychobehavioral orientation to problems that influence the client's personal-social functioning; *educational counseling and consultation,* that is, helping clients deal more effectively with learning tasks via direct contact (counseling), and indirect service through other professionals (consultation with classroom teachers); *vocational guidance and counseling,* which employs behavioral techniques yet still retains vocational-development theories and the guidance-counseling relationship; *group counseling and therapy,* which emphasizes conditioning techniques in order to facilitate the group processes; *community service,* which is directed toward confronting societal problems through psychobehaviorism; and the *influence of the setting.*

We have examined the theory, the techniques, and the research documentation. This chapter moves on to the application of the theory and techniques in a practical clinical setting.

## PSYCHOBEHAVIORAL DIAGNOSIS

"Diagnosis" generally is defined as measuring ( i.e., estimating) and describing a person's current functioning, deducing what past functionings were and what the etiology for the present problems might be, making a prognosis about the future, and setting forth a treatment plan. The central purpose of any diagnosis is to define the nature of the problem and to determine what requires treatment.

Psychodynamic diagnosis involves assessing the client's assets and liabilities, the strength and nature of defenses, and the strength and vulnerability of the ego (just to name a few of the primary dimensions). Behaviorists take a much different view of diagnosis, directing their attention to inferring the reinforcing contingencies or contingent stimuli in the past and present life of the client. The difference between the two conceptualizations of diagnosis reintroduces the differing concepts of the nature of problems to be treated and underscores a different concept of what the client needs to have treated. Or, as was illustrated by the symptom versus underlying neurotic conflict controversy, the behavior therapist would probably be likely to accept a client's statements regarding the nature of the problem in a literal manner (whether it be an interview comment or an item receiving a self-report preference on a standardized test) and would deal with the manifest problem, whereas the insight counselor-therapist would want to delve into the implicit problem, i.e., that which is, in a sense, out of the client's conscious awareness. The psychobehavioral frame of reference, however, adds a third conceptualization for diagnosis: analysis of the client's reinforcement history and social-learning contingencies, i.e., specifying the reinforcing contingencies or contingent stimuli in a behavioral manner, thereby providing supplemental data for the psychodynamically-oriented diagnosis.

Parenthetically, it should be noted that theoretical approaches to insight counseling and psychotherapy vary greatly in the amount of emphasis placed on diagnosis. For example, the client-centered therapist would probably give scant attention to diagnosis, whereas a psychoanalytically-oriented therapist would give a great deal. As has been reflected in the evolution of client-centered therapy, the value placed on diagnosis (or any facet of treatment for that matter) by any one theoretical school is subject to shifts—and at this time that seems like a scientifically healthy attribute. Moreover, as is true with so many theoretical-versus-practical comparisons, it seems probable that practitioners espousing the same theoretical approach differ significantly amongst themselves. In addition to theoretical differences, the amount of emphasis placed on diagnosis is also subject to the types of clients. In general, the counselor-therapist working with so-called "normals," such as in a college counseling center, would probably rely on diagnostic data much less than would the counselor-therapist working with more disturbed clients, such as in a mental health clinic or hospital.

The two diagnostic steps of making a prognosis and setting forth a treatment plan require that consideration be given to various possible treatment approaches. This means, in a sense, making a prognosis for each feasible treatment mode or technique and selecting the approach that seems to hold the most promise (recognizing, of course, that the treatment plan should be under constant appraisal and subject to modification at any time).

In actual practice, however, the diagnostic process all too often does not fulfill the multifaceted composition. Some diagnosticians stop with the first step, measuring and describing the current functioning. This seems to occur most often when the diagnosis is being made in conjunction with another professional. Perhaps the assumption is that the other one will carry out the remaining steps, but the result is often an incomplete diagnostic process.

When a fragmented diagnosis occurs, there is frequently an over-reliance on psychometric data. The psychological tests are useful only for describing current functioning and offering a diagnostic classification. The diagnostic classification or categorization is supposedly a means for communicating the uniqueness of the client so that professionals subsequently involved with the client can have a clearcut frame of reference as to what his characteristics are. But not even a psychiatric classification carries direct considerations of what should be done; certainly a diagnostic label provides little, if any, mainline revelations about the client as a unique human being, and it fails to yield treatment ideas that are tailored to that one individual client.

Psychobehavioral diagnosis holds as its primary goal the derivation of a treatment approach. Granted, the other steps of diagnosis are potentially of value (even inferring etiology and making a psychiatric classification), but the real value for the counseling-therapy process comes from understanding the client's charactertistics and reaction styles so that they can be translated into usable guidelines for treatment. Deriving the treatment approach might well involve the use of psychological tests, including intelligence, aptitude, perceptual, achievement, and personality measures. (Actually, any instrument that provides idiosyncratic data, which might also mean a nomothetic comparison through sample norms, can be used.)

Behaviorists believe that the use of the test data should go beyond a metrical analysis: there must also be a behavioral analysis or a behavioral diagnosis. In other words, there is an analysis of reinforcement contingencies. In accord with behavioral science, Greenspoon and Gersten (1967) note that "the behavior on any psychological test should be lawful" (p. 849), and because "the behavior therapist must resort to trial-and-error procedures to determine a contingent stimulus that may be effective with a particular patient" (p. 849), psychological tests should be used, but should be analyzed for contingencies or contingent stimuli. This means that a behavioral analysis of standard psychological test data is made to determine what kinds of reinforcers influence the client; understanding these would lead to the establishment of behavioral modification procedures that would be most likely to help the client, because they are tailored to his idiosyncratic characteristics.

In the process of behavioral analysis, the psychobehavioral diagnostician would go through the regular behavioristic diagnostic approach, perhaps even following a trait-and-factor model, but he would also subjectively analyze the responses to infer reinforcement contingencies. Greenspoon and Gersten (1967) suggest that the data be grouped into four classes of contingencies or contingent stimuli: positive verbal, negative verbal, positive nonverbal, and negative nonverbal. In other words, responses to test items that reflected verbal factors, e.g., reinforcing words, would be placed in the appropriate positive or negative verbal categories, while actions or events would be placed into the appropriate positive or negative nonverbal categories. These grouped materials would then be used to infer how behavioral modification contingencies should be scheduled to eliminate the problem being treated.

Almost any psychological test can yield material that can be analyzed for use in behavioral modification, but there are also instruments designed particularly for such use. Wolpe and Lazarus (1966) constructed a Life History Questionnaire that helps the counselor-therapist infer social learning contingencies from the client's behavioral history; Wolpe and Lang (1964) created a Fear Survey Schedule that taps a client's disturbed reactions to a variety of stimuli; and Willoughby (1934) developed a Neuroticism Schedule that is widely used by behavior therapists to gather information regarding neurotic reactions to commonly encountered situations. Wolpe (1969) presents and discusses several of these instruments for behavior therapy. For those behavioral techniques that involve suggestibility, such as clinical hypnosis and perhaps systematic desensitization, scales have been constructed by London (1962), Shor and Orne (1962), and Weitzenhoffer and Hilgard (1959, 1962). It should be emphasized, however, that unspecialized instruments, including the Wechsler and Stanford-Binet intelligence tests and inkblot and thematic projective instruments (to name but a few), can yield material that will reveal reinforcement contingencies, particularly those of a social nature.

There have been few published descriptions of behavioral diagnosis. One of the seemingly best elaborations of behavioral diagnostic processes has been offered by Kanfer and Saslow (1969). In approaching the topic, they issue the reminder that behavior therapy:

does not rest upon the assumption that (1) insight is a *sine qua non* of psychotherapy, (2) changes in thoughts or ideas inevitably lead to ultimate changes in actions, (3) verbal therapeutic sessions serve as replications of and equivalents for actual life situations, and (4) a symptom can be removed only by uprooting its cause or origin. In the absence of these assumptions it becomes unnecessary to conceptualize behavior disorder in etiological terms, in psychodynamic terms, or in terms of a specifiable disease process. (p. 428)

For a behavioral analysis, they state:

The compilation of data under as many of the headings as are relevant should yield a good basis for decisions about the areas in which intervention is needed, the particular targets of the intervention, the treatment methods to be used, and the series of goals at which treatment should aim. (p. 430)

They indicate that the methods for data collection can be quite traditional, such as via interviewing, observations, and psychological tests. The point is, of course, that the functional analysis of these data should take on a behavioral posture.

At this stage, the basic problem is how to actually conduct an analysis of the data in behavioral terms. Kanfer and Saslow (1969) set forth the following guidelines for a behavioral analytic approach:

1   A detailed description of the particular behavioral excesses or deficits which represent the patient's complaints, and of the behavioral assets which may be available for utilization in a treatment program.

2   A clarification of the problem situation in which the variables are sought that maintain the patient's current problem behaviors. Attention is also given to the consequences of psychiatric intervention on the current adjustment balance of the patient in his social environment.

3   A motivational analysis which attempts to survey the various incentives and aversive conditions representing the dominant motivational factors in the patient.

4   A developmental analysis suggests consideration of biological, sociological, and behavioral changes in the patient's history which may have relevance for his present complaint and for a treatment program.

5   An analysis of self-control, which provides assessment of the patient's capacity for participation in a treatment program and of the conditions which may be necessary to control behaviors with untoward social consequences.

6   An analysis of social relationships which provide the basis for assessing social resources in the patient's environment which have affected his current behavior and may play a role in the therapeutic program.

7   An analysis of the social-cultural-physical environment to assess the degree of congruence between the patient's present milieu, his behavioral repertoire, and the type of therapeutic goals which the therapist can establish. (pp. 443–444)

While these guidelines give much needed guidance, it must be pointed out that behavioral analysis, just like its psychodynamic counterpart, is unrelentingly dependent upon the diagnostician's expertise at making clinical judgments from the data obtained.

Psychobehavioral diagnosis, therefore, fully utilizes established assessment procedures, including psychological tests. However, emphasis is given to making the data useful, that is, translating it into treatment techniques; and when behavioral modification procedures are employed, the contingencies or contingent stimuli that have special applicability to the particular client must be identified. This requires a behavioral analysis.

## SELECTION OF BEHAVIORAL TECHNIQUES

After he makes the psychobehavioral diagnosis or analysis, the counselor-therapist selects a technical approach. It would be convenient if a well-defined set of guidelines for the selection of techniques could be offered. In view, however, of the lack of research on the matter and the idiosyncratic reactions of clients to a given technique, it would be ill-advised to set forth a restrictive system. It is possible, however, to clarify the parameters of the selection process.

Behavior therapists presume to operate on algorithms, i.e., they employ rules of procedure that lead to the solving of a problem. In the rationale for behavior therapy, it is implicit that the proper application of conditioning will produce a predictable change in behavior. This would lead one to assume that, given a specified behavior, the conditioning procedure could almost be mechanically determined, but thus far, human nature being what it is, such cut-and-dried technical prescriptions are not tenable.

There is seemingly a simplicity within behavior therapy, such as would be reflected in the delineation of the reinforcement contingencies or contingent stimuli and would presumably be operational in fitting techniques to specified contingencies or stimuli. But this simplicity is contradicted by actual practice. As Klein, Dittmann, Parloff, and Gill state (1969):

Many people suppose that the therapist begins by clearly and systematically defining the patient's problems in terms of manageable hierarchies and then selects appropriate responses to be strengthened or weakened. We found little support for this conception of behavior therapy diagnosis in our observations. Indeed the selection of problems to be worked on often seemed quite arbitrary and inferential. We were frankly surprised to find the presenting symptomatic complaint was often sidestepped for what the therapist intuitively considered to be more basic issues. Most surprising to us, the basis for this selection seemed often to be what others would call dynamic considerations. (p. 261)

This statement, aside from the support it offers to the psychobehavioral assertion that the use of behavioral techniques will be complemented by the use of insight or dynamic techniques, exemplifies how subjectivity affects the behavioral diagnosis, especially the decision of which problem should be treated, and it suggests consequently that the selection of techniques may be equally subject to the clinical judgment of the counselor-therapist.

Behavior therapists do not, in general, acknowledge this subjectivity; nonetheless they remain vague about the process of selecting techniques. Analysis of Wolpe and Lazarus' (1966) description of their procedure suggests that: if a client has a marked degree of social inadequacy, this might well receive immediate (initial?) treatment, probably by assertive training; subsequently other sources of anxiety, guilt, and depression would be explored and dealt with therapeutically, probably by anxiety-reduction techniques. They state:

In general it is expedient to give therapeutic priority to the patient's most pressing current problem. . . . In cases that display particularly distressing and debilitating reactions, one tries to subdue these reactions as rapidly as possible. (p. 28)

They go on to point out that behavior therapy cannot be "rigid behavioral engineering" (but this position is not shared by certain other behaviorists). The unfortunate thing is that for all practical purposes, the matter of selection of techniques in behavior therapy is left to nebulous generalizations about tailoring the treatment to the needs and the characteristics of the client (and one might wonder if "and of the therapist" should receive similar emphasis) and the selection process is left to the professional expertise of the behavior therapist.

Relatedly, it is lamentable that the assessment of whether a behavioral technique is producing desirable results is left to the judgment of the therapist, and often his judgments are based on circumstantial evidence:

Because behavior treatment is posited as highly specific, it follows that success depends on the patient's exact and close cooperation with the therapist's instructions. It is therefore very important for the therapist to test this cooperation repeatedly during treatment. The therapist must also constantly assess the patient's progress on hierarchy dimensions. With the possible exception of role-playing, the therapist is dependent in this evaluation upon the patient's report both of progress outside treatment and of events within the sessions themselves. Since there are no independent procedures for evaluating or verifying his report, the patient has considerable leeway to bias his report in order to please, frustrate, or otherwise manipulate the therapist, or to meet some personal expectation. And the form of much of the feedback from the patient (i.e., lifting his finger if he feels an increase in anxiety during desensitization or doing nothing if he does not) gives the therapist very few cues for distinguishing valid from invalid reports. Thus the therapist must use considerable intuition to assess progress and correct the treatment plan. This all serves to highlight a very basic discrepancy between the theoretical orientation of behavior therapy and its actual practice. (Klein, Dittmann, Parloff, and Gill, 1969, p. 262)

It seems evident that assessing the suitability or success level of a technique within the behavior-therapy model for practice has at least the potential for fostering erroneous judgments. One way of alleviating the probability of judgmental errors would be to incorporate insight-related measures, but of course this would violate the pure behavioral stance, would require acceptance of validity for psychodynamic theoretical principles and assessment instruments, and would require an eclectic theoretical posture, such as is afforded by the psychobehavioral frame of reference.

The state of affairs, then, is that while there have been some attempts to determine which techniques work best for which disorder or problem, there is no empirically-based set of rules for technique selection. This leaves the individual counselor-therapist with the task, fraught with the potential for judgmental error, of gleaning technical data from published research accounts. Other alternatives would seem to be the reliance on trial-and-error attempts, and the use of a gradually built repertoire of clinical experience, both behavorial and nonbehavioral. Obviously, none of these alternatives represents a thoroughly acceptable professional operational mode.

There have been few published attempts at matching techniques with problems to be treated. This is undoubtedly because of two clinical facts: first, clients have idiosyncratic reactions to techniques, i.e., there are subtle differences among clients with what seems to be the same problem; and second, one clinician might obtain successful results with one technique whereas another, because of personal-professional differences in preferences and skills, might not, and would have to turn to another technique.

Surveying the major published sources on behavior therapy, one finds, however, that gross matchings are possible. These matchings are derived fairly readily by perusing the research and clinical examples presented under each type of disorder or problem. To take one example, Eysenck and Rachman (1965) suggest the following groupings of problem areas and techniques: *anxiety states* (e.g., phobias, social anxiety, and pervasive or free-floating anxiety) are primarily treated by systematic desensitization; *hysterical disorders* may be treated by avoidance conditioning and operant conditioning, which involve such specific techniques as systematic desensitization, induced abreactions, negative practice, and aversive therapy; *psychomotor disturbances* (e.g., tics, tremors, writer's cramp, and spasms), which are essentially hysterical disorders, may be treated by a variety of conditioning techniques, such as avoidance conditioning, aversive therapy, systematic desensitization, relaxation exercises, and negative practice; *obsessional-compulsive disorders* may be treated by avoidance conditioning, aversive therapy, clinical suggestion (i.e., systematic psychomotor or vocal inhibition), systematic desensitization, assertive training, and satiation or negative practice; and *sex disorders* (e.g., impotence, frigidity, voyeurism, fetishism, exhibitionism, homosexuality, and transvestism) may be treated by aversive therapy and systematic desensitization, with emphasis on the use of sexual responses and assertive responses.

A somewhat encyclopedia-like source for matching a technique with a problem has been provided by Yates (1970). He offers his analysis of what techniques are suitable for specific abnormalities; he presents chapters according to behavior problem, and the reader can easily extract techniques; and he sets forth a table (see p. 71 of his book) that connects numerous abnormalities with behavioral techniques. Basically, it is comparable to the ideas derived from Eysenck and Rachman (1965), but seemingly more up-to-date and more comprehensive (if the objective is to have a reference source).

The foregoing should not be viewed as a comprehensive set of problems-techniques matchings; it is merely one subjectively established set essentially from one source. Further, it is important to acknowledge that, in addition to the previously cited restrictions placed on problems-techniques matching by idiosyncratic reactions of clients and the personal-professional differences among clinicians, professionals vary in their criteria for what they believe is adequate documentation for substantiating that a particular technique is successful when used with a certain problem area. To take a specific example, the intepretation of the efficacy for negative practice presented in Chapter 2 of this book seems, in some ways, to differ from (i.e., be less positive than) the interpretation for the same technique presented by Eysenck and Rachman (1965). Either might be considered accurate, depending upon the evaluation criteria.

With this admittedly less-than-desirable, but realistic, state of affairs, the following seem like appropriate steps that each counselor-therapist should take to assure that his technique selection is as academically astute as is possible, and is better than trial-and-error potshots. First, assuming that a psychobehavioral diagnosis has provided him with relevant data, the counselor-therapist should weigh the client's clinical information composite against more global composites illustrated by published research and clinical accounts. This would, of course, require a review of what documentation there is for the use of a given technique with a certain problematic condition, and this is the point at which the individualized interpretation of the strength of the documentation must occur, i.e., whether documentation is adequate enough to allow for an assumption of efficacy. Second, having weighed the client's characteristics against the technical documentation, the counselor-therapist must introduce his own personal-professional characteristics, giving consideration to the matter of how his unique set of preferences, skills, and attributes will influence the outcome of the use of a particular technique. Third, each feasible technique should be subjected to a prognostication for effects. And fourth, following application, every technique should be constantly assessed, with accommodations for change being possible. From this sequence of activities, the counselor-therapist will evolve his own set of (potentially transitory) algorithms.

To some behavioral scientists, the foregoing recommendations should only be offered with extreme apologies. But to the practicing clinician, who must make daily judgments that are admittedly subjective, these recommendations seem to provide the basis for at least tentative guidelines. (Note the discussion in Chapter 6 on the scientist-versus-practitioner controversy—the categories are not, of course, mutually exclusive.)

Obviously, this approach offers no concrete rules for selection and implementation, but one rule can be explicitly stated: *when using either an insight or behavioral technique, the counselor-therapist should constantly be assessing its effects and should continually be prepared to make alterations in his technical intervention.* The result of technique selection, although perhaps regrettable from a purist point of view, is unquestionably dependent upon the clinical judgment of the counselor-therapist. Perhaps some day a computer, programmed to receive data about the client and the counselor-therapist, will be able to make recommendations for techniques. While this possibility is offered somewhat facetiously, it should be acknowledged that this may not be far from reality. For example, Veldman (1967) has programmed a computer so that data from sentence-completion tests (administered to college freshmen) can be fed in and the computer will feed back "interview questions" appropriate to a particular student's set of test responses and which, if asked by the counselor, could provide diagnostic-interview clarity.

## PERSONAL-SOCIAL COUNSELING AND THERAPY

The following three sections will consider the areas of personal-social counseling and therapy, educational counseling and consultation, and vocational guidance and counseling. The purposes of the discussions are to illustrate how behavioral techniques can be integrated into already existing services, to cite research studies that both document and describe this integration, and to clarify any issues that might be unique to applications in these areas.

The first of these areas, personal-social counseling and therapy, probably requires less consideration of technical application than the other two areas. This is due to the fact that the majority of behavioral modification research, as evidenced in the materials in the first two chapters, has been directed at the problems usually associated with the personal-social area. It would seem that the applicability of these techniques has already been established. The focus, therefore, of this section will be on the unique issues that are associated with psychobehavioral counseling-therapy for personal-social problems.

Unfortunately, behavioral techniques have received a certain degree of blind acceptance from the lay public (and sometimes professionals as well), due in large extent to the accounts in popular newspapers and magazines that describe the sudden and seemingly remarkable successes of behavior therapy. The lay public, which typically looks for symptom relief more than nebulous entities like underlying emotional conflicts, reacts to these accounts with enthusiasm. They develop the belief that all their trials and tribulations will be over if they can only find a behavior therapist. This attitude can create a problem; the lay public sometimes attributes almost a mystical, if not hysterical, dedication to quick cure.

Thus it is that the counselor-therapist may encounter clients who want to prescribe their own treatment. Perhaps they have read of how a given behavior therapy technique successfully cured a group of people, and saw in themselves the ascribed characteristics of the treatment group. The psychobehavioral counselor-therapist would not, of course, be willing to give unqualified acceptance to the concept of "treat the symptom and the problem will go away" (not to mention the possible deleterious effects of allowing a client to dictate to the professional what his treatment should be; imagine a medical physician prescribing medication according to a patient's ideas about what his problems are and how they should be treated!). Granted, it may be that, after a psychobehavioral diagnosis, the counselor-therapist would conclude that the psychodynamics and the behavioral components of the situation do, in fact, allow for direct symptom treatment, pure and simple, but the most probable situation would be that even then there might be the need for other forms of counseling-therapeutic intervention.

Specifically, let us assume that an obese client seeks treatment because she wants hypnotic suggestion to stop her compulsive eating.

It is entirely possible that hypnosis or other behavioral techniques (e.g., a positive reward system or aversive conditioning) could be used to control excessive eating, but the fact remains that, in addition to the overeating's having a possible learned rewarding element, there may also be emotional conflicts that should be dealt with via counseling-psychotherapy so that the client will not need to resort to some other form of compensatory behavior. This is not to suggest that all unacceptable or problem behaviors necessarily have an underlying conflict that must be treated, or that treatment of a symptom will necessarily result in a compensatory behavior (symptom substitution); but there will be some clients who will see one symptom as being their sole problem when the fact of the matter is that they have a series of conflicts, such as faulty self-concept, that must be dealt with in an insight counseling-psychotherapy manner if they are to achieve the sort of unfettered, happy functioning that they forecast would occur if only they could lose their main problem. Therefore, returning to the example of the obese client, the proper psychobehavioral approach would be to proceed with a full diagnosis, establish a counseling-psychotherapeutic relationship, use behavioral techniques when they seemed appropriate, and retain the framework of ongoing counseling-psychotherapy, with the termination criteria being the same as those for any form of counseling-psychotherapy, i.e., agreement between the client and the counselor-therapist. It might be noted that clinical experience has shown that clients seeking a specific form of treatment usually do have other kinds of problems; this leads one to wonder if the client's having a specific idea about how treatment should be conducted is a clinical sign of defensiveness or avoidance of other psychically significant factors.

The use of an adjunct counselor-therapist is another unique aspect of the psychobehavioral approach to personal-social problems. A counselor or therapist will seldom refer one of his clients to another counselor or therapist for specialized insight-oriented services, but he will do so fairly readily when the second professional can provide behavioral therapy. Clinical experience has revealed that both psychiatrists and psychologists, regardless of theoretical orientation (including those who are psychoanalytically oriented), will, when given an orientation to behavioral modification, make referrals for adjunctive services.

Referrals are usually made for behavior therapy for a specific problem that has stymied the therapist in the course of insight treatment. What typically results (especially if the counselor-therapist receiving the referral ascribes to the psychobehavioral technical integration) is that both behavior therapy and insight counseling-therapy are provided. In other words, the adjunctive counselor-therapist treats the problems that provoked the referral, but because of his action-oriented relationship, he finds that other potential sources of problems become accessible—issues that the traditional, insight-oriented therapeutic relationship might still not (even then) be able to deal with. Therefore, the adjunct counselor-therapist forms a truly psychobehavioral relationship.

Professional protocol and ethics, of course, require that the adjunct counselor-therapist communicate relevant information to the referring primary therapist, particularly when his services move into insight counseling-psychotherapy, however different in content it may be from what the referring therapist is focusing on. At no time should the adjunct therapist allow either himself or the client to consider using their psychobehavioral relationship as a replacement for the relationship established with the initial therapist—unless, of course, the initial therapist and the adjunct therapist conclude, after consulting with the client, that this would be in the client's best interest. Clinical experience suggests that the use of an adjunct counselor-therapist, primarily for the application of behavioral-modification techniques, results in an acceleration of the therapeutic processes in the regular counseling or psychotherapy (provided by the referring therapist); this is in accord with the rationale and evidence presented for the psychobehavioral frame of reference in Chapter 1.

The use of behavioral-modification techniques in personal-social counseling and therapy does not, in and of itself, introduce any outstanding application problems. Essentially all of the considerations described in the previous two chapters are directly related to providing counseling-therapy for personal-social reasons.

## EDUCATIONAL COUNSELING AND CONSULTATION

Helping clients to deal adequately with the educational aspirations and endeavors in their lives is one of the major responsibilities of counselors, even those employed in so-called noneducational settings. The client's vocational success and personal-social happiness depend, to a large extent, upon how well he has fulfilled his educational aspirations and how well he has satisfied the requirements of the various educational experiences he has encountered during his development. Without doubt, the counseling process must, at some point, focus on educational-achievement factors.

Typically, the counselor and client strive to explore the client's attitudes, motives, and feelings as they relate to an educational choice or goal, a plan for attaining this goal, and the realistic elements (such as personal-social impingements) of both the goal and the plan. The traditional educational-counseling model tries to help the client make a partial synthesis of the numerous forms of self-concept, e.g., how he views himself, how others see him, how he idealizes his self image, and how he can realistically fulfill these self-percepts. Psychobehaviorism in no way contradicts the value of this insight model. Intra-self-dissonance must be resolved, and this can only be done through introspective exploration. However, there are many instances in which insight attempts are not sufficient by themselves, particularly when there is a significant learning disability or behavioral problem. In accord with the rationale for psychobehavioral counseling-therapy, it is in these cases that a behavioral technique can and should be introduced into the counseling-therapy relationship.

One of the most obvious uses of behaviorism in educational counseling would be the application of reinforcement for verbal conditioning. As discussed in Chapter 2, the client attempting to resolve his conflicts about educational matters could be aided by the counselor's reinforcing those classes of responses that are aligned with the determined goal. Table 2 lists several studies documenting that specific client-response classes that have relevance to educational counseling can be reinforced, e.g., self-references, verbal participation, deliberation, information-seeking, and decision-making.

Consideration of the other techniques described in Chapter 2 yields almost countless possibilities, and since each application must be tailored to the needs and characteristics of both the client and the counselor, it can be safely said that every behavioral technique has potential for facilitating educational counseling. For example, systematic desensitization could be used to reduce the anxiety that a client might experience when engaging in an educational activity, such as test-taking anxiety or fear of being assessed for educational achievement;[1] behavior rehearsal, behavioral shaping, or object and social recognition rewards could be used to help a client adapt his behaviors to the acceptable norms for the educational group to which he aspires to be a member; and clinical suggestion could be used to encourage and, in a sense, initiate educational aspiration and achievement.

Although educationally related introspection, exploration, and planning can be fostered by behavioral techniques within counseling, it would seem that the counselor skilled in behavioral techniques can find an equally important role as a consultant. Because there are many other professionals, such as classroom teachers, who have education as their primary responsibility, and who all too often lack training in behavioral techniques, the counselor trained in psychobehaviorism might best utilize his skills by functioning as an educational consultant to other educational personnel.

[1]The immobilizing effects of anxiety due to educationally related factors can be great. Most commonly, this is manifested in fear of being evaluated, as in the well-known test-taking anxiety reactions. However, it can be almost totally debilitating. For example, a highly educated, sophisticated, professionally successful man was referred to me for a psychological assessment. He had been in psychoanalysis for several years, primarily because of homosexuality and a conscious wish to become heterosexual; however, he had become progressively more anxious and less effective in his work and social relationships, and was drinking excessively. Upon the referral from the psychiatrist, the psychologist conducted a diagnostic intake interview and then started administering the Wechsler Adult Intelligence Scale. The client went through the first two subtests, Information and Comprehension, with ease, achieving scaled scores of 18 and 16 respectively; however, on the Arithmetic subtest he became openly upset, shaking and eventually sobbing, and received a scaled score of 8; on Similarities he received a scaled score of 15, but broke down again on Digit Span, with a scaled score of 10, and then regained control on Vocabulary and received a scaled score of 16; this sort of up-and-down performance continued, until he finally totally lost control and requested termination on the Block Design subtest. (For diagnostic purposes, the limits of performance were being tested, and thus the client was subject to a greater amount of anxiety than usual, i.e., obviously the scaled scores do not reflect his potential, but merely reflect how he was able to handle anxiety at that point in time.) In the discussion of his performance, he said that he had "gone through life being a fake, using intellect and verbosity to impress people, but knowing inside myself that I'm weak and not what I try to convey to others"; and he said that with the Wechsler items that he could respond to with his verbal skills, such as the Information subtest, he could handle with a mixture of intellect and distracting humor, but when the items required a clearcut objective answer, such as on the Arithmetic and Block Design subtests, he became highly anxious and would "disintegrate on things that even a third grade child should be able to answer, because there is no way around giving an answer that can be objectively evaluated."

Serving as a consultant requires both academic and personal skills. The academic expertise is fairly clearcut: the consultant must thoroughly understand the theoretical aspects of human behavior and learning, and must be able to translate these bodies of knowledge into applied recommendations, the latter typically resulting from observational analyses of behavior, such as from classroom observation. A more elusive, yet crucial, component of the consultation process is the human relationships established by the consultant. In describing a psychiatric consultation program to the schools, Mumford (1968) categorized teachers' reactions to the consultants; there were the "teacher-guides" who actively helped the consultants and expected an exchange of services, there were the "teacher-authorities" who believed that they did not need help from consultants, and there were the "teacher-friends" who believed that to accept help from consultants would be a violation of a highly personal teacher-student relationship. Mumford recommended identifying and contacting the "teacher-guides" as early as possible, because they appeared to be the best means for avoiding cleavage with the other types of teachers and for the eventual achievement of a unifying relationship between the teachers and the consultants.

In many ways, the success of a consultation project will depend upon the acceptance accorded by the ancillary professionals, and this seems especially true when new techniques, e.g., behavioral-modification procedures, are being introduced. Therefore, the psycho-behavioral counselor-therapist must give constant attention to creating a reciprocal helping relationship between himself and parents, educational personnel, and professionals in other educationally-related or supportive community agencies. The following statement suggests ways to bring these relationships into being; although it was directed to school psychologists and counselors, it is equally applicable to essentially any counselor or therapist:

In this case, as with the school counselor, the school psychologist should: first, make himself available to other educational personnel, especially the classroom teachers (accessibility is directly related to effectiveness); second, actively seek relationships with all types of educators that will allow for formal and informal consultations; and third, realize that he, the school psychologist, needs the other persons as much as or more than they need him to perform acceptably their respective functions (as history will attest, it is quite likely that the classroom teacher can function with relative success without the services of the school psychologist, but it is very unlikely that the school psychologist can function effectively without the services of the classroom teacher). (Woody, 1969, p. 67)

The counselor-therapist, who presumably is a specialist in human relations, really finds his proving ground in the area of establishing a facilitating relationship with those persons, both professional and nonprofessional, to whom he will serve as a consultant. And the success of his work with his clients makes it mandatory that consultation exist.

There is a great deal of research to document that behavioral techniques, such as object and social recognition rewards, can successfully alter the learning of children; much of this research has been reviewed in the book *Behavioral Problem Children in the Schools* (Woody, 1969), and the volume of relevant new material grows daily. Therefore, no attempt will be made to review the published accounts of uses of behavioral modification techniques for learning activities. A few generalizations, however, should help clarify the procedures.

Usually the therapist focuses upon a specific learning problem or behavior and gives some form of reinforcement to lead to a more acceptable form of learning behavior. For example, one classroom teacher wanted to eliminate some students' habit of wasting time; they would look out the window or dawdle around when they should have been studying. To eliminate this, a light was rigged up on the desks of the selected-target students, and a peer "therapist" (who was a good student already) was assigned to observe (sometimes by closed circuit television or with narrow-slitted ski glasses so the students would not know exactly when they were being observed); if a student concentrated on his study, the light would go on; if he became distracted, the light would go off. Keeping the light on for a prescribed duration would result in the selected-target student's earning a token that could later be redeemed for special privileges, such as extra time on the playground. Measurements revealed that students responded quickly to this form of reinforcement, and that their achievement increased significantly.[2] Numerous research studies document that underachievers can increase their achievement levels, that students with special reading or arithmetic problems can develop

[2]This experiment was conducted by Professor Roger E. Ulrich and his associates at Western Michigan University; it was published subsequently by Surrat, Ulrich, and Hawkins (1969).

new skills, that overt behaviors that disrupt the learning attempts of the child (as well as his classmates) can be eliminated, and that even the adequately achieving, well-behaved child can improve his performance. This has been successful with normal, behavioral problem, emotionally-disturbed, brain injured, and mentally-retarded children in regular and special education classroom and residential institutions (Woody, 1969). Generally, the educational achievement or learning processes are modified by a positive reinforcement paradigm, such as the use of redeemable tokens, candy, special privileges, or social approval or recognition.

When classroom behaviors are being dealt with, the psycho-behavioral counselor-therapist would typically not be the "therapist." Rather, he would make a direct observation of the child or the classroom or an indirect observation with the teacher serving as the source for data collection, make an analysis of the conditions within the learning situation, establish reinforcement contingencies, and help the teacher understand how to implement the reinforcement, assess its effects, and evaluate the effectiveness of the procedure. He would then monitor for uncontrolled sources of reinforcement that might counteract the desired outcome, and being prepared to recommend alterations in the behavioral-modification procedures.[3] In other words, he would be serving as a consultant to educational personnel. Stephens (1970) and Toews (1969) provide further elaboration on behavioral consultation for school-related problems.

## VOCATIONAL GUIDANCE AND COUNSELING

As with educational counseling-consultation, vocational guidance and counseling are directed at an area that has monumental importance to the overall functioning of the individual; educational

---

[3]Many trainees in counseling and psychology have seemed dismayed that agencies and schools do not provide behavior therapy. What many of them do not seem to realize is that the agencies and schools do, in fact, provide behavior therapy, but that it does not take the classical form of one-to-one treatment, which occurs primarily in clinic and hospital settings where services are provided to clients or patients with major disorders. Most agencies and schools, and most recipients of behavioral modification, have a behaviorally controlled environment, such as a classroom where only acceptable behaviors are rewarded. This is just as much "therapy" as is the one-to-one "therapy" in the clinical setting, and trainees should realize that their therapeutic ambitions can be fulfilled by serving as a behavioral-modification consultant.

achievement and vocational satisfaction have inestimable influence on a person's inner satisfaction, his ability to relate to others, and his self-fulfillment. Therefore, a client's vocational attitudes, choices, and aspirations should justly receive consideration during counseling-therapy, essentially regardless of the basic therapeutic goal, because inevitably the vocational self-concept will enter into his other forms of self-concept, and relationships in his employment setting will be of utmost importance to his social role.

Underlying vocational guidance and counseling is the assumption that there are theoretical constructs to the series of vocational choices, whether real or fantasized, that every human being makes tion that there are theoretical constructs to the series of vocational development theories have been posited; these generally give importance to such theoretical constructs as inherent proclivities, social-environmental press, maturational development, familial influences, experiential variables, and self-concept development (Holland, 1966; Roe, 1956; Super, 1953). In addition, psychoanalytically-oriented psychologists have attempted to explain vocational choices as the manifestations of emotional conflicts and unfulfilled needs. Although there has been a great deal of theorizing about vocational choices and development theory, some professionals seriously doubt that there currently exists a defensible theory of vocational choice that meets the rigorous demands of theory building (Carkhuff, Alexik, and Anderson, 1967). Stefflre (1966), however, has offered a series of propositions that, although admittedly not a comprehensive theory, account for vocational choices and development in terms of personality, occupational persona, needs, and societal forces.

The psychobehavioral counselor-therapist might well accept any of the vocational-development theories if he believed that they were logical and defensible on academic grounds, but he would augment the theory with the following proposition: vocational choices result, in part, from habituated behavior that can be modified. In other words, a person may be led into a vocational choice because some of his previous behaviors, which have been compensatory for needs that are unrelated to the vocational choice, have been rewarding, and were therefore generalized into an employment setting. An example is the music student who begins to study music because it allows him a mode of expression and is a potential vehicle to social acceptance, and who, after having achieved a degree of virtuosity, finds himself a professional musician not because he needs social acceptance but because a skill developed to fulfill a need can also unexpectedly be turned into a wage-earning profession. Although this kind of vocational choice can be explained by psychoanalytic concepts, it is also explainable by reinforcement theory, namely that the person gets reinforced for certain behaviors and that these behaviors affect his vocational choice. Accepting that interests, attitudes, and behaviors are reinforced (as exemplified by the father who gets upset when his son says he wants to be an artist, but who beams when the son says he "will follow in his dad's footsteps and become a lawyer too"), the psychobehavioral counselor-therapist can then adopt the tenets of the vocational-development theory of his choice and enter into vocational guidance and counseling with the integrated insight-behavioral armament.

Many of the arguments used against behavioral-modification techniques as a whole could probably be lodged against their use for vocational purposes, but the arguments are generally oversimplified. For example, some professionals maintain that vocational counseling requires that the client go through a series of introspective activities, and that behavioral techniques would deprive him of the decision making; in other words, there is concern that behavioral techniques would mean total manipulation of the client and the deprivation of his individuality:

This position might even be extended hypothetically to the point that government-conducted research would be fed into a computer, the names of potential candidates with suitable characteristics would be spewn out, and behavioral counselors would be assigned clients to interview and to reinforce them into accepting and even liking a vocational choice made for them by the Establishment: the manpower needs of the society would be met at the expense of individuality. (Woody, 1968, p. 100)

This is really a naïve, misinformed, and alarmist position. Psychobehaviorists would probably be the first to raise the cry of dissent and condemnation, even louder than the nonbehaviorists, if the impersonal approach of "Big Brother" were implemented. It is the psychobehaviorist's concern for the optimum happiness, fulfillment, and well-being of his clients that leads him to be willing to assume responsibility for the outcome of his counseling-therapeutic interventions and to apply his knowledge of behavioral science. Being a humanist, the psychobehavioral counselor-therapist does all that he can, including assuming the personal responsibility of helping clients overcome and eliminate difficulties. Therefore, fear that behavioral techniques will make Orwell's and Huxley's fictional prognostications come true is irrelevant and is, in fact, conservative defensiveness against innovation. Vocational guidance and counseling can be facilitated by behavioral techniques without violating the personal integrity of the client and the humaneness of the society.

As has been discussed elsewhere (Woody, 1968), most of the primary behavioral techniques have been or can be used in vocational guidance and counseling. The following few examples will suffice. *Social recognition and object rewards* could be used in a junior high school career-planning class:

If the student carried out certain assigned tasks, such as reading a number of career pamphlets or writing the required essay on a job or talking to an adult employed in the position he was studying, then he would receive a reward to give positive reinforcement for productivity in the class (the reward might be extra time in the school library for free-reading or permission to go on a special field trip). If he did not perform well or if he misbehaved, the reward would be withheld. The careers teacher might use social recognition by ignoring the student when he did not apply himself and by smiling, praising, and showing approval when he worked diligently in the class. (Woody, 1968, p. 98)

*Social modeling,* using a recorded or filmed model of a desired behavior to influence a client's behavior, could be used to shape the client's attitudes toward careers:

In a sense this principle is involved when a careers teacher presents a film describing a job and depicting a worker in his daily activities; the viewer, the student in the class, is being figuratively asked to project himself into the role of the worker in the film and feasibly to pattern his own behavior after that of the model. (Woody, 1968, p. 98)

Films might be used to orient and influence regarding specific careers, or filmed models of vocational counseling sessions could lead new vocational clients to more initial counseling productivity than would be true if they received no model-preparation. Jones and Krumboltz (1970) provide one behavioristic vocational counseling example involving social modeling. They offered special film treatments about banking jobs to high school males and females from diverse subcultures. The experimental films depicted five different banking jobs to a point that a problem had been raised and a decision had to be made: the first group would then write their solution and receive immediate feedback as to how bank employees actually solved the problem; the second group was asked "to think about" a solution but not to write it down, and they received feedback; and the third group simply saw the problems raised and solved and were not requested to try to solve it themselves. The first experimental group, which was deemed the most overtly active in participation requirements, seemed to make the most gain. Of major importance, when contrasted to control interventions (e.g., regular banking career films, printed banking career information, printed general career information, and filler films), these experimental film methods (which were behavioristic and involved social modeling) were the most effective in influencing interest in banking occupations, attitudes toward banking, and vocational exploratory activities. *Verbal conditioning* via reinforcements from the counselor, e.g., praise and acceptance responses, could lead to increased exploration, information-seeking, and other kinds of in-counseling and out-of-counseling behaviors that would result in improved efficacy for the vocational guidance and counseling. Studies cited in Table 2 exemplify how verbal conditioning has been used in vocational counseling; relevant studies include those by Ryan and Krumboltz (1964), Krumboltz and Thoresen (1964), Krumboltz, Varenhorst, and Thoresen (1967), Krumboltz and Schroeder (1965), and Thoresen and Krumboltz (1967, 1968). Reference to Table 1 will clarify the kinds of responses that might be made to reinforce in vocational counseling. *Systematic desensitization* can be used to facilitate work adjustment. This approach has been used successfully with numerous on-the-job situations that have provoked anxiety or fear in an employee and thus impaired his productivity; for example, Folkins, Lawson, Opton, and Lazarus (1968) used systematic desensitization with adults with anxiety over industrial accidents. *Assertive practice* or *behavioral rehearsal* can be used to foster improved personal skills in work settings:

The client could be trained to show positive assertion during a job interview or in meetings of a labor union or in his interpersonal relations with his work-colleagues; the client could develop new personal characteristics that would qualify him for job advancements, e.g., promotion into a leadership role; or the client could gain assertive skills that would foster improved self-respect or self-concept reformation. (Woody, 1968, p. 99)

Essentially, many of the management development programs employ a modified version of behavioral-modification techniques, such as assertive practice or behavioral rehearsal. These techniques have also been useful for eliminating certain phobic reactions. For example, a combination of insight therapy, systematic desensitization, and behavioral rehearsal might be used to help an employee-client overcome his dread of going to work because of fear of criticism from his fellow workers. *Clinical suggestion and hypnosis* can also be applied to a variety of work-related problems; most commonly, however, these techniques would be adjunctive to other techniques in vocational counseling.

It should be pointed out that a vocational concern will frequently develop from other goals in counseling and psychotherapy:

One example of special relevance occurred in a psychiatric project on sexual deviations where electric shocks were being used in an aversive conditioning format to eliminate sexual problems, e.g., sexual fetishes and transvestism; it was not unusual to find the patient re-examining his vocational attitudes (losing such a chronic and influential behavior could, of course, have far-reaching implications in the patient's personal-vocational adjustment). (Woody, 1968, p. 100)

The point is that vocational guidance and counseling might evolve in the midst of an ongoing session, insight and/or behavioral techniques could be applied, and the primary reason for counseling-therapy could then be resumed. Parenthetically, this also gives credence to the argument that every counselor and psychotherapist should have familiarity with vocational development theory and guidance (or have a close referral source); even if his specialty seems unrelated to vocational problems per se, the possibility of a need for vocational guidance and counseling cannot be ruled out.

Theoretically, there is no reason why any of the behavioral modification techniques could not be used in vocational guidance and counseling. The techniques are adaptable and, conversely, vocational theories and services do not preclude their use. There is certainly adequate documentation, particularly for such techniques as verbal conditioning and behavioral rehearsal, to justify their immediate application in vocational guidance and counseling.

## GROUP COUNSELING AND THERAPY

There has recently been a distinct movement toward the use of group counseling and therapy. Like so many trends, this one has taken on the flavor of a fad (it seems that some professionals and clients seek group involvement because "it is the thing to do"), but beneath it all is a solid foundation of behavioral science. Individual psychotherapy in the beginning was based on a limited amount of knowledge about the psychology of the person, as witnessed by Freud's extensive analysis of individual cases as a means for positing constructs for generalization to the total species; but group counseling and psychotherapy has the benefit of not only a more thoroughly evolved psychology of the individual, but also of well thought-out, systematically organized research about collective behavior. From collective behavior came knowledge of small group dynamics, the sequences of experiences and phenomena that occur in variously structured groups of persons. With this theoretical base, group counseling-psychotherapy could justly emerge as a treatment approach that is well within the bounds of behavioral science.[4]

It is logical that when a treatment approach achieves clinical success in individual therapy, it should be considered for use in group treatment, and this is the case with behavioral-modification techniques. Conditioning-based procedures have been tried experimentally in laboratory groups and subsequently investigated in applied clinical groups; in both formats, they have, in general, survived their experimental tests and have earned a validity that justifies their use with counseling and therapy clients.

[4]The context does not accommodate an exhaustive review of group materials; rather, emphasis is on the use of behavioral techniques in a counseling or therapy group. If the reader is interested in more detailed material, the following are worthwhile sources: Cartwright and Zander (1960) have provided what many view as the "classic" text on group dynamics, and similarly good books have been written by Bonner (1959) and Olmsted (1959); group guidance and counseling have been dealt with by Lifton (1966) and Muro and Freeman (1968); and an overview of group psychotherapy is presented by Rosenbaum and Berger (1963).

Verbal behaviors are, of course, the primary mode for communication within counseling and psychotherapy. As was mentioned in previous chapters, there is evidence that counselors and psychotherapists reinforce certain classes of their clients' verbal responses, whether it be done consciously or unconsciously, and that the counselor-therapist's responses can serve as powerful reinforcers to decrease the client's use of certain kinds of responses and to increase his use of other kinds of responses; i.e., verbal conditioning occurs.

On this base of planned and unplanned reinforcements' influencing the client's verbal responses, we encounter the area of accomplishing verbal conditioning in groups. In a study involving guesses as to what color the group leader had selected, Shapiro (1963) found that positive verbal reinforcement from the experimenter-leader would lead individual members to alter their responses, regardless of the group consensus. Similarly, Endler (1965) divided subjects into three groups—conformity, neutrality, and deviancy—and reinforced each subject according to his experimental placement relative to the group consensus (e.g., if a given subject was in the deviancy subgroup, he would be praised for disagreeing with the total group consensus, while a conformity subject would be praised only when he conformed with the consensus). The subjects did not know their assigned placement. Endler found that subjects could be verbally conditioned into agreeing with a contrived group consensus, thereby promoting conforming behavior, or could be conditioned into dissenting behavior in the group.

In addition to being able to influence any given group member's acceptance or rejection of his group's norms, as reflected in a group consensus on a particular topic, it has been found that the same verbal-conditioning procedure can influence the order or sequence of speakers in a group. For example, Shapiro (1964) found that when he reinforced the occurrence of a certain sequence of speakers in a group by telling the subjects that their responses were correct only when the previously determined (but unannounced) sequence occurred, the subjects began modifying the order of speakers, and were thus unconsciously trying to obtain the praise-reward from the experimenter. The order of speakers in the group was thus brought under partial experimental control.

The implications of these laboratory studies for group counseling and therapy are apparent. With planned, or even unplanned, reinforcement, the group counselor-therapist could structure the response styles of the individual members or establish the overall group atmosphere. Given a proper psychobehavioral diagnosis, such as having clearly distinguished what were the appropriate counseling-therapy goals and what were the response contingencies that would lead to the desired behaviors, the psychobehavioral counselor-therapist could change the entire sequence of counseling-therapeutic processes in order to increase efficacy.

The foregoing is what could be assumed from laboratory research, and, as is well known, these deductions may or may not enjoy fruition in the applied clinical setting. These laboratory studies have, however, had comparable clinical counterparts. Although there are a number of group behaviors, particularly verbal responses, that can be reinforced by the experimenter or counselor-therapist in a group setting, let us focus on two aspects that have not previously received reference; these are: controlling the amount of verbalization in a counseling-therapy interview (as contrasted to controlling specific kinds of verbal responses) and the effects of different personal characteristics on the part of the counselor-therapist.

The importance of the amount of verbalization or its opposite —silence—is a function of the theory espoused. For example, psychoanalytically-oriented counselor-therapists might view silence as a particularly destructive portion of the interview (especially for adolescents), because it is at that time that the ego has fewer means for defending itself and anxiety may flood forward; conversely, the client-centered counselor-therapist might maintain that "silence is golden," because the client, by being silent, is finding that he can still be accepted (by the counselor-therapist) without having to fulfill external criteria, e.g., talking in the session. Another view, which might ironically be either psychoanalytic or behavioral in orientation, would hold that the client who is not verbalizing in counseling or therapy is being resistant or withholding or reflecting a lack of motivation to make therapeutic gains. Obviously, the psychobehaviorist would accept any of these positions, but would go on to say that there may be times when the counselor-therapist will, via diagnostic methods, conclude that silence (or talkativeness) is not in the best interest of the counseling-therapy and will want to take steps to bring the silence or the amount of verbalization under control; at this point he would turn to a behavioral technique.

Although it would be feasible to use various behavioral techniques to modify the amount of verbalization in a group setting, for the sake of variety let us consider the application of a mildly aversive technique. Heckle, Wiggins, and Salzberg (1962) conducted group psychotherapy in which they wanted to control the amount of silence that occurred; specifically, they wanted to see if they could eliminate it. A baseline of silences was determined by monitoring the first fifteen minutes of four successive group-therapy sessions. During the first quarter-hour of each of the next four sessions, a hidden speaker sounded an unpleasant noise (which went unexplained to the participants) whenever a silence exceeding ten seconds occurred. And during the first quarter-hour of the next set of four sessions, the frequency of silences was again counted. (There was no aversive noise during this set of sessions.) It was found that the aversive auditory stimulus successfully reduced the number and duration of silences. In other words, the group therapy members were unconsciously conditioned to avoid silences by talking.

In the early stages of research on verbal conditioning, it was found that the characteristics of the experimenter have a definite influence on the subject's response to the reinforcers; a particular subject might react differently to a big burly Marine-type male experimenter than he would to a petite, attractive female experimenter (Binder, McConnell, and Sjoholm, 1957). That is, in behavioral counseling or behavior therapy it might be expected that various counselors and therapists would have differing levels of reinforcing powers, depending at least in part on the client's reactions to certain characteristics that the counselor or therapist might possess (Ryan and Krumboltz, 1964).

To determine the effects of different personal styles of therapists, Drennen and Wiggins (1964) subjected a group of chronic schizophrenic patients to a gruff-hypercritical therapist and to a congenial therapist who gave the group members object rewards (candy and cigarettes), encouragement, suggestions, and verbal praise. This latter therapist's behavior led the majority of the schizophrenic patients to increase their verbal interaction; in other words, they responded to positive reinforcement with more verbalizations with each other. On the other hand, the gruff-hypercritical therapist's behaviors resulted in the group members' initially decreasing their verbal activity, but then increasing it. This pattern is interesting from a behavioral point of view. The negativism of the therapist initially produced withholding; one might wonder whether this was to punish or attack him (in other words, they might have used their participation as a way of saying, "I won't play your therapy game because you aren't nice to me") or whether it was done out of fear. Regardless, the intriguing part is the shift to increased verbal activity. This shift might have been due to an avoidance reaction paradigm: initial withdrawal resulted in continued or further punishment, so talking developed (i.e., increased) to avoid even more punishment—if the patients were talking, the therapist could not make his negative statements. Here again it is recognizable that a therapist's behaviors, whether verbal or nonverbal, may have reinforcing properties.

Another behavioral technique that has received group usage is systematic desensitization (see Chapter 2). One of the earliest studies of the use of systematic desensitization was conducted by Lazarus (1961) in a group therapy setting. In working with phobic disorders, Lazarus found that systematic desensitization could indeed be used in a group context and that it was significantly more effective in alleviating and eliminating the phobic problems than conventional insight-oriented group psychotherapy. Similar results were obtained by Paul and Shannon (1966): a group of males who became highly anxious when confronted with a public speaking task was effectively treated with group systematic desensitization. Paul and Shannon (1966) also concluded that there was no significant difference between individual and group desensitization, as measured by various psychometric instruments. Woody and Schauble (1969a, 1969b) found that systematic desensitization could be effectively presented to groups via video tapes, and that clinical suggestions could beneficially supplement the standard systematic desensitization procedure, i.e., the suggestions had a significant effect on the group's reactions to the fear-provoking stimulus. Likewise, Donner and Guerney (1969) found that audio-taped group desensitization (as well as regular desensitization in groups) led to significant improvement in grade point average with college students who had test-taking anxiety.

Systematic desensitization and other behavioral techniques have been integrated into group counseling and therapy. Hedquist and Weinhold (1970) studied socially anxious and unassertive college students; two behavioral groups (social learning and behavioral rehearsal) were compared to a traditional counseling (group interaction) group, and it was found that the two behavioral groups produced more verbal assertive responses than the control group. Warner and Hansen (1970) provide another integrative study; in a group context, alienated high-school students received either verbal reinforcement to reduce their feelings of alienation of models participating in the groups (without knowledge that they were "models") who would presumably foster imitative behavior. It was found that both behavioral approaches were effective in reducing the students' feelings of alienation, with no difference between the two treaments, as contrasted to the no change found in the placebo group (where the counselor met with them but did not try to focus the discussion or to reinforce any statements) or the control group (who received no treatment or intervention). Cohen (1969) provided desensitization for college students with test-taking anxiety; all subjects in the desensitization groups had a significantly greater reduction in test-taking anxiety than the control subjects, but those who also had an opportunity to interact verbally reported greater anxiety reduction than those who had no interaction (regular desensitization). This supports the value of supplementing systematic desensitization with some sort of relationship factors, such as might be gained from counseling or psychotherapy. Such an integration was also supported by the Katahn, Strenger, and Cherry (1966) study (cited in Chapter 2), which exemplified how combined group counseling, relaxation training, and systematic desensitization (via visual imagery) can be effectively used to deal with groups of test-anxious college students.

Programmed groups constitute another approach to using behavioral techniques in an insight-predicated group setting. A programmed group is structured, in that the counselor-therapist analyzes what sorts of contents should be explored and dealt with in the group sessions and then creates programmed materials to help the group members better accomplish their task. Thus far, programmed groups have not been extensively investigated, but there is both direct and indirect evidence that supports that such an approach can have potential benefits. For example, Solomon, Berzon, and Weedman (1968) compared the value of self-directed groups, i.e., groups without a professional leader, with professionally directed groups. A programmed approach was used in the self-directed groups; at each session the members received a message about interpreting relationships, a review of cognitive material, and/or concepts for understanding interactions, and then the group was given an assigned inter-active component, i.e., a task or exercise designed to structure their discussion or exploration of the stimulus message. The results were not strikingly significant, but it was found that the self-directed pro-grammed and the professionally directed nonprogrammed groups had about the same amount of therapist-rated movement toward the therapeutic goal, i.e., rehabilitation. Relatedly, Jaffe and Reed (1969) found that the popular "rap group" approach was most effective when it was structured in a behavioral manner.

Although programmed groups have not been adequately in-vestigated to date, the approach seems to hold promise. The use of programmed self-directed problem-solving groups, if the proper pro-gram could be developed, would seem to be a much needed aid to meeting the supply-and-demand crisis encountered in mental health. To extend the idea hypothetically, it would seem feasible that problem-solving groups in the community could be programmed by professionals so that their interactions, whether with or without pro-fessional leaders, would result in insights and understanding of criti-cal issues. Possible issues might include improving of parental atti-tudes toward raising children, facilitating communication between spouses or between parents and children, eliminating the compensa-tory value derived from certain questionable behaviors (e.g., exces-sive drinking, use of drugs, hostile or inappropriate teenage actions), creating acceptance of handicapped persons, and fostering motivation to resolve conflicts between minority groups. These are but a few examples; the hypothetical applicability of the programmed group concept seems limited only by the ingenuity of the group programmer.

The use of video tapes for stimulated recall of counseling and psychotherapy sessions, described in detail in Chapter 2 and else-where (Woody, 1969), has ready application in a group setting. For example, Berger, Sherman, Spalding, and Westlake (1968) used es-sentially the same procedure as used in the Interpersonal Process Recall project with groups of persons in a community mental health service program.

Participating in a therapeutic group, regardless of the theo-retical orientation, places a client under a certain amount of social pressure. In other words, group members tend to pressure each other toward appropriate behavior. This group principle has been evi-denced in a behavioral-group format. For example, Harmatz and

Lapuc (1968) report how overweight psychiatric patients were either (1) penalized by loss of money for failure to lose weight, i.e., withdrawal of a positive object reward, (2) subjected to social pressure and social reinforcement in a group therapy setting for weight loss, or (3) placed only on a diet. After six weeks of treatment, the first two groups (both behavioral-modification in rationale) produced weight loss, but only the first group of subjects continued to lose weight in a four-week follow-up nontreatment period.

Intrinsic to the integration of behaviorism into counseling and psychotherapy is the idea that there will be more than one theoretical orientation operating. This was, of course, enunciated in the rationale in Chapter 1. In focusing on the group setting, a review of published accounts suggests that most (if not all) insight theories, such as those with a psychoanalytic or a client-centered orientation, work well with behavioral techniques in a group format. There has been, however, little written specifically on the theoretical integration for groups. One exception is a presentation by Mayer, Rohen, and Whitley (1969) that provides a technical description of combining Bandura's social learning theory and Festinger's cognitive dissonance theory for elementary school group counseling; they conclude that such a theoretical and technical integration is potentially highly effective for promoting attitudinal and behavioral changes in group counseling.

To summarize, there have been enough published accounts of the successful use of behavioral techniques in a group setting to justify the conclusion that group counseling and psychotherapy can be facilitated by supplementing the insight format with conditioning-based techniques. The technical integration in groups would follow essentially the same psychobehavioral guidelines set forth for the individual counseling-therapy (see Chapter 1), but the counselor-therapist would also need to give proper consideration to group dynamics.

## COMMUNITY SERVICE

Contemporary crises and societal needs have created a powerful press for all mental health workers to adopt a stronger commitment to community service. In fact, some counselor-therapist educators are predicting that, because of the pressure created by the events of our era, counselors and therapists are having to become involved with problems much different from those toward which their academic training was directed, and that counselors and therapists are, in a sense, moving toward the role of "community counselor-therapist," as opposed to what may soon be the outdated role of "personal counselor-therapist." Since there are numerous ramifications within this issue that relate directly to professional training, this will receive further consideration in subsequent chapters. Suffice it to say here that a preponderance of research documents that human behavior can be beneficially influenced by reinforcement, and that behavioral techniques can be used with both therapy groups and community groups. In view of the community-societal problems, counselors and therapists must extend their services into the community, forsaking if need be the romanticized notion of the walnut-paneled offices of the psychotherapist in favor of a "let's-get-the-job-done-where-the-action-is" approach. Behavioral science documentation more than adequately justifies the counselor-therapist's assuming responsibility for community change and for applying his professional skills; and there is evidence that behavioral techniques are applicable to community problems (Burgess and Bushell, 1969; Woody, 1970). Certainly the individual client will never achieve actualization or optimal functioning if he has to exist in a disordered community; man is a social being, and the conditions of today require that counseling and therapy services be directed toward alleviating social stress. The humanist and actionist elements of psychobehavioral counseling and therapy provide a combination that should enhance the chances of achieving marked community change through mental health services.

## INFLUENCE OF THE SETTING

Although it would be fair on theoretical grounds to say that behavioral techniques do not, at least in general, involve factors that lead to reservations about their use in certain settings, it is only realistic to acknowledge that there may well be differences in their acceptance according to the setting. Restrictions may be created because a particular setting may not have adequate staff; for example, Marks (1968) believes that aversive therapy frequently evokes rather deep-rooted emotional reactions, and thus should be done only when psychiatric consultation is available—some settings might not have a psychiatric consultant and would not, if they accepted Marks' view, be in a position to provide aversive therapy. Other restrictions may result from opinions about a technique; for example, there is certainly reason to question whether the philosophical constructs associated with public education would allow for the use of aversive therapy with children in the schools, and Woody and Herr (1966) found that even experienced doctoral-level psychologists had more reservation about using clinical hypnosis in the public school than they had about using it in a college or university.

Queries are frequently raised as to whether a rehabilitation counselor-therapist employed in a medical or psychiatric setting can be technically innovative, particularly in the use of behavioral-modification techniques. The implication is that physicians, and particularly those, it seems, who are psychoanalytic in orientation, would resist endorsing the use of unusual (and especially behavioral) procedures. This kind of query may itself be a defense; that is, it may be a rationalization to avoid having to take the responsibility for therapeutic action. When there are opposing medical attitudes, there is always the possibility of dealing with them. Experience has shown that two things must be avoided: first, the counselor-therapist must not allow himself to be drawn into an interprofessional status contest, and second, the counselor-therapist must not get trapped into a theoretical debate, which is unlikely to be won by either side. Both points involve a warning against defensive behaviors that can only serve to block the real challenge, helping the client. Therefore, the only logical approach is to begin providing colleagues, in a non-threatening and nonhostile fashion, a progressive orientation to one's theories and techniques. The behaviorist might want to practice what he preaches, and condition or shape his colleagues into accepting his ideas. There is reason to believe that ego defense can be kept out of the picture, and if there is, in fact, a solid academic rationale, professionals of any discipline and in any setting will be accepting enough to allow the counselor-therapist to utilize his preferred approach.

Professionals in mental health clinics or hospitals, including those affiliated with colleges and universities, usually do not have to operate under stringent restrictions and can thus proceed in a manner that is sanctioned by their colleagues and peers in the professional community; the public schools, however, present a different situation. Public education is unique in many ways, not the least of which is the fact that professionals must answer directly to the lay public. This is quite defensible, since this is well within the realm of our democratic society. However, the fact remains that professionals in the schools *are* influenced by public opinion about their practices.

The basic issue probably is: should clinical services, such as counseling and psychotherapy, be provided in the schools? In the past, it was probably correct to believe that school personnel were not prepared to enter into clinical service. For example, Moore (1961) opposed school counselors' being involved in anything that remotely resembled therapeutic counseling, primarily on grounds that they were not prepared for such a function. But this situation has changed. Particularly because there are more school psychologists and, because school counselors have been receiving more advanced training than they did a decade ago, there are now many counselors and psychologists in the schools who should, can, and do provide a high quality of clinical service, including counseling and psychotherapy.

A more important issue is whether the educational setting is appropriate for mental health services, and whether the public schools are charged by the public to make such provisions. The answer in both instances is: Yes! The social-economic-technological-cultural developments within our society have led to new responsibilities for the public schools. The concept of "educating the total person" has moved well beyond cultivating the individual's academic aptitudes, and into his psychological structure and involvement with social systems, be it the family or the cultural subgroup. Logically, the schools have been thrust into an ever-increasing responsibility for both the development of the child and the influencing of societal development.

This shift in responsibilities has been recognized by professional associations. For example, the American School Counselor Association (1965), in describing the recommended functions of secondary school counselors, states that it is "essential that the majority of a school counselor's time be devoted to individual or small-group counseling." Numerous counselor educators have stated their belief that counseling, as provided by school counselors, is on a continuum with psychotherapy, and that the school counselors, therefore, should be prepared, both academically and in terms of role definition, to provide mental health services like counseling and psychotherapy (Patterson, 1966; Woody, 1969b).

Aside from the need for school counselors and school psychologists to provide mental health services because of the supply-and-demand factor, the schools also provide, by virtue of their being the designated representative of public attitudes and needs, an unmatched opportunity to provide mental health aid. Patterson (1966) sees the schools as being able to void the stigma that is occasionally still erroneously attached to mental health problems. Even professionals from other disciplines, such as psychiatrists and public health workers, are eyeing the school as a most ideal launching pad for their mental health services. For example, Stickney (1968) maintains that the schools possess unique opportunities for preventive efforts, casefinding, and crisis intervention; he has headed a project in Pittsburgh that has successfully supplied the schools with the essentials in attempts to provide mental health services: proper personnel and facilities. There have been numerous other productive programs in which professionals representing interdisciplinary community mental health sources have joined with the school staff to upgrade the available services and to implement their noneducational services through the facilities of the school system, the results of which have been superior to the quality of service that would have been possible if there had not been this unification of institutional efforts (Condell, Anderson, and Ebinger, 1966; Cowen, Zax, Izzo, and Trost, 1966; Mumford, 1968; Stickney, 1968). These successful endeavors provide part of the basis for the pressure that counselors and psychologists are experiencing to move their personal commitment away from isolated individual services toward a community orientation. (This does not, of course, mean total abandonment of individual service, but rather more emphasis on societal-community service, particularly of a preventive nature.) These factors will receive further consideration when implications for training are presented in subsequent chapters.

Both the implementation of counseling-psychotherapy and mental health services in the schools and the use of new, sometimes publicly unfamiliar techniques, e.g., behavioral modification procedures, mean that the counselor-therapist must at some point deal with the philosophical side of public education. Many elements of educational philosophy such as administrative regulations, can only justify their existence by longevity. That is, they have existed or worked in the past, and so they are continued. Unfortunately, these pseudo-respectable myths abound in some school systems, and rather than serving as safeguards (which is their proponents' typical rationalization), they only hamper progress. This results in failure to meet the educational and personal needs of the students and the community.

This means in practical terms that the professional involved in the schools, regardless of assigned role and theoretical orientation, must at some time be prepared to accept the fact that he is a professional (and perhaps he is not really one until he can make such an assertion). This means that he must be personally willing to be involved; he must be willing and able to make his own assessment of conditions, use his professional competencies to suggest improvements, and offer these forthrightly to his colleagues and the public. This sort of responsible action means simply that: in taking an assertive, professional action, he is saying in effect, "My professional training suggests that these changes are necessary, regardless of what might have been true in the past, and I am willing to take responsibility for the results of these recommendations."

Many educators, particularly classroom teachers and special pupil services personnel, acknowledge that conditions need to be changed and can even envisage better alternatives, but they are hesitant to take the initial, responsible step, because this usually means a confrontation with existing administrative policies. There seems to be the perception that the abstract "administration" is an awe-inspiring, all-powerful body that could, if offended, snuff out the professional who raises an idea contrary to its preferences. This is, of course, ridiculous. The administration is merely the product of the attitudes, opinions, and ideas offered by the public and the profession, and the individual educator's integrity as a person and as a professional rests on his being able to take, state, and support a position on issues vital to the outcomes of education. Undoubtedly, there will come a time when the proffered ideas run counter to existing policies, but a stand must be taken. "Token progress" has no place in our contemporary society, whether it be affording all persons human dignity, civil rights, or good educational services.

An essential element of psychobehavioral counseling and therapy is that the counselor-therapist assume responsibility for professional actions, both in the counseling-therapeutic relationship and in the setting in which he is employed. If there are administrative barriers to effective service, he must try to alter them; if there are public opinions that restrict his meeting the needs of his client, he must be willing to exert an effort to bring about modification and public acceptance. In short, he must be a true professional, constantly working to improve his knowledge and his technique. Practically, this means that he spends a major portion of his energy on program development; this takes the form of relentlessly orienting other professionals and the community to the various needs and modes for their fulfillment. The justification for any service rests solely on the professional's ability to achieve, via an academic rationale, acceptance from others. Finally, the psychobehavioral counselor-therapist must be well entrenched in the ongoing process of becoming a better professional person. This will mean much more than academic knowledge. It means being in the process of achieving greater degrees of self-understanding, particularly about how his personal characteristics affect his professional functioning; this leads us to the critical area of professional training.

## REFERENCES

American School Counselor Association. Guidelines for implementation of the ASCA statement of policy for secondary school counselors. In J. W. Loughary, R. O. Stripling, and P. W. Fitzgerald (Eds.), *Counseling: A growing profession*. Washington, D. C.: American Personnel and Guidance Association, 1965, 100–106.

Berger, M. M., Sherman, B., Spalding, Janet, and Westlake, R. The use of videotape with psychotherapy in a community mental health service program. *International Journal of Group Psychotherapy*, 1968, *18*, 504–515.

Binder, A., McConnell, D., and Sjoholm, Nancy A. Verbal conditioning as a function of experimenter characteristics. *Journal of Abnormal and Social Psychology*, 1957, *55*, 309–314.

Bonner, H. *Group dynamics: Principles and applications*. New York: Ronald, 1959.

Burgess, R. L., and Bushell, D., Jr. (Eds.). *Behavioral sociology: The experimental analysis of social process*. New York: Columbia University Press, 1969.

Carkhuff, R. R., Alexik, Mae, and Anderson, Susan. Do we have a theory of vocational choice? *Personnel and Guidance Journal*, 1967, *46*, 335–345.

Cartwright, D., and Zander, A. *Group dynamics: Research and theory* (2nd ed.). Evanston, Ill.: Row, Peterson and Co., 1960.

Cohen, R. The effects of group interaction and progressive hierarchy presentation on desensitization of test anxiety. *Behaviour Research and Therapy*, 1969, *7*, 15–26.

Condell, J. F., Anderson, R. L., and Ebinger, R. D. Providing school psychological service through a community mental health center. *Community Mental Health Journal*, 1966, *2*, 82–85.

Cowen, E. L., Zax, M., Izzo, L. D., and Trost, Mary Ann. Prevention of emotional disorders in the school setting. *Journal of Consulting Psychology*, 1966, *30*, 381–387.

Donner, L., and Guerney, B. G., Jr. Automated group desensitization for test anxiety. *Behaviour Research and Therapy*, 1969, *7*, 1–13.

Drennen, W. T., and Wiggins, S. L. Manipulation of verbal behavior of chronic hospitalized schizophrenics in a group therapy situation. *International Journal of Group Psychotherapy*, 1964, *14*, 189–193.

Endler, N. S. The effects of verbal reinforcement on conformity and deviant behavior. *Journal of Social Psychology*, 1965, *66*, 147–154.

Eysenck, H. J., and Rachman, S. *The causes and cures of neurosis*. San Diego, Calif.: R. R. Knapp, 1965.

Folkins, C. H., Lawson, Karen D., Opton, E. M., Jr., and Lazarus, R. S. Desensitization and the experimental reduction of threat. *Journal of Abnormal Psychology*, 1968, *73*, 100–113.

Greenspoon, J., and Gersten, C. D. A new look at psychological testing: Psychological testing from the standpoint of a behaviorist. *American Psychologist*, 1967, *22*, 848–853.

Harmatz, M. G., and Lapuc, P. Behavior modification of overeating in a psychiatric population. *Journal of Consulting and Clinical Psychology*, 1968, *32*, 583–587.

Heckel, R. V., Wiggins, S. L., and Salzberg, H. C. Conditioning against silences in group therapy. *Journal of Clinical Psychology*, 1962, *28*, 216–217.

Hedquist, F. J., and Weinhold, B. K. Behavioral group counseling with socially anxious and unassertive college students. *Journal of Counseling Psychology*, 1970, *17*, 237–242.

Holland, J. L. *The psychology of vocational choice*. Waltham, Mass.: Blaisdell, 1966.

Jaffe, A., and Reed, Alice. Involving the turned-on generation through structured "rapping." *Personnel and Guidance Journal*, 1969, *48*, 311–315.

Jones, G. B., and Krumboltz, J. D. Stimulating vocational exploration through film-mediated problems. *Journal of Counseling Psychology*, 1970, *17*, 107–114.

Kanfer, F. H., and Saslow, G. Behavioral diagnosis. In C. M. Franks (Ed.), *Behavior therapy: Appraisal and status*. New York: McGraw-Hill, 1969, 417–444.

Katahn, M., Strenger, S., and Cherry, Nancy. Group counseling and behavior therapy with test-anxious college students. *Journal of Consulting Psychology*, 1966, *30*, 544–549.

Klein, Marjorie H., Dittmann, A. T., Parloff, M. B., and Gill, M. M. Behavior therapy: Observations and reflections. *Journal of Consulting and Clinical Psychology*, 1969, *33*, 259–266.

Krumboltz, J. D., and Schroeder, W. W. Promoting career planning through reinforcement. *Personnel and Guidance Journal*, 1965, *44*, 19–26.

Krumboltz, J. D., and Thoresen, C. E. The effect of behavioral counseling in group and individual settings on information-seeking behavior. *Journal of Counseling Psychology*, 1964, *11*, 324–333.

Krumboltz, J. D., Varenhorst, Barbara B., and Thoresen, C. E. Nonverbal factors in the effectiveness of models in counseling. *Journal of Counseling Psychology*, 1967, *14*, 412–418.

Lazarus, A. A. Group therapy of phobic disorders by systematic desensitization. *Journal of Abnormal and Social Psychology*, 1961, *63*, 504–510.

Lifton, W. M. *Working with groups: Group process and individual growth* (2nd ed.). New York: John Wiley, 1966.

London, P. *The children's hypnotic susceptibility scale*. Palo Alto, Calif.: Consulting Psychologists Press, 1962.

Marks, I. M. Aversion therapy. *British Journal of Medical Psychology*, 1968, *41*, 47–52.

Mayer, G. R., Rohen, T. M., and Whitley, A. D. Group counseling with children: A cognitive-behavioral approach. *Journal of Counseling Psychology*, 1969, *16*, 142–149.

Moore, G. D. A negative view toward therapeutic counseling in the public schools. *Counselor Education and Supervision*, 1961, *1*, 60–68.

Mumford, Emily. Teacher response to school mental health programs. *American Journal of Psychiatry*, 1968, *125*, 113–119.

Muro, J. J., and Freeman, S. L. (Eds.). *Readings in group counseling*. Scranton, Pa.: International Textbook, 1968.

Olmsted, M. S. *The small group*. New York: Random House, 1959.

Patterson, C. H. Psychotherapy in the school. *Journal of School Psychology*, 1966, *4*, 15–29.

Paul, G. L., and Shannon, D. T. Treatment of anxiety through systematic desensitization in therapy groups. *Journal of Abnormal Psychology*, 1966, *71*, 124–135.

Roe, Anne. *Psychology of occupations.* New York: John Wiley, 1965.

Rosenbaum, M., and Berger, M. (Eds.). *Group psychotherapy and group function.* New York: Basic Books, 1963.

Ryan, T. Antoinette, and Krumboltz, J. D. Effect of planned reinforcement counseling on client decision-making behavior. *Journal of Counseling Psychology,* 1964, *11,* 315–323.

Shapiro, D. The reinforcement of disagreement in a small group. *Behaviour Research and Therapy,* 1963, *1,* 267–272.

Shapiro, D. Group learning of speech sequences without awareness. *Science,* 1964, *44,* 74–76.

Shor, R. E., and Orne, Emily C. *Harvard group scale of hypnotic susceptibility.* Palo Alto, Calif.: Consulting Psychologists Press, 1962.

Solomon, L. N., Berzon, Betty, and Weedman, C. The programmed group: A new rehabilitation source. *International Journal of Group Psychotherapy,* 1968, *18,* 199–219.

Stefflre, B. Vocational development: Ten propositions in search of a theory. *Personnel and Guidance Journal,* 1966, *44,* 611–614.

Stephens, T. M. Psychological consultation to teachers of learning and behaviorally handicapped children using a behavioral model. *Journal of School Psychology,* 1970, *8,* 13–18.

Stickney, S. B. Schools are our community mental health centers. *American Journal of Psychiatry,* 1968, *124,* 101–108.

Super, D. E. A theory of vocational development. *American Psychologist,* 1953, *8,* 185–190.

Surratt, P. R., Ulrich, R. E., and Hawkins, R. P. An elementary student as a behavioral engineer. *Journal of Applied Behavioral Analysis,* 1969, *2,* 85–92.

Thoresen, C. E., and Krumboltz, J. D. Relationship of counselor reinforcement of selected responses to external behavior. *Journal of Counseling Psychology,* 1967, *14,* 140–144.

Thoresen, C. E., and Krumboltz, J. D. Similarity of social models and clients in behavioral counseling: Two experimental studies. *Journal of Counseling Psychology,* 1968, *15,* 393–401.

Toews, J. M. The counselor as contingency manager. *Personnel and Guidance Journal,* 1969, *48,* 127–133.

Veldman, D. J. Computer-based sentence-completion interviews. *Journal of Counseling Psychology,* 1967, *14,* 153–157.

Warner, R. W., Jr., and Hansen, J. C. Verbal-reinforcement and model-reinforcement group counseling with alienated students. *Journal of Counseling Psychology,* 1970, *17,* 168–172.

Weitzenhoffer, A. M., and Hilgard, E. R. *Stanford hypnotic susceptibility scale, form A and B.* Palo Alto, Calif.: Consulting Psychologists Press, 1959.

Weitzenhoffer, A. M., and Hilgard, E. R. *Stanford hypnotic susceptibility scale, form C.* Palo Alto, Calif.: Consulting Psychologists Press, 1962.

Willoughby, R. R. Norms for the Clark-Thurstone inventory. *Journal of Social Psychology,* 1934, *5,* 91–95.

Wolpe, J. *The practice of behavior therapy.* New York: Pergamon, 1969.

Wolpe, J., and Lang, P. J. A fear survey schedule for use in behaviour therapy. *Behaviour Research and Therapy,* 1964, *2,* 27–30.

Wolpe, J., and Lazarus, A. A. *Behavior therapy techniques.* New York: Pergamon, 1966.

Woody, R. H. Vocational counseling with behavioral techniques. *Vocational Guidance Quarterly,* 1968, *17,* 97–103.

Woody, R. H. *Behavioral problem children in the schools: Recognition, diagnosis, and behavioral modification.* New York: Appleton-Century-Crofts, 1969. (a)

Woody, R. H. Psychobehavioral therapy in the schools: Implications for counselor education. *Counselor Education and Supervision,* 1969, *8,* 258–264. (b)

Woody, R. H. Behavioral techniques in community service: A psychobehavioral perspective. *Journal of School Psychology,* 1970, *8,* 82–88.

Woody, R. H., and Herr, E. L. Psychologists and hypnosis. Part II. Use in educational settings. *American Journal of Clinical Hypnosis,* 1966, *8,* 254–256.

Woody, R. H., and Schauble, P. G. Desensitization of fear by video tapes. *Journal of Clinical Psychology,* 1969, *25,* 102–103. (a)

Woody, R. H., and Schauble, P. G. Videotaped vicarious desensitization. *Journal of Nervous and Mental Disease,* 1969, *148,* 281–286. (b)

Yates, A. J. *Behavior therapy.* New York: John Wiley, 1970.

# II

# Implications for Training

# 4

# History of Program Development and Trainee Selection

During the past twenty years, the period that has seen the main developmental thrust of guidance, counseling, and psychological services, the professional training programs could probably be justly characterized as the product of the opinions of the professors at the training institution.[1] Their opinions, no doubt, were formed by the subjectively assumed implications of relevant research, the perceived success or failure of training efforts across the country, and the objectives (and recommendations for role functions and training) offered by the professional associations with which they identified. The two primary professional organizations that have devoted frequent and rigorous efforts to upgrading training are, of course, the American Psychological Association (A.P.A.) and the American Personnel and Guidance Association (A.P.G.A.). But this entire approach to developing training guidelines remains subject to the potential for strong personal biases. Without a system for assessing the needs of the service recipients, or the efficacy of particular training procedures, or the factors (such as faculty and facilities) unique to each training institu-

[1]Professionals interested in training, and particularly, it seems, those in the field of counselor education, have progressively been debating the appropriateness of the terms "preparation," "training," and "educating" as they relate to the professional development of trainees. At times, this seems more like "lexical gamesmanship" than an academic effort to make training improvements. The rationale, regardless of which term is being defended, is rooted in philosophy (e.g., as might relate to an educational philosophy tenet or to the overused term "nature of man") and in the theory of counseling or psychotherapy being espoused, rather than on any creditable behavioral-science evidence. Because the psychobehavioral approach is an eclectic one, philosophically, theoretically, and technically, unless specified for a special reason, terms like preparation, training, and education of would-be counselors and psychologists are used synonymously throughout this book.

tion, it is virtually impossible to assume a scientific basis for training.

There have been several notable sets of recommendations that affect training practices. After the rapid growth of the "war years baby"—clinical psychology—counseling psychology emerged as a distinct specialty in the early 1950s. In 1952, the Committee on Counselor Training of the A.P.A.'s Division of Counseling and Guidance (which was renamed the Division of Counseling Psychology later that year) offered two reports, one on the recommended standards for training doctoral-level counseling psychologists and the other on the practicum training of counseling psychologists (American Psychological Association, 1952a, 1952b). These were followed in 1956 by the report of a special Divisional Committee on Definition, which viewed the counseling psychologist as giving emphasis to three areas:

(a) the development of an individual's inner life through concern with his motivations and emotions, (b) the individual's achievement of harmony with his environment through helping him to develop the resources that he must bring to this task (e.g., by assisting him to make effective use of appropriate community resources), and (c) the influencing of society to recognize individual differences and to encourage the fullest development of all persons within it. (American Psychological Association, 1962, p. 16)

During this period, leaders in the profession offered their ideas about how counseling psychology should be structured; for example, Super (1955) gave emphasis to helping the client deal with the way he functions in a variety of settings (as contrasted to a specialized segment such as education) and pointed out that counseling psychologists are concerned primarily with normal persons; that is, in contrast to the clinical psychologist's concern with psychopathology, the counseling psychologist is concerned with hygiology. Even with abnormal persons, the focus would be on their normalities.

During this same period, there was a marked increase in the provision of counseling services in schools, and again there was little empirical evidence for role definitions and guidelines. Rather, they continued to be based on such things as personal opinions from proven professional experts or leaders, e.g., Arbuckle's (1958) early paper on the generalities of educating a school counselor, and professional organizations' recommendations for minimum standards for counselor preparation (American Personnel and Guidance Association, 1958) and for the involvement of psychology in the preparation of school counselors (American Psychological Association, 1962).

There was another flurry of activity when professionals began to delineate what should be the criteria for trainees in counseling and counseling psychology. Initially, counselors were defined as those persons trained in educational guidance activities, usually with, at most, one year of graduate-level training, and counseling psychologists were defined as those persons with two years of graduate training and a strong background in psychological and behavioral science. This was found to be too simple a differentiation, and is no longer applied in this sense.

The selection problem for counseling is more ambiguous than for even closely related psychological specialties. When the functions of the professional counselor are vague or poorly defined, and the ultimate criteria for his performance are essentially nonexistent, it is understandably difficult to set up meaningful selection procedures. This was definitely the case in the early years of counseling; fortunately, the evolution of the specialty has been accompanied by progressive functional distinctions, and the selection ambiguity has been somewhat eased.

There was little, if any, solid experimental evidence as to how to select trainees. Essentially, what was accepted was what was already in vogue, as derived from the personal opinions of respected professionals. Occasionally, these opinionated analyses of the ideal personal characteristics of counselors were based on surveys, such as descriptions by school principals of the professional and personal qualities of the counselors in their schools and ratings of their effectiveness. It is surprising that it was seldom questioned whether a nonpsychologically oriented administrator could validly assess characteristics or counseling effectiveness. Dismaying as it may be, this sort of practice still exists.

There were studies that were more oriented to research that related measures from standardized instruments to counseling effectiveness, but these seemed to provide meaningless diffusion rather than meaningful clarity. As an example of the kinds of characteristics that supposedly could be attributed to counselors, Cottle (1953) reviewed the literature to that date and found that a few selected "counselor characteristics" were fairness, sincerity, personality, good character and wholesome philosophy, common sense, health, emotional stability, interest in guidance and personnel work, integrity, sense of humor, vitality, and on and on. Looking back over those terms, the contemporary professional is apt to respond with a cynical, "Isn't that sweet!" In fairness to Cottle (1953), his review of the research (or quasi-research) led him to conclude, with some understatement, that "many of the reports are based on subjective judgment of a questionable nature," and that additional scholastic aptitude and personal trait measures were needed.

The next, and more scientific, step was to apply psychometric measures to the therapeutic relationships. In other words, consideration was given to the measurable personal characteristics of the counselor-therapist that contribute to the relationship. Thus began a series of significant research studies that focused on the personality of the counselor-therapist. Fiedler (1950) found that is was the therapist's expertise that was critical to achieving an "ideal therapeutic relationship," not the theory or orientation of psychotherapy that he endorsed. Strupp (1955) studied the therapeutic responses of psychologists, psychiatrists, and social workers, and found in contrasting the disciplines that difference in technique was most closely related to the factor of experience (not professional discipline), and that an analysis of therapist response profiles revealed "a considerable degree of similarity" among the three professional groups. He concluded that the professional affiliation—that is, whether the therapist is a psychologist, psychiatrist, or social worker—"exerts a relatively minor influence upon the kinds of techniques used." Weitz (1957), in a subjective analysis of the influence of the counselor's personality, concluded that there were three counselor personality patterns that were of critical significance to the counseling interaction: security, sensitivity, and objectivity.

It was at about this time in the evolution of counseling and psychotherapy that Betz and Whitehorn (1956) published research showing a significant statistical relationship between the personality types of therapists and the success of psychotherapy with schizophrenics. In 1958, the American Psychological Association conducted the first of a series of conferences on research in psychotherapy. Snyder (1959) summarized the relevant research and acknowledged that "our findings are rather scattered"; however, he stated that the following characteristics of therapists seemed to influence client behavior "to some extent":

(a) self-insight, (b) insight into others, (c) adaptability, (d) emotional control, (e) social interaction, (f) dependence, (g) negative attitudes toward the client, (h) preference for a given type of therapy (active or passive), and perhaps the following three characteristics: (a) concern with conformity, (b) concern with sex, and (c) concern with aggression. (p. 253)

The second conference, in 1961, gave even more emphasis to the psychotherapist's contribution to the treatment process, with much of the material being centered on the personal qualities (as opposed to professional technical skills). Levinson (1962) proposed seven classes of variables or events: (1) relatively stable personal-social characteristics of the therapist, (2) relatively stable personal-social characteristics of the patient, (3) characteristics of the patient-therapist pair (the matching effects), (4) stages in the treatment career (i.e., the various stages that therapy progresses through), (5) overall treatment outcome (i.e., the criteria for therapeutic change, such as symptom-reduction, improved social adjustment, general living comfort, improved self-esteem, or any other criteria that unquestionably depend upon the particular theory underlying the treatment), (6) the institutional setting of treatment, and (7) the social context of the patient's life. While each of these seven points could feasibly have an effect on the therapeutic relationship, of particular relevance herein is the very first one, about which Levinson (1962) remarks:

(c) The therapist's character traits, values, and affective qualities. Of interest here are such variables as emotional warmth, capacity for empathic relationship, obsessiveness, impulsiveness, authoritarianism, tolerance for various kinds of value-violating behavior, values relating to achievement, creativity, sensuality, work, honor, and the like. . . .
(d) The therapist's psychosocial characteristics: class origin and mobility, ethnicity and ethnic identity, marginality, religion, age, sex, political outlook, and the like. . . . (p. 15)

Although quite relevant, one must acknowledge that these adjectives are still largely the result of deductive reasoning. Still, there is a definite focus on the personality of the therapist. Of great importance is the fact that in the same conference, Strupp (1962) gave a scholarly discussion of the "vagaries" of a research program on these matters, and noted that there were many methodological problems plaguing experimental and quasi-experimental studies. Also in the second conference, Betz (1962) presented the previous and continued findings of the studies that she and her colleagues conducted on the relationship between the therapist's personality type and the success of his psychotherapeutic treatment of schizophrenic patients.

In summary, this period produced a number of research studies (although not cited individually here, they are referred to in the aforementioned sources) that brought unprecedented attention to the importance of the therapist's (or counselor's) personal characteristics to the outcome of his therapeutic interventions. It should be noted that the A.P.A.-sponsored Conferences on Research in Psychotherapy, of which there are three at this writing (Rubinstein and Parloff, 1959; Strupp and Luborsky, 1962; Shlien, Hunt, Matarazzo, and Savage, 1968), provide the professional interested in counseling and psychotherapeutic processes with a wealth of reference materials.

Along with these research investigations of the influence of the counselor-therapist on the therapeutic relationship, there developed a heightened degree of professional interest in new approaches to treatment. The advent of Carl R. Rogers' (1951, 1961) client-centered counseling and psychotherapy had an immeasurable influence on treatment behaviors and on personal and professional attitudes, philosophies, and identities.

The impact of client-centered procedures led to new definitions of the ideal counselor-therapist and of the characteristics necessary to make the therapeutic relationship meaningful. As with its theoretical counterparts, client-centered counseling and therapy had, for well over a decade, a minimal amount of evidence that any particular set of counselor-therapist characteristics did, in fact, affect the treatment processes. Instead, the rationale was again limited to speculations (admittedly, from sagacious theorists). Rogers (1959), for example, attempted to define the characteristics of a "helping relationship" by posing very personal questions to himself, such as "Can I *be* in some way which will be perceived by the other person as trustworthy, as dependable or consistent in some deep sense?" Although these pronouncements were based on an extremely limited amount of experimental study, most professionals (this author included) found worth in Rogers' personalized delineations of the help-ing characteristics (it is always comforting to identify with a warm, human experience, even if only through an article in a professional journal), and they received a large amount of clinical, philosophical, and religious support.

The client-centered school and its related existential approaches flourished, and behavioral scientists, many of whom were tormented by the ambivalent feelings of wanting to reject the tenets on aca-demic-experimental grounds, but accept them because of the philo-sophical-personal-charismatic properties, breathed a sigh of relief when there was a flurry of research efforts on facilitating conditions. These efforts might best be exemplified by the studies conducted by Truax, Carkhuff, Berenson, and their colleagues, as summarized in Truax and Carkhuff (1967) and Carkhuff and Berenson (1967). Many of the studies produced within this client-centered or facilitat-ing-relationship realm are impressive; many of them yield results that say, in effect, "If the counselor or therapist possesses $X$-amount of characteristic $I$, then he will be able to facilitate his clients' achiev-ing factor $Q$ significantly better than the counselor or therapist who only possesses (a smaller) $Y$-amount of characteristic $I$." Because mental health professionals are entrusted with a great societal re-sponsibility, and because the counseling-therapy movement is still embryonic and in search of an impeccable scientific stature (al-though this is hard to admit consciously), such positive statistical results provide a much needed salve for our professional egos. But then, much to our dismay, the same messianic sources present simi-lar evidence that nonprofessionals can get the same (and occasionally better) results as we professionals (Carkhuff, 1968; Guerney, 1969).

After the initial traumatic effects have subsided, the behavioral science armament again becomes visible. It would seem that the proper perspective would be to be pleased that the clients can be helped through another person's creating and communicating facili-tating conditions, whether he be a professional or a layman. If care-fully selected laymen with limited training can get *some* of the same beneficial results as a highly trained professional, then we may be getting closer to solving the mental health services' supply-and-de-mand problem. Moreover, the professional's responsibility to help fulfill society's mental health needs should provide ample justification, indeed a mandate, for the mental health professions to give increased attention to optimal use of lay and technician-level persons. This would include efforts to improve orienting and training procedures, and to assure that they receive proper supervision.

Another factor that worries some professionals is that the so-called "facilitating conditions" are not in themselves sufficient to effect cures, and thus should not be held up as the prototype for all counselors and therapists to achieve. The documentation fails to confirm a relationship between facilitating conditions and a positive outcome (e.g., Bergin and Jasper, 1969: Truax, Carkhuff, and Kodman, 1965; Truax, Frank, Imber, Battle, Hoehn-Saric, Nash, and Stone, 1966; Truax, Wargo, and Carkhuff, 1966); because these studies have generally found that at least one of the therapeutic conditions failed to have a significant correlation with a positive outcome (at one time or another, the major conditions of genuineness, nonpossessive warmth, and accurate empathy have each received such a contradiction), Truax and Carkhuff (1967) developed a new principle: "When any two therapeutic conditions are sufficiently high, positive patient or client change will occur." (p. 91)

This kind of atmosphere surrounding the research on facilitating conditions leads some professionals to question whether unwarranted assumptions have been made about the purported established importance of the currently defined conditions. There are some professional "facilitators" who would maintain that: "Unless you have a score of $X$ on the facilitating characteristic of $I$ scale, you will not be able to help your client achieve self-understanding." To the behavioral scientist, the obvious position is: "Yes, it is nice to score high on these scales, but we cannot say it is essential, because there is still reason to question that these facilitating characteristics scales are actually valid, that is, that they actually measure all (or enough) of the factors that are essential to changes in the disordered behaviors presumably being treated—not to mention the fact that there is reason to question the reliability of such simplistic rating scales and the methods used for sampling the behaviors that provide the purported experimental basis for the facilitating approach."

Although these issues could be debated at great length, the following statements seem to be justifiable summary assertions about the issue of "facilitating conditions": (1) even if it is granted that the definitions are clear, there is not, *at present,* adequate experimental evidence based on high-quality research designs to accept that these conditions have been validated as leading to change; (2) the methods for measuring change are limited, and while they provide valuable evidence, they should not be construed to possess an infallibility, especially in the area of reliability, that would negate the value of contradictory evidence; (3) in some instances, the criteria for outcome seem readily disputable; and (4) these conditions unquestionably represent a single approach to counseling and psychotherapy, and thus far there is no scientific reason to believe that this theory is significantly stronger than (or, for that matter, weaker than) numerous other theories. The psychobehavioral position is that the counselor-therapist has the goal of using his relationship with his clients as part of the therapeutic process, but that this constitutes only a portion of the total composite of the therapeutic influences.

The foregoing discussion, because of the emphasis on scientific documentation, may create the impression that relevant writings must be primarily experimental to have value. This is not so. It is true that experimentation is necessary if counseling-psychotherapy is to claim status as a behavioral science, but certainly much can be gained from personal-philosophical writings.

From a number of such writings that could make beneficial contributions to the training process, there are four sources that seem to have special value. Grater, Kell, and Morse (1961) made a subjective analysis of how counselors and therapists seem to be highly nurturant individuals (this need is viewed as having a positive value), and they state that counselors and therapists

have developed long standing patterns of relationships with others which in many ways are emotionally satisfying but tend to produce a certain amount of isolation and emotional distance and resulting loneliness. Their nurturant behavior serves to maintain a certain equilibrium between their needs to relate to people and the distance-producing behavior patterns which they have learned. However, the counseling relationship reduces the rewards one may expect from the pattern and tends to produce greater emotional distance. (p. 11)

In view of these speculations about the counselor-therapist's search to fulfill his needs, in this case his nurturance need, the comments offered throughout this book about the counselor-therapist's use of conscious or unconscious reinforcers gain credence. Farson (1962) used a provocative article title, "The Counselor is a Woman," to point out the masculine and feminine elements in being a counselor; on the nurturant need in counselors, he said:

By and large, in our American society, the male is expected to be clever, tough, strong, courageous, independent, more concerned with things than with people, whereas the female should be tender, gentle, loving, dependent, receptive, passive, more concerned with family and inter-personal relationships than with things. If we were to say which of these roles best matches the kind of behavior it is important to embody as a counselor, we would no doubt agree that the female role comes closer. In this sense the counselor is a woman. (p. 44)

Parenthetically, more recent research and trends in counseling practice have led Carkhuff and Berenson (1969) to point toward the fact that the counselor initiates communication and is action-oriented and to assert that "the counselor is a man and a woman." A third personal document worthy of special note is offered by Kell and Mueller (1966); after analysis of therapeutic interventions, they propose that the process of counseling-psychotherapy is a highly dynamic reciprocal relationship, which produces impact on and changes in both the counselor-therapist and the client. And finally, Hobbs (1962) stated what he believed were the components of the "Compleat Counselor"; in his opinion, this counselor should first be a good general psychologist who realizes the societal implications of his work, the uniqueness of working in an educationally-oriented area, and the importance of research in practical issues. (Note that this article was originally published in 1958.) There is one especially interesting statement:

Four things should happen to the candidate in his first week in graduate school: (1) he should be handed a detailed list of concepts which the faculty considers essential knowledge of psychology and counseling in general, with the injunction that he master the concepts within the year; (2) he should be involved in a research project of contact with a client; (3) he should have some kind of contact with a client; and (4) he should do some work in a public school. (Hobbs, 1962, p. 54)

The one amendment that might logically be made, and which will be elaborated later, is that the "work in a public school" should be altered to be "work in a service setting compatible with his professional aspirations," but Hobbs was, of course, giving major consideration to the counselor in the schools. It might also be added that training should not be limited solely to the employment setting to which the trainee aspires, because there is no doubt that there is much to be gained from involvement in a variety of service settings, and it is not unusual for a counselor or therapist to change his aspirations significantly during his training.

A closely related approach to trainee selection is the analysis of the functions of the counselor-therapist and speculation, hopefully with some degree of academic reasoning, on what the desirable characteristics would be. Hill (1961) prescribed several steps that would presumably lead to a sensible pattern for selecting persons for an occupation such as counseling. He discussed the influences, merits, and liabilities of the following issues: certification, the supply-and-demand problem, use of standardized tests, and the pooling of opinions from professional organizations. Aspects like interdisciplinary training, courses in a variety of areas, and supervised clinical experience seemed to merit particular importance, but Hill acknowledged that criteria for selection were anything but clear cut, and that "selection" was one of the most integral and important aspects of the quest to make the counseling profession an effective vehicle of educational (and, one might add, societal) progress. Cottle (1953) followed much the same format as Hill, but gave more emphasis to reviewing published accounts about what should be the characteristics of counselors; his review included numerous studies, each using its own set of descriptive adjectives. As a result of nebulously defined (if defined at all) terminologies, the sophisticated reader must wonder how much overlap there is and just what the characteristics that really merit incorporation into a training program's selection processes are. Of course, these uncertainties do not even approach the overriding issue of measuring the characteristics in such a way as to guarantee fairness to the applicant, the training program, the profession, and society.

In an attempt to shed some light on the selection problem, the American Psychological Association's (1954) Counselor Training Committee produced a subcommittee report that included an analysis of practices in counselor trainee selection. Questionnaires were sent to thirty-three universities that were engaged in counselor training;

it was later found that only twenty-eight of these universities in fact had people enrolled in these programs. Of the twenty-eight, 75 percent responded, providing descriptions of the department in which the counselor training programs were located, the different levels of training that were open to students, the number of applicants for counselor education and other forms of training in the same department, the number of students who actually enrolled in counselor education and the other programs within the department, and the entrance requirements. It is interesting to note that: departments differed considerably in their requirements regarding the applicant's undergraduate major; grade point average was the most frequently cited entrance factor; some training departments recommended work experience (e.g., teaching experience); letters of recommendations and interviews were used clinically or intuitively (one intriguing statistic, derived from a supposedly behavioral-science-based field striving for objectivity, is that 57 percent of the respondents used interviews, but 62 percent of these had no standard form, i.e., prescribed information was not obtained from all of the applicants interviewed); and finally, psychometric tests, such as the Graduate Record Examination and the Miller Analogies Test, played a major role in the selection process. The report concludes that even with so-called objective data "there would appear to be a lot of 'intuiting' going on."

A selection bugaboo that has plagued counselor education for years is whether trainees, particularly those preparing to be counselors in educational settings, should be required to have had classroom teaching experience. It should be noted that this sort of teaching requirement is considerably different from the requirement of work experience, which is based on the assumption that a person who is to be a counselor should have had to assume independent responsibility for fulfilling a task, have had to make decisions related to the desired outcome of the work activity, and have been cast into a goal-seeking endeavor where cooperation, communication, and interaction are required for successful performance. This type of would-be counselor will have had experiences that should facilitate maturity, self-understanding, and responsible actions. Obviously this is not always the case, but without defending work experience as a selection criterion per se, it seems to have a sounder rationale than the too-often-used requirement that the counselor first be a classroom teacher. State departments of public instruction have, through the years, required teaching experience before permanent certification is granted. This was designed to be a quality-control check over the instructional personnel, but the concept got extended to all those working with the students. This, in turn, meant that counselors were required to have teaching experience before they got their training in counseling. Granted, the school counselor must be aware of the philosophical, administrative, and instructional context of education, but the question is: Could not a counselor trainee acquire these educationally oriented knowledges and skills in ways other than spending one or more years as a classroom teacher? Some professionals would maintain (on the basis of learning-theory reasoning rather than personal opinion) that if these so highly prized educational knowledges and skills could be specified (discounting for the time being whether, in fact, they are necessary) then a curriculum could be developed that would transmit them to trainees without the requirement that they spend one or more years as a classroom teacher. It should be acknowledged, however, that during a teaching experience, the trainee would be forced to confront problems and acquire knowledges of matters that might in some instances complement his future work as a counselor, but these very actions might also deflect his personal energies and resources from counseling and provide him with apperceptive materials that might be of no future benefit and might be even a negative influence.

Although a few writers in the field of counseling have endorsed teaching experience for counselor trainees, it should be noted that most recommendations of this kind were made in the early 1950s. There have been many changes since that time: changes in the educational systems and responsibilities within the public schools, changes in training methodologies in colleges and universities, and, perhaps most important, changes in the pressing needs of society. These conditions combine to produce an ever expanding role definition for counseling services.

Recent writers have been moving away from the teacher-counselor position, or as Strowig (1967) titled one of his articles, ". . . And Gladly Teach (That I May Counsel)." Rossberg (1967) notes that there is a dilemma about whether counselors should be put into a bureaucratic mode, in which the counselors follow confidently accepted training requirements that are *implemented* (but the word "enforced" seems more accurate) by the bureaucratic organization (state certification and university requirements), or into a professional mode, in which the counselors become paramount, and the organizational system is subordinate to, and in service to the development of, individual activities and colleague relations.

It is difficult to imagine that any requirement, and especially one that relates counseling certification to a year of satisfactory classroom teaching experience, could foster the individuality that is the all-important characteristic of an effective counselor. Selection criteria should be guidelines that can be fulfilled directly, or that can be compensated for indirectly by possession of a composite of human-professional qualities that will, in many instances, lead to a degree of competence surpassing that prescribed by hard-and-fast, rigid requirements (which are of unproven validity anyway).

Issues of trainee selection and the contents of counselor education remain nebulous, and in the face of such ambiguity, one's first inclination is to search for a comparable model in a related area. Clinical psychology might be the hoped-for panacea, particularly because it has similar service functions, it has had greater longevity as a specialty, and it is rather clearly differentiated from its general-experimental counterparts. We find, however, that trainers of clinical psychologists are confronted by the same kinds of training problems as those facing trainers of counselors, school psychologists, and counseling psychologists. In fact, there is striking similarity between the sequence and contents of efforts and the resulting outcomes in these psychological specialties.

In addition to the committees discussed above, there have been several conferences that have analyzed functions, evaluated training practices, and set forth recommendations. Perhaps the most notable are: for clinical psychology, the 1950 Boulder Conference (Raimy, 1950), the Springfield-Mount Sinai Conferences on intern training (Finn and Brown, 1959), and the 1965 A.P.A. Conference on professional preparation (Hoch, Ross, and Winder, 1966); for school psychology, the Thayer Conference (Cutts, 1955); for counseling psychology, the Greyston Conference (Thompson and Super, 1964); and for general applied psychology, the Miami Conference (Roe, Gustad, Moore, Ross, and Skodak, 1959) and the Stanford

Conference (Strother, 1956).[2] Each of these conferences has, in a sense, become a historical milestone in the training of psychologists. Despite the fact that the products undeniably represent subjective appraisals of training factors, it is of some comfort to know that these published proceedings represent the learned thoughts of some of the most astute psychologists-educators of our era.

One regrettable fact, especially because counseling-therapy and all psychological specialties lay claim to being scientific, is that training procedures have not been subjected to more experimentation. For example, the use of simulated conditions is one of the most frequently used methods for experimental research on behavior, whether it be such things as the socialization of animals in a laboratory colony, perceptual and sensory-motor reactions to controlled impinging stimuli, or human behavior in problem-solving groups. This method has, of course, been used in a variety of quasi-counseling (and therapy) situations, as evidenced by the numerous verbal-conditioning studies. It has seldom been applied, however, to the selection of trainees or training principles and methodologies. Strupp's (1962) quasi-experimental studies on the therapist's influence in psychotherapy and the innovative efforts of Kelly and Fiske (1951) in which numerous contrived situations, e.g., deliberately provoked stress, were applied to applicants and trainees as a means for predicting the eventual performance of graduate students in clinical psychology are the only general studies. There have been a fairly sizeable number of studies using this form of research on what seem to be isolated training variables, e.g., having professors screen counselor trainee-applicants by watching a video-tape recording of them conducting a simulated counseling interview with a model

[2]It is acknowledged that the conferences cited are but a few of those that have been conducted. While those mentioned were some of the most important according to certain criteria, it should go without saying that many of the unmentioned conferences undoubtedly produced equally valuable training materials, which were assimilated into training practices. Further, at the time of this writing, there have been very recent conferences for which the published outcomes are not available, and there are others planned for the near future. The discussion on conferences should be interpreted as exemplary of a process for analyzing training. It was not intended to evaluate the specific contents of any of the conferences, nor should it be inferred that this is not a respectable means for developing training procedures; but there should be no apologies for the fact that this approach has limitations, and that there may well be more systematic and scientific ways to analyze and improve training in the mental health specialties.

client (usually an advanced graduate student or a hired actor). Occasionally, various scales of dimensions presumed to be valid indices of counseling effectiveness have been incorporated.

It appears, however, that these efforts have been fragmented, and that techniques are used that have not been validated (such as scales of dimensions presumed to be intrinsic to counseling-therapy effectiveness). There is therefore a distinct need for a comprehensive, systematic experimental analysis of selection and training procedures. There is a lack of experimentation and necessary replication for many of the individual training techniques and requirements, and the total area of selection and training of counselors and psychologists has thus far neglected the very essence of its existence—documentation.

It would be ill-advised and pretentious to attempt to offer a single, definitive answer for these selection and training problems. The following points, however, seem entirely justified.

Every training program, without reservation and regardless of its specialty or the status previously earned or accorded to the department and even to the university, should: (1) be aware of the needs of the recipient of their products, namely society, recognize the responsibility to fulfill these needs, and tailor the structure, contents, and model of their training program accordingly; (2) assess the in-training and post-training functionings of their trainees and graduates; (3) constantly analyze and evaluate the training components; and (4) attempt to validate each specific training procedure used in the program (recognizing, of course, that the appropriateness of any procedure will depend upon a multiplicity of factors, such as the faculty, resources, and desired student-product). All of this implies that there can never be a *final* training model, but that it will vary with changes in societal needs; the so-called "ideal" model may differ greatly among training programs because of the idiosyncratic needs of the segment of society for which the training program is assuming responsibility, and toward which it is directing its efforts. Each of the four points in this recommendation requires a *system* for its accomplishment, and this, in turn, means that there must be as much *objectivity* as is possible.

If the concept of applied psychobehaviorism is to have any sense of totality, it is appropriate and necessary to offer a recommendation on the training of psychobehavioral counselors and therapists. In view of the current state of affairs in professional training, it would appear that the best approach would be to clarify the training specialty of the psychobehavioral counselor-therapist. In other words, should he be trained as a clinical psychologist, a counseling psychologist, an educational counselor, or something else? Consideration should be given to what kinds of academic knowledges are necessary, what sorts of learnings are prerequisite to and requisite for the use of behavioral techniques, and what kind of supervised clinical experiences can best accommodate the uniqueness of psychobehavioral counseling and therapy.

Intrinsic to these ideas is the implication that there will probably have to be curriculum changes, and one can readily see the relationship of this to the necessity of improving training programs. To support both the idea of tailoring training to psychobehaviorism and the idea that curriculum development is an undeniable necessity for every training program, Chapter 5 offers guidelines for curriculum revision.

Regarding format for the rest of the chapters, it has seemed prudent to give attention to selected critical issues related to training. The issues particularly important to both the psychobehavioral frame of reference and professional training in general are: (1) helping the trainee to achieve self-understanding, so that there will be relative compatibility between his professional and personal self-concepts, and his personal characteristics will aid rather than hinder his counseling-therapeutic services; (2) enabling professional trainers, whether in counselor education or in one of the other psychological or mental health specialties, to make meaningful their involvement in the trainee's practicum-internship; and (3) motivating mental health professionals to assume increased responsibility and take greater, more efficacious *actions* to fulfill all of the functions of their profession. This writer believes strongly that the profession, and consequently the functions therein, is much more encompassing, both philosophically and practically, than has heretofore been acknowledged.

It has been directly and/or indirectly implied throughout this book that the need for an expansion and more clearly delineated professional perimeter is dictated by the needs of our contemporary society. This has led to the humane mandate for greater responsibility and action from mental health workers and to the concept of psychobehavioral counseling and therapy. Needless to say, although this societally dictated humane mandate is succinctly directed at the mental health professions, stereotypic historical antecedents all too often create a counter-valence that places the professional in the ambivalent position of being pulled toward conservatively safe but relatively ineffective functioning rather than moving deliberately with his behavioral science armament toward responsible action.

But this mandate must be fulfilled—for the welfare of the individual, the professions, and the society! The final segment of the last chapter will therefore focus on the psychobehavioral counselor-therapist's responsibility to the community, and how certain aspects of his image must be discarded or altered. One of the best examples is the need for alteration in the idea that "treatment" must follow the outdated "medical model" of treating the existing illness via conventional therapeutic techniques. This is opposed to a position that retains technical aspects of the traditional "medical model" for "treatment," but puts the main emphasis on preventive efforts for mental health via technical innovations that capitalize on behavioral-science-based shaping consultations. These consultations should facilitate circumventing problems within the individual and within the community and/or society. In view of the cultural crises plaguing contemporary society, one might maintain that the individual, the society, and indeed humanity, are dependent upon responsible action from all who have something to offer. While some of these comments might justly be labeled "alarmism," there are, in fact, real problems that must be confronted—and sometimes there are justifiable reasons for being "alarmed." Inevitably, any consideration of the foregoing factors will also imply certain prognostications about the future role definitions and functions of the mental health professions.

## REFERENCES

American Personnel and Guidance Association. Professional Training, Licensing and Certification Committee. Counselor preparation: Recommendations for minimum standards. *Personnel and Guidance Journal,* 1958, 37, 162–166.

American Psychological Association. Committee on Counselor Training, Division of Counseling and Guidance. Recommended standards for training counseling psychologists on the doctoral level. *American Psychologist,* 1952, 7, 175–181. (a)

American Psychological Association. Committee on Counselor Training, Division of Counseling Psychology. The practicum training of counseling psychologists. *American Psychologist*, 1952, 7, 182–188. (b)

American Psychological Association. Counselor Training Committee, Division of Counseling Psychology. An analysis of practices in counselor trainee selection. *Journal of Counseling Psychology*, 1954, 1, 174–179.

American Psychological Association. Committee on Definition, Division of Counseling Psychology. Counseling psychology as a specialty. *American Psychologist*, 1956, 11, 282–285.

American Psychological Association. The scope and standards of preparation in psychology for school counselors. *American Psychologist*, 1962, 17, 149–152.

Arbuckle, D. S. Five philosophical issues in counseling. *Journal of Counseling Psychology*, 1958, 5, 211–215.

Bergin, A. E., and Jasper, L. G. Correlates of empathy in psychotherapy: A replication. *Journal of Abnormal Psychology*, 1969, 74, 477–481.

Betz, Barbara J. Experiences in research in psychotherapy with schizophrenic patients. In H. H. Strupp and L. Luborsky (Eds.), *Research in psychotherapy, volume II*. Washington, D. C.: American Psychological Association, 1962, 41–60.

Betz, Barbara J., and Whitehorn, J. C. The relationship of the therapist to the outcome of therapy in schizophrenia. *Psychiatric Research Reports*, 1956, 5, 89–105.

Carkhuff, R. R. Differential functioning of lay and professional helpers. *Journal of Counseling Psychology*, 1968, 15, 117–126.

Carkhuff, R. R., and Berenson, B. G. *Beyond counseling and psychotherapy*. New York: Holt, Rinehart and Winston, 1967.

Carkhuff, R. R., and Berenson, B. G. The counselor is a man and a woman. *Personnel and Guidance Journal*, 1969, 48, 24–28.

Cottle, W. C. Personal characteristics of counselors: I. *Personnel and Guidance Journal*, 1953, 31, 445–450.

Cutts, Norma E. (Ed.). *School psychologists at mid-century*. Washington, D. C.: American Psychological Association, 1955.

Farson, R. E. The counselor is a woman. In J. F. McGowan and L. D. Schmidt (Eds.), *Counseling: Readings in theory and practice*. New York: Holt, Rinehart and Winston, 1962, 43–45.

Fiedler, F. E. The concept of an ideal therapeutic relationship. *Journal of Consulting Psychology*, 1950, 14, 239–245.

Finn, M. H. P., and Brown, F. (Eds.). *Training for clinical psychology*. New York: International Universities Press, 1959.

Grater, H. A., Kell, B. L., and Morse, Josephine. The social services interest: Roadblock and road to creativity. *Journal of Counseling Psychology*, 1961, 8, 9–12.

Guerney, B. G., Jr. (Ed.). Psychotherapeutic agents: New roles for nonprofessionals, parents, and teachers. New York: Holt, Rinehart and Winston, 1969.

Hill, G. E. The selection of school counselors. Personnel and Guidance Journal, 1961, 39, 355–360.

Hobbs, N. The compleat counselor. In J. F. McGowan and L. D. Schmidt (Eds.), Counseling: Readings in theory and practice. New York: Holt, Rinehart and Winston, 1962, 45–54.

Hoch, E. L., Ross, A. O., and Winder, C. L. (Eds.). Professional preparation of clinical psychologists. Washington, D. C. American Psychological Association, 1966.

Kell, B. L., and Mueller, W. J. Impact and change: A study of counseling relationships. New York: Appleton-Century-Crofts, 1966.

Kelly, E. L., and Fiske, D. W. The prediction of performance in clinical psychology. Ann Arbor: University of Michigan Press, 1951.

Levinson, D. J. The psychotherapist's contribution to the patient's treatment career. In H. H. Strupp and L. Luborsky (Eds.), Research in psychotherapy, volume II. Washington, D. C.: American Psychological Association, 1962, 13–24.

Raimy, V. C. (Ed.). Training in clinical psychology. Englewood Cliffs, N. J.: Prentice-Hall, 1950.

Roe, Anne, Gustad, J. W., Moore, B. V., Ross, S., and Skodak, Marie (Eds.). Graduate education in psychology. Washington, D. C.: American Psychological Association, 1959.

Rogers, C. R. Client-centered therapy. Boston: Houghton-Mifflin, 1951.

Rogers, C. R. The characteristics of a helping relationship. Personnel and Guidance Journal, 1958, 37, 6–16.

Rogers, C. R. On becoming a person. Boston: Houghton-Mifflin, 1961.

Rossberg, R. H. To teach or not to teach: Is that the question? In C. H. Patterson (Ed.), The counselor in the school: Selected readings. New York: McGraw-Hill, 1967, 188–192.

Rubinstein, E. A., and Parloff, M. B. (Eds.). Research in psychotherapy, volume I. Washington, D. C.: American Psychological Association, 1959.

Shlien, J. M., Hunt, H. F., Matarazzo, J. D., and Savage, C. (Eds.). Research in psychotherapy, volume III. Washington, D. C.: American Psychological Association, 1968.

Snyder, W. U. Some investigations of relationship in psychotherapy. In E. A. Rubinstein and M. B. Parloff (Eds.), Research in psychotherapy, volume I. Washington, D. C.: American Psychological Association, 1959, 247–263.

Strother, C. R. Psychology and mental health. Washington, D. C.: American Psychological Association, 1956.

Strowig, R. W. . . . And gladly teach (that I may counsel). In C. H. Patterson (Ed.), *The counselor in the school: Selected readings*. New York: McGraw-Hill, 1967, 182–188.

Strupp, H. H. Psychotherapeutic technique, professional affiliation, and experience level. *Journal of Consulting Psychology*, 1955, *19*, 97–102.

Strupp, H. H. The therapist's contribution to the treatment process: Beginnings and vagaries of a research program. In H. H. Strupp and L. Luborsky (Eds.), *Research in psychotherapy, volume II*. Washington, D. C.: American Psychological Association, 1962, 25–40.

Strupp, H. H., and Luborsky, L. (Eds.). *Research in psychotherapy, volume II*. Washington, D. C.: American Psychological Association, 1962.

Super, D. E. Transition: From vocational guidance to counseling psychology. *Journal of Counseling Psychology*, 1955, *2*, 3–9.

Thompson, A. S., and Super, D. E. *The professional preparation of counseling psychologists*. New York: Bureau of Publications, Columbia University, 1964.

Truax, C. B., and Carkhuff, R. R. *Toward effective counseling and psychotherapy: Training and practice*. Chicago: Aldine, 1967.

Truax, C. B., Carkhuff, R. R., and Kodman, F., Jr. Relationships between therapist-offered conditions and patient change in group psychotherapy. *Journal of Clinical Psychology*, 1965, *21*, 327–329.

Truax, C. B., Frank, J. D., Imber, S. D., Battle, Carolyn C., Hoehn-Saric, R., Nash, E. H., and Stone, A. R. Therapist empathy, genuineness, and warmth and patient therapeutic outcome. *Journal of Consulting Psychology*, 1966, *30*, 395–402.

Truax, C. B., Wargo, D. G., and Carkhuff, R. R. Antecedents to outcome in group psychotherapy with outpatients: Effects of therapeutic conditions, alternate sessions, vicarious therapy pretraining, and patient self-exploration. Unpublished manuscript, University of Arkansas, 1966.

Weitz, H. Counseling as a function of the counselor's personality. *Personnel and Guidance Journal*, 1957, *35*, 276–280.

# 5

# Curriculum Revision and
## Special Academic Knowledge

The training of counselors and psychologists is unjustifiably restricted by establishmentarianism in related professions. This topic was touched upon in the last chapter in the reference to the need for clarifying the training specialty location of the psychobehavioral counselor-therapist. In other words, disregarding its applicability in all of the other mental health disciplines, and confining the discussion to the field of psychology, the question is posed: With which of the psychological specialties (clinical, counseling, or school) should training be aligned? This creates an unnecessary restriction, because such subdividing of psychology into specialties, each with its own set of clinical techniques and responsibilities, is essentially invalid in view of a contemporary application of mental health services. The only defense would be that at one time the field of psychology was struggling to evolve a professional status and a professional identity for a group of highly trained psychologists who were probably more divergent in training and interests than the members of most other professional groups; at that time, subdividing into specialty areas served an evolutionary purpose.

At this point in the evolution of psychology, it is clearly evident that professional stature has been assured, although there is a continuing process to upgrade by reevaluating and restructuring, and those psychologists engaged in applied mental health services share more commonalities than they do differences. Aside from sharing the same "helping" objectives, there is a common basis of behavioral science in their techniques, and the main distinction is the site in which these techniques are employed. Granted that there are substantial differences in training experiences, but to a large extent these could be eliminated, and the thrust turned toward assuring that all trainees acquire a core of behavioral-science learnings. Differences in training should result from accommodations made to each trainee's personal characteristics and aspirations rather than from any prescribed specialty model that the trainee begins in and is confined to despite professional and personal growth that might lead him beyond the confines of his beginning specialty. Such restrictions do not provide safeguards to the profession or to the societal recipients; they only create frustrations that lead to a loss in much needed professional manpower.

In approaching the issue of training in psychobehavioral counseling and therapy, there is support for two postulates: (1) there should be a core of learnings, and (2) specialties produce overlap and unnecessary confinement. Support is evident in the definitions of the various applied psychological specialties.

Clinical psychology, one of the most firmly entrenched specialties and, presumably, one of the best defined, is actually one of the most nebulous. As Ross (1959) states in regard to clinical child psychology:

The present status of the psychologist engaged in clinical work with children is largely that of a man without a country. His doctorate is usually in philosophy, sometimes in education, with the parenthetical understanding that what it really means in clinical psychology. . . . Once the psychologist has become specialized, the lack of definition continues to be a source of confusion. He has to search out articles relevant to his activities in a variety of professional journals devoted primarily to work with adults and containing in their titles such nonspecific adjectives as *abnormal* and *social, consulting,* and *clinical.* (p. 4)

He goes on to cite the "confusing" aspects of the clinical child psychologist's attempt to find identity through association with professional organizations. Although Ross advocates specialty training, in this case clinical child psychology, his discussion notes that the clinician may have training from any number of university programs (e.g., from such departments as psychology, educational psychology, human development, counselor education, and special education), that much of the shaping comes on the postdoctoral level, and that specialization, which indeed is eventually necessary, comes not from university training but from the professional person's experiences and interests after he has entered the profession.

In the American Psychological Association's Chicago Conference on the preparation of clinical psychologists, Rodnick (1966) notes that the existing model (usually called the "Boulder" model because it had its derivations from the 1949 Boulder Conference) is

designed for training a generalist in clinical psychology who possesses foundations for *entry* into a subsequent career as a clinical psychologist at a journeyman's level—who matures and develops postdoctorally into a competent and seasoned professional. Because of the emphasis on breadth of training and experience within a 4- or 5-year period, only part of which is devoted specifically to professional aspects, it cannot hope to equip the student at the time he earns the degree to function independently with diagnostic and therapeutic sophistication and mature clinical judgment. That can come only after intensive on-the-job experience, in association with mature clinical psychologists. During this period he can develop, as needed, more intensive specialty preparation in specific areas of clinical practice through either professional growth or specialized postdoctoral training. (pp. 21–22)

The key point is, again, the need for a broad academic behavioral-science background, followed by continuing applied experience culminating in a specialty identity achieved after entering the real work world—if indeed "culmination" ever occurs.

One of the most striking similarities is that between clinical psychology and counseling psychology. Most attempts to differentiate seem rather gross, such as reflecting the employment setting or the clientele served (and their characteristics); this point is clearly exemplified in Super's (1955) often-quoted statement that clinical psychology is concerned with psychopathology and counseling psychology is concerned with hygiology. For the issue of training, this dichotomy provides little direction. Even if the primary concerns are psychopathology and hygiology respectively, there is no reason to assume that the academic and experiential contents of the two training programs should be different. This is particularly true if any value is attributed to the view that the "compleat" counselor-therapist should, as in Hobbs' (1958) statement, first and foremost share with all psychologists the quality of being a "good general psychologist." Hobbs emphasized that his idea was offered not to gain "dubious respectability" for specialties or to preserve the "unity of psychology," as is so often used as a rallying cry, but that it was based on "the sheer utility value of a solid foundation in general psychology." Support for Hobbs' position comes when the confusions of two types of definitions are inspected: definitions of specialties and definitions of counseling and psychotherapy. A few samples from the many definitions of each area will illustrate this point.

Regarding definitions of specialties, consider the following rather lengthy definition of the counseling psychologist adapted from the U. S. Department of Labor's 1965 *Dictionary of Occupational Titles.* This definition was used by a project of the Professional Affairs Committee of the A.P.A.'s Division of Counseling Psychology (Jordaan, Myers, Layton, and Morgan, 1968) which was designed to define and describe the uniqueness of the specialty of counseling psychology:

PSYCHOLOGIST, COUNSELING. Provides individual and group guidance and counseling services in schools, colleges, and universities, hospitals, clinics, rehabilitation centers, and industry, to assist individuals in achieving more effective personal, social, educational, and vocational development and achievement. Collects data about the individual through use of interview, case history, and observational techniques. Selects, administers, scores, and interprets psychological tests designed to assess individual's intelligence, aptitudes, abilities, and interests, applying knowledge of statistical analysis. Evaluates data to identify cause of problem and to determine advisability of counseling or referral to other specialists or institutions. Conducts counseling or therapeutic interviews to assist individual to gain insight into personal problems, define goals, and plan action reflecting his interests, abilities, and needs. Provides occupational, educational, and other information to enable individual to formulate realistic educational and vocational plans. Follows up results of counseling to determine reliability and validity of treatment used. May engage in research to develop and improve diagnostic and counseling techniques. (unnumbered page)

Analysis of this definition reveals the following: (1) the person providing these services would have to be highly educated and would have to have training in the psychosocial behavioral sciences, and (2) a person in any psychological specialty—be it clinical, counseling, or school (or other related ones)—should be potentially able to perform each of the above services, and probably would provide each

of them regardless of employment setting or the departmental affiliation of his university training program. The major differences would
come from the differing emphasis given each area according to his
work setting, his clientele, his professional skills, and his personal interests and aspirations. In other words, the definition does not define
a unique psychological specialty per se, but defines an emphasis that
might be accepted by any psychological specialist who provides applied clinical services.

If we move to definitions of counseling and psychotherapy, it
again becomes clear that a specialty cannot lay sole claim to
either. Nor can any specialty distinguish itself simply because it
applies the intrinsic elements in a particular setting or because of a
particular training program title. Brammer and Shostrom (1968) use
the term "therapeutic psychology" to denote those functions shared
by school psychology, clinical psychology (hospitals, clinics, private
practice), counseling psychology (schools, hospitals, industries), social work, pastoral counseling, and psychiatry. To extend their model,
we might also include numerous other specialties, such as psychiatric
nursing and special education, assuming that the professionals in
them had the relevant personal and professional characteristics and
skills. In surveying definitions of counseling and psychotherapy,
Brammer and Shostrom (1968) present two continua: first is the
therapy continuum between medicine (psychiatry and neurology)
and psychology (counseling-clinical), with medicine having unique
functions for the treatment of severe neuroses or psychoses (surgery,
electroshock, and medication), medicine and psychology sharing or
overlapping in responsibility for psychotherapy or reeducation services, and psychology having the unique functions of planning and
problem solution (e.g., use of psychological tests for diagnostic and
predictive purposes); the second continuum views counseling as
progressing uninterruptedly into psychotherapy, with the transition
point not being clear cut—this continuum is, of course, maintained
throughout this book. From analysis of definitions, Brammer and
Shostrom conclude that "counseling" involves factors and functions
related to education, support, situation, problem solving, conscious
awareness, and normalcy, and "psychotherapy" involves factors and
functions related to support (more focused than in counseling), re-
construction, depth emphasis, analysis, the unconscious, and neu-

roticism and other severe emotional problems. This continuum between counseling and psychotherapy is essentially supported, although perhaps articulated somewhat differently, by numerous theorists and researchers. Patterson (1966a, 1966b), for instance, tends to view "counseling" and "psychotherapy" as two terms for much the same functions, and Albert (1966), with the exception of strictly information-giving types of advisement and guidance, believes that the potential of counseling cannot be confined to the conscious, rational layers of personality, and may well move into the realm of psychotherapy. Analysis of the multitude of definitions of counseling and psychotherapy, as available in several composite reviews (e.g., Arbuckle, 1965; Brammer and Shostrom, 1968; McGowan and Schmidt, 1962; Woody, 1969), reveals evidence that there are differences among the definitions, but that these differences seem to be based mainly on the employment setting and the type of audience for which the writings were designed; that the elements within the processes for the two terms are, for the most part, identical or closely comparable; and that in actual practice a continuum between counseling and psychotherapy is inevitable and indisputable. Certainly the definitions of counseling and psychotherapy have enough in common to justify the position that the title of a specialty training program cannot prescribe the applied functioning of the practitioners, and that the contents of the various training programs must, therefore, have a common core of related learnings.

Much of the foregoing is centered around the technical similarity and comparable efficacy of different specialists in accomplishing the same goals. However, the commonalities also extend into other areas, such as philosophy. Dole, Nottingham, and Wrightsman (1969), for example, found that trainees in counseling, clinical psychology, and rehabilitation seemed to share common beliefs about the nature of man.

In considering the justification for specialization, there is also the question of whether a trainee actually knows what specialty he should prepare for when he is in graduate school. And there is evidence for the view that many trainees do not know. In studying graduate students who received advanced degrees in psychology from the Pennsylvania State University between 1950 and 1965, Kirchner (1969) found that about half indicated that their eventual employment positions were substantially different from their goals at the time they began graduate study. This would obviously support the view that training, particularly on the lower graduate levels, should be relatively unspecialized (or that more efforts should be directed at preparing trainees to make more adequate employment choices earlier in their training).

It has been adequately established that a particular psychological specialty and the departmental location of a given training program make little if any beneficial contribution to the preparation of counselors and therapists. In fact, such establishmentarianism can definitely hinder the efficacy of the training if it imposes unjust or arbitrary barriers to other training programs, whether within the same university or in other universities.

The various psychological specialties share a psychosocial behavioral science frame of reference for their applied clinical services. To facilitate their professed "helping" objective, all related specialties and departmentalized training programs within a given university should attempt to complement rather than compete with one another. There is benefit in specialization and departmentalization, but primarily in focusing the trainee's attention on specific service functions and employment settings.

Specialization is necessary, but it should not be allowed to become a source of professional isolationism, which can only lead to inefficiency in training and service; rather, it should tailor a trainee to fulfill his aspirations. For the most part, however, training should be generic. All trainees, regardless of specialty or specific program, should share "core" learnings, and their specialization experiences should be geared not only toward initial employment in a chosen role, but also toward enabling them to evolve in generic psychology, possibly (depending upon innumerable variables and circumstances) to move into another specialty quite different from the one entered upon completion of formal academic training. Likewise, it seems logical that training, regardless of specialty or academic degree attained, is an ongoing responsibility that should never cease; of course, how this development is accomplished will vary greatly according to such factors as amount and quality of academic training (of which the "degree" is only one sign), supervised clinical experience, personality, and environment.

There is certainly room for mental health workers who do not have a doctorate. The needs of society and the research evidence combine to justify that there should be persons providing certain mental health services at all levels of preparation. Preparation of counselors should range from short-term training of lay persons, to two-year junior college training for mental health technicians and counseling aids, to the A.B. and M.A. levels (and possibly other intermediary levels below the doctorate), and then through doctoral and postdoctoral training. Obviously, the amount of training will have to be fitted to role functions and responsibilities, and professional supervision should always be available, if not mandatory, for subprofessionals or paraprofessionals serving the mental health needs of the public. Care should be taken to avoid false barriers; it should be possible for a given person, regardless of level of training or degree held, to satisfy the requirements for particular roles or functions. There are many ways to acquire learning and skills besides accumulating university credits and degrees. This situation creates a challenge of paramount importance to the mental health professions. It will remain the responsibility of the professionals to continue developing criteria and measurement-assessment methods for ascertaining the qualifications and suitability of a practitioner (at any level). At this time there has been neither adequate professional attention nor empirical research directed to these matters.

## CURRICULUM REVISION

Training programs must be continually examined, assessed, validated, and revised. This task could be performed with more assurance if there were empirically established methods, but despite the scientific stature of the field, there is little research evidence from which to draw definitive guidelines for curriculum development and revision. Most evaluative methods have been derived from "expert opinion" (e.g., American Psychological Association, 1958). One promising alternative is the use of reasonably objective assessment procedures. Gerken (1969) has presented a scale of attributes important for the training of counseling psychologists that is designed to be a method for objectively assessing training programs in that specialty. Perhaps it is from methods like this that trainers will eventually derive better means for curriculum development and revision, but at present there is not enough evidence to allow for an unquestioned format.

There are, however, certain logical steps that can be suggested as a guide for approaching curriculum development. Many of the following comments reflect the processes (largely subjective) used in one effort to analyze and revise a graduate-level training program.[1]

### Defining the Product

One of the first steps in curriculum revision is to determine what is the desired training product. In other words, it must be decided what the responsibilities of the training program are, although this decision may be substantially determined by administrative regulations imposed by the university. (A given department, when it was founded, may have had to submit a rationale and organizational structure that clearly delimited the training product.) Aspects that will have to be considered include: What are the public needs? (e.g., How do school administrators define what they need from pupil personnel workers?) How well are other training programs in the state and elsewhere meeting certain needs? What does the profession view as the preferred functional products? What is the master plan for the state system of higher education? What physical and personnel resources are available and will be available to the training program? What implications do societal and educational projections have for training? What do the students' personal aspirations and

[1]Many of the ideas set forth in this section result, in part, from a year-long Curriculum Revision Task Force in the Department of Counseling and Personnel Services, College of Education, the University of Maryland. Appreciation is expressed to the participants of the Task Force for the contributions each made to this author's conceptualizations. In addition to this author, who served as Chairman and represented the Psychological Services in the Schools training program, the participants and the training programs they represented were: Raymond A. Ehrle (Rehabilitation Counseling), Kenneth R. Greenberg (Elementary School Counseling), Thomas M. Magoon (Student Personnel Administration), George L. Marx (Department Head), Mark B. Peterson and Thomas M. Stipek (Secondary School Counseling), David J. Rhoads (Community Counseling), and Gail S. Bradbard (Recorder). Obviously, the foregoing Task Force members should, in no way, be viewed as sharing responsibility for the interpretations set forth herein; individually, they may or may not agree.

views of the profession suggest should be the training contents?[2]

Answering these questions or issues is a highly idiosyncratic process, and the chances are that answers would vary greatly among training programs, as well they should. However, the primary goal of this initial step, no matter what method is used to gain the informational backdrop (be it a survey of current practices and opinions or an analysis of past graduates or any other measurement procedure), is to apply evaluation techniques that are as objective as possible to yield data that will lead to a description of the graduates of the program. From this description, which obviously is couched in generalizations and does not prescribe that all graduates must present the same image, the core learnings for the curriculum can be extrapolated.

[2]In a survey of graduate students in A.P.A.-approved clinical training programs, Clement and Sartoris (1967) found that the majority of student-respondents favored placing primary emphasis on applied training and secondary emphasis on experimental-theoretical training, and favored changing degree requirements accordingly. It appeared that they believed that existing training programs did not, in general, present learnings that correspond with their professional goals. On the practical-versus-theoretical point, there might well be reason to question the suitability of program components; perhaps certain requirements, such as foreign language competency for doctoral degrees, should be reevaluated for relevance to contemporary service, particularly for the practice-oriented Doctor of Psychology degree, as opposed to the research-oriented Doctor of Philosophy degree with a major in psychology (Peterson, 1966, 1968). However, when it comes to who determines what should be the components and requirements, the supposition is, by virtue of the students' being enrolled to study, that professors have, by virtue of advanced training and professional experience, a degree of expertise for guiding and developing their students. It would seem illogical, when earnestly soliciting the students' views about what a training program should encompass, to allow the untrained views and personal aspirations to dictate totally the curriculum and the resulting product. From personal experience, it is obvious that many graduate students fail to recognize the dependency of applied techniques on theory, and (particularly, it seems, in the first two years of graduate training) feel strongly that more emphasis should be placed on techniques and applied experience. As they increase their level of training, however, there seems to be a progressive appreciation of the importance of theory, so that by the time they complete doctoral training they are advocating general-theoretical knowledge as a foundation for subsequent practice. This progressive change is readily seen in both informal and formal-class discussions and in differences between statements made on master's-level and doctor's-level comprehensive examinations. Student views are important and deserve attention—serious attention—but their developmental level also merits consideration when curriculum revisions are being made.

## Core Learnings

Determination of the core learnings, unfortunately, rests on the consensual validity of the so-called experts, the professors. They, naturally, should reflect a national (or even international) scope in their thinking, should be in tune with the ideas of the profession, the practitioners, and the students, and should be anything but parochial in their motives—while at the same time justifying the parochial role that the training program must play.

Core learnings should be the knowledge and skills that all trainees should possess. Specialized learnings, reflecting the employment setting or individual aspirations of the trainees, constitute a separate criterion. The concept of core learnings requires scientific frame of reference; that is, the training of psychobehavioral counselors and therapists requires a psychosocial behavioral science curriculum model.

There are five major categories of core learnings: human behavior (normal-abnormal, developmental, sociocultural, and personality), theories and methods of behavioral change (counseling, psychotherapy, and behavioral modification), theories and methods of research, theories and methods of individual and group assessment, and practical application of generic techniques (such as observational analysis, interviewing, guidance, consultation, counseling, psychotherapy, behavioral modification, test administration, diagnosis, interpretation, communication of information, and professional interaction). While these five categories seem adequately inclusive, at least for the current state of affairs in counseling-therapy, the exact contents of any or all of them might alter significantly according to research advances and changes in professional responsibilities. In all probability, however, the bulk of the contents will remain fairly stable. It should also be noted that preparation for a particular specialty might add content to any or all of the core areas, but the true core learnings cut across all psychological specialties. Thus, when an experimental psychologist scrutinizes the core learnings for the psychological counselor-therapist and finds many aspects of his specialty missing, it is not because the core concept is faulty. The groundwork for future specialization can be laid by adding new areas and objectives to the core concepts, but to add the specialty knowledge itself would be to move beyond the boundaries of the core learnings.

### Specialty Learnings

The third step in curriculum revision is the determination of how specialization should be accommodated. This step might mean accommodation of different academic emphases within the same program, or of different functions among several specialties administratively placed in the same university department, or of differences among students. Trainees in a specialty would be expected to fulfill a set of specialty training objectives that uniquely characterizes the specific role-functions they hope to perform. Just as is the case with core learnings, the determination of specialty learnings is a highly subjective process and relies almost exclusively on the expertise and clinical judgment of the responsible faculty members.

### Training Objectives

Numerous areas of education seem to be infatuated with the use of behavioral objectives, and the infatuation may really be justifiable affection. These are a form of presenting a specific bit of knowledge and stating the process by which it can be acquired, manifested, and reliably documented as having been achieved. For example, "Based on the material in the textbook, the student will be able to list in writing the names of four persons who have developed theories of counseling or psychotherapy" is a behavioral objective that may be broken down as follows: the textbook material provides the means for acquisition of the knowledge, writing a list provides the process by which the knowledge will be manifested, and checking the number and names of theorists against the content of the book provides the criterion for passing or failing.

The use of behavioral objectives works very well for factual materials, but it is difficult to fulfill the requisite elements when the knowledge being measured pertains to human behavior, a nonfactual realm (at least at times). For example, although it would no doubt be possible to develop numerous behavioral objectives around a concept about rapport-building, it would be difficult to make statements in this form that would adequately measure or estimate the quality of rapport-building that a trainee should demonstrate in an internship interview. Likewise, particularly in this day of academic freedom for professors and the importance of considering the opinions of and maintaining the individuality of students or trainees, it seems that the best approach for curriculum revision in counseling-therapy is to change "behavioral objectives" to "training objectives," or perhaps "training outcomes."

Training objectives (outcomes) would be more general than behavioral objectives, but would still define the basic skills that a trainee should demonstrate in any given core or specialty area. For example, "In a simulated relationship, the trainee will be able to obtain desired information from the model-client" does not fulfill the criteria for a behavioral objective, but it could serve as a training objective. The exact specification of how the knowledge relevant to this objective is acquired, manifested, and documented is not prescribed, but the basic training objective of "obtaining desired information from a model-client" is spelled out. As might be inferred from the previous sentence, a single training objective could contain numerous behavioral objectives, and such a subdividing transformation is a necessary part of curriculum development.

The idea would be to develop as many categories of core and specialty learnings as could be consensually validated, transform these into specific bits of information, and then make the final transformation into training objectives or training outcomes. To accommodate academic freedom, the statement of behavioral objectives could be left to the professors involved with a particular set of training objectives. The specificity and the number of the training objectives for any given category would, of course, be dependent upon the emphasis given various curricular aspects by the particular training program, but, hopefully, when the training objectives for a given category or subcategory were considered together, the informational-experiential contents would be comprehensive.

### Sequencing and Packaging

Most colleges and universities are unnecessarily dedicated to the use of courses and credits. Similarly, accreditation and certification boards, such as state departments of public instruction, often seem to be more concerned with checking for particular course titles and tabulating the number of university credits than they are with ascertaining whether the student has actually achieved the knowledge relevant to the approval he is seeking. In all fairness, it must be admitted that this method is as logical an index as is probably possible, at least for the present, but its existence is not really justified. The critical goal is to guide the student to achievement of relevant learnings, and the educator-trainer should not adhere unnecessarily to false structures, including rigidly prescribed course sequences.

The alternative, which is definitely more complex and demanding to administer in this "rush to a college degree" era, is the sequencing of learnings, which would involve giving more importance to the interrelationships among bits of learnings, disregarding their major categorization, and forsaking staid packaging concepts (such as a course that meets once per week for three hours for fifteen weeks). As one feasible example, it may be that catgory A has fifteen training objectives, and that three of those should be taught before the first training objective from category B could be presented, and in turn the first seven of the B training objectives should preface the fourth A training objective. . . . In other words, the emphasis is on presenting specific learnings when their acquisition could optimally be achieved; this requires consideration of the interrelationships among the categories of learnings. Reality dictates that some form of recording, such as course titles and credit hours, is necessary, but the issue here is that such forms should service the learning processes, not the opposite. Part of any curriculum revision should focus on how learning can best be facilitated and packaged, even if it means voiding traditional procedures.

One might wonder why more has not been said about teaching methodology. Here again the uniqueness of the training program, meaning primarily the capabilities of the faculty and the educational resources at their disposal, makes the selection of a teaching technique highly individualized. The one point that should be made is that, as was the case with packaging, consideration must be given to each training objective or, to reduce the focus even further, to each bit of information involved in a training objective, and the teaching technique or presentation procedure should be geared to its uniqueness. It might be that all of the training objectives in category A could best be accomplished solely by the lecture method, given the characteristics of the professor assigned the responsibility for those training objectives and the students pursuing them; but it might also be that while Professor Jones could teach category A objectives 1, 2, and 3 best by lecturing, he could accomplish objectives 4, 5, and 6 best by using another technique, such as programmed materials on microfilm. The point is that, just as is the case with counseling and therapy techniques, no teaching technique has universal efficacy, and there must be instructional-technical eclecticism.

Such issues as the length of time required to earn a particular degree, the specialties that should be offered as "majors," the administrative structure, examination practices, and personnel policies all have relevance to curriculum revision, and at some point would have to be determined. However, it is unlikely that universality has any logical support. It may well be, however, that such issues as minimal required training objectives for a particular specialty can eventually be studied and "recommended" by appropriate professional organizations, such as education and training boards or committees in the American Psychological Association and the American Personnel and Guidance Association; but this would necessarily follow many applied efforts and experiments.

### Curriculum Planning in the Future

This is the age of the computer. It would seem logical that curriculum revision for training in counseling and therapy should benefit from its use. For example, there is no reason why computers could not be programmed to record, weight, and analyze data from sources relevant to the training product; produce criteria for the selection of students; prescribe evaluation techniques for applicants based on the individual's characteristics; extrapolate core and specialty learnings from research results and quantified practical data, and transform them into training objectives; synthesize faculty and institutional resources and responsibilities and the needs of the given students in order to sequence the learnings and recommend the presentation approach; assess the trainee's accomplishments and (if necessary) offer remedial developmental ideas to help him fulfill the training objective; and offer the trainee's professor various topics that he might wish to pursue with his student in tutorial or supervisory sessions. The computer age might well bring a return to the professor-student tutorial relationship of several centuries ago, with the programmed materials (presented by either machine or human) being used to present basic information and the professor-student relationship regaining a long overdue personal tutorial quality. But these are prognostications which do not solve the present problem of using sheer manpower to develop the training program's curriculum.

## SPECIAL KNOWLEDGE FOR BEHAVIORAL MODIFICATION

The importance that the psychobehavioral frame of reference gives to behavioral modification might be interpreted as suggesting that the training of professionals who will adopt psychobehaviorism into their practice should have knowledge and skills that are quite different from those adopting a traditional insight approach. Two points should therefore be made: first, regardless of the theoretical and technical approaches adopted after training, the preparation processes should expose all trainees to a core of learning in the counseling-therapy spectrum, and behavioral modification does not get adequate attention in many training programs; and second, there should be some discretely specifiable learnings included in the training program of the would-be user of behavioral modification.

In view of the amount of impressive research that has been amassed, it is surprising and regrettable that training programs have not moved more quickly to include new knowledge about behavioral modification. The realist must acknowledge the too-often-present reliance on tradition (apparently for "safety's sake," or because of professional lethargy) that abounds in training programs. It is an unfortunate state of affairs, especially because the philosophical stance of higher education is that the opposite should be true, i.e., that training programs should be highly flexible and experimental—

closer to "experiment for experiment's sake" than "tradition for tradition's sake."

There is some indication of a trend toward including courses in behavioral modification training programs. These are still relatively few and far between; but several programs in counselor education, special education, and clinical, counseling, and school psychology have didactic courses on principles of behavioral modification; occasionally, usually because of the supervisor's interests, trainees in a practicum or internship experience are able to try out some behavioral techniques with clients. While this trend is to be commended, one can only pose the following question: If the contents of a training program are to be based on empirical research evidence, and emphasis given to any particular theory or technique determined accordingly, are our training programs giving just weight to each theory of counseling and therapy? Clearly, behavioral modification does not typically receive the amount of emphasis that its research base would support, which means in turn that other approaches are receiving far more emphasis than their respective research bases justify.

In an approach comparable to that of the supporters of separate specialty-training programs, there are some behaviorists who would maintain that behavior therapy, or, to use the broader term, behavioral modification, should be taught as an almost independent entity; in other words, it should be taught via a separate training system, distinctly apart from other approaches that some behaviorists condemn, seemingly in order to justify their own existence. The preferred position, from the standpoint of both simple logical reasoning and the psychobehavioral frame of reference, is that behavioral modification should be integrated with the learnings from other theoretical approaches. There is, then, a double barrier to this integration: the reluctance of training programs to move ahead and incorporate behavioral modification, and the conscious or unconscious desire of some behaviorists to maintain a special identity.

There are several behavioral-modification training programs and centers in the United States. The usual format is for trainees, who have already been trained in their psychological specialty, to undergo either a short term of intense training in applied behaviorism or a year as an intern (on either the pre- or postdoctoral level). In addition, workshops (generally lasting a few days) are frequently sponsored by professional organizations (and occasionally by an enterprising professional) to provide accelerated training in specific behavioral-modification methods. These training opportunities "take up the slack" for the professionals already in the field who have not received formal training in behavioral modification, and it is to this group that they should continue to be directed (as part of the ongoing professional development concept). But only integrationist training opportunities will properly prepare present and future trainees to make their own weightings of the appropriateness of the various theoretical approaches for their own practices.

In delineating the specific learnings relevant to applied behavioral principles that should be provided to the trainees, it is necessary to specify the level of functioning. For example, there might be four levels: level 1 would be lay (or paraprofessional) behavioral-change agents who would have little or no formal education in human behavior, but who would provide certain reinforcers under the programming and supervision of a professional; level 2 would be behavioral technicians (again, probably paraprofessionals) who would have certain special knowledge about human behavior, specifically about the application aspects of behavioral modification techniques, but who would need the supervision-guidance of a professional. (This level might include graduates of two-year junior or community college programs for mental health technicians and counseling or rehabilitation aides, or undergraduate students in the behavioral sciences); level 3 would include those professionals who, assuming the availability of consultation, could provide general or basic behavioral modification techniques autonomously or semi-autonomously. (This level might include such professionals as classroom teachers and subdoctoral counselors and psychologists; it should be recognized that some subdoctoral persons might be equally competent to use the full range of behavioral procedures as the doctoral-level professional, depending upon individual qualities); and level 4 would include professionals in the behavioral sciences, usually holding the doctorate, who have had training in applying the spectrum of behavioral modification procedures autonomously and who can serve as consultants and supervisors to the other levels. The first level might be characterized as the agent-technician, the second level as the basic behavior modifier, and the third and fourth levels as the behavioral counselor or the behavior therapist. It should be noted that persons on the first two levels would potentially be able to be involved directly with both behavioral counseling and behavior therapy, as well as (and more probably) with the general kinds of situational reinforcement, such as the use of positive rewards to increase the occurrence of a particular behavior.[3] In one of the few writings available on the training of behavior therapists, Poser (1967) describes the use of two levels: trainees who serve as technicians or co-therapists with a professional therapist, and those trainees who are advanced enough to be independent professional personnel.[4]

[3]Since the material in this book is concentrated on the counseling and therapy functions, which would mean primarily levels 3 and 4, no attempt has been made to ascribe the specific techniques appropriate for levels 1 and 2. Those who are interested in other aspects will find some of them discussed in detail in *Behavioral Problem Children in the Schools* (Woody, 1969). In that source, the techniques were divided into two sections, general and specialized, and attention devoted to the specific competencies necessary for using a particular procedure; the materials in that book were devoted primarily to persons who would fit into levels 2 and 3, with reference being made to the use of level 1 persons, e.g., parents and peers. This source cites evidence that peers can be used as reinforcers, or, to stay within the categorization system, level 1 behavioral-change agents. For example, the applied work of Professor Roger E. Ulrich and his colleagues at Western Michigan University has involved training elementary and even preschool children to administer a behavioral technique (Surratt, Ulrich, and Hawkins, 1969). An elementary school child can be trained to monitor the behaviors of peers and, when a specified class of behavior occurs, to administer a positive reward, e.g., a signal that a token redeemable for special privileges has been earned by apt study behavior. And a child of about five can be trained to help a younger child (a sibling of about three), develop his sight-reading vocabulary via the flash-card method by giving verbal praise or an object reward when the younger child makes a correct response and withholding it when the response is incorrect. Actually seeing children involved with the application of behavioral techniques creates several very personal reactions; after the amazement has died away, it becomes somewhat amusing and definitely gratifying to see children constructively interacting and truly fulfilling the often quoted but too seldom practiced "help thy brother"—not to mention the benefit that professional manpower saved allows for improved educational and behavioral services.

[4]In numerous places the expression "independent professional personnel" is used. In accord with the earlier discussion on the professional's responsibility to be involved in an ongoing training process, in no instance should it be implied that total "independence" is being endorsed, but rather that the professional has achieved a stature where he has the preparation to assume responsibility for taking action on his own. Hopefully, any professional, regardless of competence, would always have available and would seek consultative and supervisory reactions from other professionals. It should be clearly understood that this does not mean having a formal supervisor; the "consultative and supervisory reactions" could very well come from informal exchanges between professionals, but these exchanges would accommodate a professional "checking out" of ideas and practices. This is critically important, because it has been found that therapists experience marked changes in attitudes toward providing treatment after they are practitioners, e.g., Anthony (1967) found that therapists reported a feeling of increased insecurity in the psychotherapeutic setting despite four years of applied experience. Certainly this demonstrates the need for continued postgraduate

Because the emphasis throughout this book is on the counseling-therapy functions, consideration of the academic knowledge necessary for the use of behavioral modification procedures should be confined primarily to levels 3 and 4. In attempting to find precedents on which to base statements, one is struck by the sparsity of writings in the area. Even behavior therapy, despite being clinically practiced a great deal, has not been adequately analyzed for determining what and how the would-be behavior therapist should be taught. In approaching the issue of knowledge, there seem to be three main aspects: training models, academic knowledge, and supervised clinical experiences.

### Training Models

There are few training programs in behavioral modification, and those that exist are often relatively unsystematic; in fact, Wolpe and Lazarus (1966) state that, at the time of their writing, there was "no institution in the world where a systematic schooling" in the theory and practices of behavior therapy could be obtained. Since then there have, of course, been several specialized training programs inaugurated which have been consistently developing their own systems, but at this point there is still virtually no proven model.

When there is a sequence of behavioral-modification training available in a college or university, it might be described as a three-fold system: first, the student is exposed to general learning theory; second, he takes a survey course, typically rather didactic, in the applied techniques; and third, he uses a few of the techniques, usually systematic desensitization and positive reward, during the course of a practicum or internship (if there is a supervisor available who appreciates behavioral modification). Certainly such a sequence does not fulfill the rigorous standards for scientific use of the terms "system" or "model." In other words, at the present time there is no defensible single model, and one might wonder if there are even any quasi-models, for training in behavioral modification.

### Academic Knowledge

A discussion of necessary academic knowledge requires consideration of the levels. For the level 1 person, the knowledge is as

---

training of some kind; particularly it would seem an experience that would allow for working through conflicts and feelings about the role of the psychotherapist, i.e., the integration of the professional self and the personal self.

much or little as the supervising professional believes will accommodate the application of the technique. For level 2 there would necessarily be a knowledge of basic principles of general psychology and learning theories in particular, but again the restrictions of the role make the amount of knowledge subject to the supervising professional's objectives.

In analyzing the academic knowledge generally necessary for classroom teachers and other psychoeducational personnel, presumably on levels 2 and 3, to use the basic or general behavioral-modification procedures, it would seem that the following areas would be requisite: general and experimental psychology, with special emphasis on learning theory; psychopathology, with emphasis on the psychology of exceptional children (particularly those with behavior problems and learning disabilities); personality theory; and guidance and counseling theories and techniques. For these levels, the academic knowledge could be quite basic, and could probably be obtained on the undergraduate level, with level 3 persons acquiring advanced knowledge and skills in the same areas and in other complementary areas on the graduate level of training.

As for those who are going to engage in behavioral counseling or behavior therapy, such as levels 3 and 4 persons, there is some question about exactly what would be best. For example, Poser (1967) believes that behavior therapists should be exposed to diverse theories, not just the behavioral ones, in their training; and similarly, Woody (1968) has stated that

there should be no such specialty as a "behavioral counselor," but rather that there should be counselors educated in comprehensive counseling services, which would include behavioral counseling. This is compatible with . . . an integrative theoretical position. (p. 360)

On the contrary, Wolpe and Lazarus (1966) indicate that the behavior-therapy trainee need not be familiar with psychoanalytic knowledge, and that, in their opinion, such knowledge might prove to be a "positive hindrance." They set forth three areas of knowledge that behavior therapy trainees should have: knowledge of scientific methodology, knowledge of modern learning theory, and knowledge of relevant research.

From the psychobehavioral viewpoint, there seems no doubt that trainees should have the same core of relevant knowledge. This would mean that all trainees, not just those interested in behavior therapy, would be taught what Wolpe and Lazarus would deem the rudiments of scientific methodology, modern learning theory, and relevant research on behavior therapy; but likewise they would be given a comparable exposure to the other theoretical positions. At this time, there is less knowledge about behavioral modification than about most other theories of comparable stature, but there is no reason for this, and it should not be used as a basis to rally separatism by eliminating certain learnings, such as those related to psychoanalytic psychotherapy, from the generic core of knowledge for trainees who prefer, and may eventually apply, behavior therapy.[5]

### Supervised Clinical Experiences

The one training issue about which there is little disagreement is the importance of supervised clinical experience. Differences do emerge, however, when it comes to determining the clinical context and the points at which applied experience should begin and end.

There are those trainers who are proponents of starting the trainee in experiencing "helping" human relationships from the first moment he enters the program, while others believe that the experience can be most productive, in a *professional* sense, if it is prefaced by certain academic knowledge. The former group would maintain that, under guiding supervision, the embryonic trainee, without any academic preparation, could engage in an interaction with someone, say an elementary-school child, and benefit professionally from the experience. The latter group would maintain that the former might be right, in part, if a trainer would, in fact, follow through by providing adequate guiding supervision (because some academic knowledge would be transmitted in the process), but that trainers too often bypass this responsibility. This point of view assumes that a more efficacious training approach would be to arm the trainee with academic knowledge, particularly in the psychosocial behavioral sciences and basic counseling techniques, and then expose him—as early in his training as is feasible—to interactions with persons who can make the academic knowledge practical and meaningful.

Because behavioral-modification techniques can be applied at quite divergent levels of sophistication, this is one approach that lends

[5]Another neglected training area, and one that is not confined to any one specialty or discipline or theoretical orientation, is the equipping of the nonmedical counselor-therapist to assess his clients' complaints, symptoms, case history, and clinical signs to determine whether medical intervention is necessary. This is a crucial problem for any professional involved with counseling or psychotherapy and merits primary attention by trainers.

itself nicely to the first view. That is, a trainee could interact with a person-client with little or no formal academic knowledge (but with proper guiding supervision), but if he wanted to increase his level of involvement with behavioral modification, he would have to have academic knowledge of the matter before he could attempt to perform the more specialized procedures. Thus it would seem that training in the behavioral aspects of psychobehavioral counseling and therapy encompasses both views.

As to the point at which supervised clinical experience should end, it depends upon how much the trainee hopes to achieve academically and what sorts of services he hopes to provide. Moreover, he must realize that some form of supervised clinical experience will always be within the role of the professional counselor-therapist.

The supervised clinical experiences in the behavioral aspects of psychobehavioral counseling and therapy can be distinguished from experiences in other theoretical aspects. Poser (1967) emphasizes that behavior-therapy trainees should be trained in a setting that *actually* provides behavioral-modification services, that they should cultivate an awareness of the necessary relationship of experimental research (particularly that related to learning principles) to clinical behavior therapy, and that they should experience presenting their behavioral work to nonbehavioral professionals. This last experience would create a situation in which a trainee would have to give special emphasis to his defense of his technical services, which is compatible with the assertion made in Chapter 3 that the justification for any service rests solely on the professional's ability to achieve, via an academic rationale, acceptance from others.

The supervised clinical experiences that are part of the training for the psychobehavioral counselor-therapist provide the stage for developing more than academic knowledge. These factors will receive further consideration, but for the present it need only be pointed out that the practice of behavioral-modification procedures, particularly on the more advanced levels and with the more specialized techniques, makes it mandatory for the trainee to develop some highly personal factors. Lazarus (1966) notes that students of behavior therapy tend to restrict their technical applications to a narrow range of the available stimuli, thereby omitting stimuli that might greatly increase the overall efficacy of the treatment; he concludes that *flexibility* and *versatility* are two personal, yet professionally related, characteristics that must be cultivated. These two factors relate quite directly to the factor of *responsibility,* and in responsibility lies, to a large extent, the key to the manifestation of responsible, innovative professional action. Another personal factor that is of major import for the treatment outcome is *self-understanding;* this too will receive more detailed discussion at a later point. The ill-advised view of certain behaviorists that the therapist's relationship with the client is not really important to behavior therapy was, it is hoped, adequately answered in Chapter 1; the rationale for the psychobehavioral position more than adequately substantiates the view that the successful use of behavioral-modification procedures, regardless of level, depends to some degree on the counselor-therapist's understanding of his own dynamics and need system and his ability to control the influence of his personal characteristics when he is providing counseling-therapy services. Since behavioral techniques are not immune to these influences, part of the supervised clinical experience should focus on how the trainee's personal characteristics affect the application of the techniques.

In summary of the special knowledge necessary for the use of behavioral modification within the psychobehavioral frame of reference, the following recommendations can be made:

1   The psychosocial behavioral science core and specialty learnings should be maintained for all trainees, and should include knowledge of how experimental-general psychology, personality theories, and psychopathology can be interpreted from a behavioral point of view.

2   Counseling-therapy trainees should acquire knowledge about learning theories and principles, with special emphasis on how they can be transformed into applied techniques, such as verbal conditioning.

3   Trainees should be able to state counseling-therapy goals as behavioral objectives.

4   Trainees should be able to analyze traditional sources of diagnostic data, such as psychometric tests, and identify reinforcement contingencies.

5   The trainee should be oriented to the full range of behavioral-modification techniques and should have supervised clinical experience in using a representative sample of them; emphasis should be given to integrating these applications into a regular, insight-oriented counseling-therapy format.

6   The trainee should be able to analyze a recording of his interviews or counseling-therapy sessions and reliably identify the following: the types or classes of client responses, planned and unplanned reinforcements within his own responses, the effects of his responses-reinforcers on the client's behavior, and ways he could alter his response style to influence the client's responses in a desired direction.

Without doubt, the implementation of behaviorally oriented training requires that the training program have an adequately prepared professional trainer available; there are, unfortunately, many training programs that lack such personnel. This points to the necessity for the trainers already in the programs to take steps to acquire knowledge and skills related to behavioral modification. This process can be accomplished in various ways, such as through reading, consultation, attending workshops or seminars, or obtaining tutorial-type supervision from an experienced professional who is already trained in behavioral modification.

## REFERENCES

Albert, G. If counseling *is* psychotherapy—then what? *Personnel and Guidance Journal*, 1966, *45*, 124–129.

American Psychological Association. Education and Training Board. Criteria for evaluating training programs in clinical and counseling psychology. *American Psychologist*, 1958, *13*, 59–60.

Anthony, N. A longitudinal analysis of the effect of experience on the therapeutic process. *Journal of Clinical Psychology*, 1967, *23*, 512–516.

Arbuckle, D. S. *Counseling: Philosophy, theory and practice*. Boston: Allyn and Bacon, 1965.

Brammer, L. M., and Shostrom, E. L. *Therapeutic psychology* (2nd ed.). Englewood Cliffs, N. J.: Prentice-Hall, 1968.

Clement, P. W., and Sartoris, P. C. Clinical students evaluate present APA approved training programs and make suggestions for changes. *Journal of Clinical Psychology*, 1967, *23*, 57–62.

Dole, A. A., Nottingham, J., and Wrightsman, L. S., Jr. Beliefs about human nature held by counseling, clinical, and rehabilitation students. *Journal of Counseling Psychology*, 1969, *16*, 197–202.

Gerken, C. An objective method for evaluating training programs in counseling psychology. *Journal of Counseling Psychology*, 1969, *16*, 227–237.

Hobbs, N. The compleat counselor. *Personnel and Guidance Journal,* 1958, *36,* 594–602.

Jordaan, J.-P., Myers, R. A., Layton, W. L., and Morgan, H. H. *The counseling psychologist.* Washington, D. C.: American Psychological Association, 1968.

Kirchner, Elizabeth P. Graduate education in psychology: Retrospective views of advanced degree recipients. *Journal of Clinical Psychology,* 1969, *25,* 207–213.

Lazarus, A. A. Broad-spectrum behaviour therapy and the treatment of agoraphobia. *Behaviour Research and Therapy,* 1966, *4,* 95–97.

McGowan, J. F., and Schmidt, L. D. (Eds.). *Counseling: Readings in theory and practice.* New York: Holt, Rinehart and Winston, 1962.

Patterson, C. H. Psychotherapy in the school. *Journal of School Psychology,* 1966, *4,* 15–29. (a)

Patterson, C. H. *Theories of counseling and psychotherapy.* New York: Harper and Row, 1966. (b)

Peterson, D. R. Professional program in an academic psychology department. In E. L. Hoch, A. O. Ross, and C. L. Winder (Eds.), *Professional preparation of clinical psychologists.* Washington, D. C.: American Psychological Association, 1966, 143–146.

Peterson, D. R. The doctor of psychology program at the University of Illinois. *American Psychologist,* 1968, *23,* 511–516.

Poser, E. G. Training behavior therapists. *Behaviour Research and Therapy,* 1967, *5,* 37–41.

Rodnick, E. H. Comments on the "Boulder" model. In E. L. Hoch, A. O. Ross, and C. L. Winder (Eds.), *Professional preparation of clinical psychologists.* Washington, D. C.: American Psychological Association, 1966, 21–23.

Ross, A. O. *The practice of clinical child psychology.* New York: Grune and Stratton, 1959.

Super, D. E. Transition: From vocational guidance to counseling psychology. *Journal of Counseling Psychology,* 1955, *2,* 3–9.

Surratt, P. R., Ulrich, R. E., and Hawkins, R. P. An elementary student as a behavioral engineer. *Journal of Applied Behavior Analysis.* 1969, *2,* 85–92.

Wolpe, J., and Lazarus, A. A. *Behavior therapy techniques.* New York: Pergamon, 1966.

Woody, R. H. Preparation in behavioral counseling. *Counselor Education and Supervision,* 1968, *7,* 357–362.

Woody, R. H. *Behavioral problem children in the schools: Recognition, diagnosis, and behavioral modification.* New York: Appleton-Century-Crofts, 1969.

# 6

# Development of the Professional Person

In *any* form of counseling or therapy, it is crucial that there be
extensive development of the personal qualities of the trainees. The
key terms are "self-understanding" and "responsibility." In approaching these topics, one must acknowledge, without apologies but with
due respect for the needed scientific documentation, that there is
little from behavioral science that would provide empirical guidelines, and that the comments therefore present deductive reasoning.
Recognizing that these subjective views expressed lack experimental
verification, the goal is to have the ideas serve as stimulation for introspection. Even with mountains of statistical data, the final process of
accentuating and continuing to develop self-understanding and responsibility remains within the bounds of the highly personalized
process of introspection and self-derivations of meaning.

## SELF-UNDERSTANDING

Divergent theoretical positions have maintained that a trainee
should experience, as an integral part of his training, the processes
that he will eventually, as a professional, guide others through. The
classic prototype is psychoanalysis. From its inception, a would-be
psychoanalyst's training has not been complete until he has successfully completed his own analysis. Klauber (1968) notes that "the psychoanalyst's personality must inevitably influence considerably the
direction taken by the analysis" (p. 321), and he emphasizes the
need to give "increased recognition of the influence on the psychoanalytic transaction of the structure of the ego in analyst and patient"
(p. 322). Despite the attempts to remove the therapist's personality
from the process (such as by having the analyst sit behind the re-
clining analysand), psychoanalysis has always recognized that the

therapist's personal qualities could be influential and that successful analysis should thus be part of training. It has been only more recently that the neoanalytically oriented therapists (or quasi-analysts) have recognized that regardless of their own analysis, their personalities are influential, i.e., therapy is an interpersonal transaction (and many therapists are relinquishing their couches in favor of face-to-face confrontations).

The importance of a therapeutic experience for trainees is by no means limited to psychoanalysis or the psychoanalytically oriented psychotherapies. Because of the facilitating conditions that the client-centered counselor hopes to impart to his clients in the counseling relationships, trainers in this theoretical vein have held that counselor trainees can be helped to develop the necessary qualities by experiencing the client-centered relationship, either by formal counseling or by turning their supervised clinical experiences (practicum or internship) into the basis for transforming the supervisory relationship into a model client-centered relationship. Those trainers who are more existential believe that the counselor or therapist must have achieved a certain "experiential wisdom" that helps his clients develop and learn from existential sharing; this would probably mean having been engaged in a similar existential sharing relationship. Behaviorism seems to be the only clinical approach that has not looked on such experiences as a necessary part of training. Presumably, this is due to some behaviorists' belief that behaviors and personality develop from social reinforcers, and that if the behavior therapist does not have maladaptive habits or behaviors that interfere with his professional abilities to analyze reinforcement contingencies and to create interventions that will administer reinforcers for conditioning or counterconditioning, then he need not have experienced the therapeutic process firsthand. The position favored herein, of course, is that behaviorism is no more immune to the influence of the personal characteristics of the therapist than are most other forms of therapy.

There seem to be two postulates behind the practice of having trainees participate in a therapeutic experience. First, and most legitimate from an academic point of view, is the postulate that, if the trainee is to appreciate the emotional as well as the technical concomitants of counseling or therapy, he should have participated in the process as a recipient. In other words, participation as a client is thought to lead to increased academic knowledge of the theoretical and technical components of his eventual service functions. The second postulate, which is aligned with a philosophical-ethical concern, is that, in order to assure that counseling-therapy is meeting the needs of the client rather than the needs of the counselor-therapist, trainees should have self-understanding of their own feelings, conflicts, needs, and values, and should be able to hold them in abeyance during their service functions. In the early days of counseling and psychotherapy, there was an abundance of writings that emphasized the commitment of the counselor-therapist to his clients, and one of the central themes was that the counselor's own mental health influenced his professional functioning, that he must strive to "know himself" and be aware of his values in order to avoid ethical dilemmas, and that while he would undoubtedly satisfy some of his needs by his professional participation, the counseling process was for the client's needs, not the counselor's.

Both of these postulates seem sound, but they are obviously more the products of introspection than of research. In taking a stand one must decide between inductive and deductive reasoning.

The practical necessity of providing clinical services makes it justifiable to accept (temporarily) the subjective deductive logic underlying both postulates, and as research accumulates, it appears that there is a relationship between the outcome of counseling and therapy and the personal characteristics of the counselor-therapist; note, for example, the evidence presented in Chapter 4 on the role of the therapist's personality in treatment. At this point in the evolution of counseling and psychotherapy, it seems possible to defend on philosophical and practical grounds, if not experimental evidence, the position that the counselor-therapist should have an awareness of the relationship his personal self-concept has to his professional self-concept and the resulting services. This means that professional training should accommodate the trainee's quest for self-understanding.

There may be several ways to achieve this goal. Perhaps the most obvious is for the trainee to participate in counseling or therapy, regardless of some trainers' belief that the supervisory relationship can serve the same purpose. In many ways, the exact manner in which the trainee tries to achieve self-understanding should be, and no doubt will be, a product of both the theoretical orientation of his primary mentor and the trainee's own needs and defense system. As will be discussed in the section on supervision, there is reason to believe (and any experienced trainer can attest) that the trainees tend to adopt the facilitating characteristics of their primary advisor or supervisor, not only in terms of technical and theoretical preferences, but in terms of personal value systems as well. It is sometimes amusing to observe how graduate students alter their behaviors toward those of the professor with whom they most identify—and sometimes vice versa. For example, a professor grows a beard and suddenly the students are growing beards; or a professor advocates a particular form of therapy, and overnight a group of disciples materializes, sometimes to the chagrin of the professor. And it should be noted that a professor's influence is often more personal than academic; Kirchner (1969) found that former trainees believed that professors were extremely influential in their career and academic decisions, and that professors' personal qualities were slightly more influential than their intellectual qualities. (The trainees, incidentally, placed a high value on a mentor-trainee relationship.) Whether this mentor-trainee influence is desirable must remain conjecture, but it certainly points up the importance of giving careful consideration to the assignment of advisees to advisors, and also to the recruitment of new faculty members. (Undoubtedly, future training programs will be able to solve both the assignment and recruitment issues by computerizing the relevant data, but for the time being these are the sorts of issues that department heads have to mull over in darkness —perhaps this matter is important enough to merit research attention.)

Before discussing the role of self-understanding in the training of counselors and therapists, there are two sources of ambiguity that should be acknowledged. First, part of the rationale for self-understanding is that the professional person should be "mentally healthy." Yamamoto's (1966) review shows that, although generalizations can be drawn from the research, there is considerable diversity of opinion about the components of the "mentally healthy" composite. Thus, even after extensive self-understanding efforts, both the trainee and trainer might be left with little to document successful achievement. Of course, others would counter that "mental health" is not prerequisite to effective professional functioning, and this introduces the second source of ambiguity: there is uncertainty about whether the training goal should be the achievement of a high level of self-understanding or an intensive and extensive examination of self-characteristics, with the actual achieved level of self-understanding considered secondary to the ongoing ability to be involved in self-examination. Shoben (1965) asserts that the most desirable approach would be to strive for a relatively high degree of *personal involvement,* which would not be insight or problem-solving ability per se, but the cultivation of the "examined life" (i.e., personal development).

Subjectively, Shoben's position seems to be the best frame of reference. It is improbable that trainees could be fairly assessed for how their mental health relates to their professional functioning. From a training standpoint, it would appear that the goal would be to implant in all trainees the seeds of personal involvement. In other words, trainees should be helped to learn to accept the "examined life" concept, with the recognition that no particular degree of "health" would be required,[1] that there will be some variable amount

[1]As is well known to experienced trainers, there are trainees who, either upon entry to the program or during the course of their training, are so disturbed that their own welfare (as well as the welfare of their future clients) requires that they receive therapy. None of the comments should be interpreted as suggesting that the trainer does not have a responsibility in these matters. In fact, the opposite is true. If anything, too many trainers are fearful or negligent in assessing the mental health of their trainees, and there needs to be more systematic action and assumption of responsibility for this matter. It is paradoxical that a profession that has a major commitment to psychodiagnostic assessment does not include this more often in its screening and evaluation of applicants and trainees; the test of this is for the reader to ask himself how many training and certification programs require evidence (psychometric or otherwise) of mental health. It is a matter of fact that there are few. Seldom does an applicant or trainee find his professional aspirations directly dependent upon his mental health, with the exception of some professional organizations and licensing and accreditation boards who solicit information from other professionals about the applicant, including opinions about his personal characteristics. Certainly for the typical student pursuing a one- or two-year degree program in any of the "helping" professions, there is no systematic procedure for evaluating mental health. There seems little doubt, if one attributes validity to the assessment procedures used in clinical services, that such evaluations would be possible and that, indeed, the trainer has a responsibility to the public, the student-trainee, and the profession to be involved in this matter. It might mean that some trainees would be excluded from the field, or that they would be counseled to seek more appropriate areas, or that they might be required to undergo treatment if they wanted to remain in the training program (with presumably some sort of attestation from the therapist treating the trainee as to his suitability to be graduated). This issue opens up numerous considerations that could and should be debated among professionals.

and degree of insight and problem-solving, and that introspection should be a part of a never-ending professional development. The term *self-understanding*, as used in this book, should be interpreted from the personal-development frame of reference.

There is evidence that persons choosing counseling as a vocation have a relatively high degree of self-insight (Mezzano, 1968), but there is not enough research to draw conclusions. Arbuckle (1966) states that counselors generally have greater difficulty in examining their own "self" than in entering into introspection with their clients, and he sees the self of the counselor as being important to the "counselor freedom" variable, which he relates to the counselor's ability to establish an empathic relationship with his client, to operate within the client's frame of reference, and to be genuine and honest in the counseling relationship (very much a client-centered style of functioning).

There have only been a few good accounts of the empirical outcome of providing trainees with counseling or therapy, and inferences could be drawn from them about the effectiveness of different styles of supervision. These inferences would have limited value, however, because the criteria for efficacy of supervisory styles are quite different among the studies and do not allow for valid comparisons.

In selecting relevant research, one of the basic questions is: Does the self-understanding of the counselor-therapist really have effects in the counseling-therapy per se? As has been pointed out, much of the argument in favor of self-understanding is practical logic, often predicated on the hindsight of a clinical veteran, who says, in effect, "After all these years, I can see how my own personality could have adversely influenced my counseling and therapy, and I therefore feel that training programs should try to develop self-understanding." And examination of countless research studies on counseling and psychotherapy shows that results vary with counselor or therapist characteristics. The control of counselor-therapist influence has been, of course, one of the plagues of counseling-therapy research. Of more direct relevance are the studies that examine the possible relationship between the counselor-therapist's degree of self-understanding and the quality of his clinical services. As in most areas of behavioral science, there are conflicting findings;

in general, however, it seems that this relationship does exist. Foulds (1969) for instance, found that self-actualization correlated significantly with empathic understanding and genuineness (facilitative conditions) in interpersonal processes (the counseling interview). He interpreted his findings to mean that counselor-education programs "should provide the kinds of experiences which will facilitate personal growth and self-actualization of counselor candidates" (p. 132).

There are several noteworthy studies on the use of self-understanding methods in training. Foreman (1967) presents a subjective analysis of one training program's use of so-called "T groups"; he concludes that the group experience is a useful adjunct to the practicum section of a training program because

the T Group represents an economical means through which members may develop observational and diagnostic skills. . . . Group members have the opportunity to participate in fashions akin to clients and counselors as well as participant observers. . . . The T Group enables students and staff to relate to each other in a more genuine, open fashion than is usually attempted. . . . Much of the quality of the relationship formed within the T Group is continued in the counseling practicum. (p. 52)

It should be noted that this study analyzed a program in which there was considerable openness between faculty and students. There are reasons why this might not be advisable. For example, Arnold (1967) recommends that individual counseling should be available for entering trainees in order to provide them the opportunity to work through problems of choice and self-understanding, but he maintains that the counseling should not be conducted by the trainee's advisor or instructor. This view presumably is based on the belief that the trainee will not receive maximum benefit from the experience if he feels that it could jeopardize his academic standing; therefore, to involve his advisor or faculty members would create a barrier to progress.[2] War-

[2]This author has conducted both individual and group therapy with trainees from the same department in which he taught and which included some of his advisees, and has experienced the conflicting feelings that can result from having to play multiple roles in the lives of students. The conflicts seem to be present in both the therapist-faculty member and the student-trainee. However, given a certain degree of self-understanding and almost didactic role delineation at the outset, it appears that this role conflict can be handled adequately and can, in fact, provide

kentin (1955) subjectively describes his proported successful use of group psychotherapy as a means of "developing the therapeutic capacity" of teachers and medical students, but again there were no data that provided a reasonable estimate of the effects of the intervention.

A slightly more sophisticated level of investigation, although still short of the level of scientific rigor that is needed, is the use of questionnaires. In an initial study, Gazda and Ohlsen (1961) found that trainees in counseling who had a group-counseling experience reportedly reflected improved functioning as a result; the findings of this self-report follow-up were generally supportive, but not conclusive. Bonney and Gazda (1966) did a similar follow-up questionnaire study on trainees who had met for group counseling for an hour and a half, twice a week, for eight weeks; the groups were designed to be therapeutic. As is too often true with questionnaires, the findings represent crude estimations and are, therefore, difficult to interpret. In general, however, when the trainees considered the influence of the group-counseling experience on personality dimensions (concept of self, professional relationships with colleagues, and professional relationships with clients) and the factors commonly associated with group counseling (understanding of intrapersonal dynamics, understanding of how others perceive you, understanding of how others

---

valuable material to work through in the course of therapy. For example, if it becomes an issue after several months of the relationship, one can examine about why it came in focus at that particular time. For the training programs providing self-understanding experiences, with the exception of sensitivity-group exchanges to foster improved communications between faculty and students, it seems that the wisest approach in most instances would be to have these services provided by nonfaculty professionals. And as relates to the therapist-faculty member's responsibility for assessing the mental health of the trainee, and yet not hampering the experience by allowing it to jeopardize the trainee's academic standing, the author adopted the position that when a student-trainee with whom he has been involved therapeutically is discussed for administrative-academic reasons in faculty meetings, he will maintain the confidentiality of the therapeutic relationship and will not present therapeutically revealed information that will either help or hurt the trainee's academic standing. If it emerges in the therapy that the student-trainee is so disturbed that the advisability of his remaining in the program or progressing at the present rate through training is questionable, this can be handled in the therapy relationship. Thus far, the approach seems to have worked out well on both sides. While it is clearly evident that this position can still create complexity and conflict, and that it creates a dual responsibility for the therapist-faculty member, the benefits seem to outweigh the disadvantages.

react to you, and learning of new interpersonal roles), they believed that it had had positive effects, and all of them recommended that it be available to other counselor trainees. Using a modified version of the Bonney-Gazda questionnaire, Woody (1971a) did a one-year follow-up study of graduate trainees who had been in psycho-analytically oriented group psychotherapy for training purposes (see subsequent discussion of Woody, 1971b). It was found that the trainees deemed the group psychotherapy to be a beneficial experience, as would relate to influencing both their personal characteristics and their personal attributes. It was also found that 60 percent of the trainees had sought further counseling or psychotherapy within the one year following the group experience; the comment was made:

Whether this was due to the uncovering of psychic material in the Seminars that necessitated further exploration and therapeutic resolution or whether it was because the trainees attracted to volunteering for the Self-Understanding Seminars were in particular need of a therapeutic experience in the first place must remain conjecture. In either case, however, it would seem that the Self-Understanding Seminars provided an experience that potentially alleviated the possibility of inept or disturbed functioning when the trainees became practicing counselors. According to the results of this questionnaire follow-up, it appears that trainees react favorably to the inclusion of a group psychotherapy training experience as part of their professional preparation. (Woody, 1971a, manuscript p. 5)

While this form of documentation may seem to hold "face validity," it still does not provide the research rationale that is necessary if training programs are to practice what they preach—the use of behavioral science to justify professional actions.

There are a few research studies that use psychometric instruments to estimate the effects of counseling-therapy experiences for trainees, but they often have design limitations that restrict generalization. Using self-concept as the criterion, Wirt, Betz, and Engle (1969) studied the effects of fourteen weekly one-hour group counseling sessions on graduate students enrolled in a counseling practicum. Design limitations led to ambiguous results: it was found that the experimental subjects were not significantly different from the control (no treatment) subjects on post-treatment measures, but there was significant change on the measured real and ideal self-concept scores for the experimental group.

In a more extensive study, Woody (1971b) matched twenty counseling trainees who had volunteered for self-understanding seminars with twenty trainee-controls from the same specialty, with the same number of graduate hours of credit, and the same sex. The experimental subjects received thirty one-and-a-half-hour psychoanalytically oriented group-therapy sessions. Pre- and post-treatment measures were obtained from the Edwards Personal Preference Schedule, the Tennessee Self Concept Scale, the Elmore Psychological Anomie Scale, and the Porter Counseling Inventory. The objective was to see whether group psychotherapy would lead to significant changes in areas relevant to professional training and competency. A computerized discriminant analysis revealed that the groups could not be distinguished by their set of subtest scores for any of the individual criterion instruments, either pre- or post-treatment. A test for homogeneity of regression showed that the experimental and control groups were indeed comparable. On the Edwards Personal Preference Schedule, there were only three scales that revealed what might be noteworthy change: the experimental subjects had a greater change in Deference ($p < .03$) and had a lowering of Exhibition ($p < .19$) and Change ($p < .09$) scores. The Tennessee Self Concept Scale, which estimates self-concept factors that would presumably be influenced by counseling-therapy processes (Physical Self, Moral-Ethical Self, Personal Self, Family Self, and Social Self, among others), did not yield any notable differences between the two groups. The Elmore Psychological Anomie Scale provides estimates of Meaninglessness, Valuelessness, Hopelessness, Powerlessness, Aloneness, and Closed-mindedness; only on Valuelessness ($p < .18$) was there a notable difference, with the experimental subjects being higher in valuelessness. The Porter Counseling Inventory is composed of excerpts from counseling sessions; the respondent makes forced multiple-choice responses, thereby giving indications (presumably) of the way he would respond in an actual counseling situation. Obviously this instrument has direct implications for training. From the various possibilities of types of responses (Evaluative, Interpretive, Supportive, Probing, Understanding, Content, Shallow or Partial, and Reflection), the experimental subjects increased their use of Evaluative ($p < .11$) and Interpretive ($p < .03$) responses (but it should be noted that a second estimate of Interpretive responses within the Scale was $p <$ .45) and decreased their use of Understanding ($p <$ .08) responses, as compared to the control subjects. These psychometric data provide only limited support for the value of providing counseling-therapy to trainees.

There seem to be three important generalizations that can be derived from the Wirt, Betz, and Engle (1969) and Woody (1971b) studies. First, there are not clearcut, pronounced psychometrically based values for training via counseling-therapy experience. (Of course, it is possible that the kinds of instruments used do not measure adequately the effects of such an experience; but the tests do work for clients, and surely trainees and clients are not so different that the rationale for the instruments can be totally discounted. It may be that these instruments are not sensitive enough to measure the effects of counseling and psychotherapy; but this supposition is then applicable to assessing the effects in both training and clinical service.) Second, there are psychometric differences that merit consideration, such as evidenced in the Porter Counseling Inventory scores in the Woody (1971b) study. Third, it seems important to note the scores that were not significantly different. For example, in the Woody (1971b) study, there was no significant difference between the experimental and control groups on the Intraception and Nurturance scales of the Edwards Personal Preference Schedule, to name but two of several seemingly relevant scores; such factors as these have at least face validity for desirable outcomes of training and an inherent relationship to presumed counseling and psychotherapeutic processes, yet statistical differences were not found.

The research results cited in this section do not negate the value of using counseling and psychotherapy to cultivate self-understanding (both for trainees and for clients), but they give no support, either. It is evident, however, that there is room to question whether self-understanding should be part of training and if so to what extent; how it should be assessed; and whether counseling and psychotherapy are the best means to accomplish such a goal. Subjectively, it seems that self-understanding is highly important, that it is critical that training programs develop personal factors along with academic factors, and that counseling-psychotherapy has a greater potential for increasing self-understanding than other training methods. But this is subjective logic and opinion.

## RESPONSIBILITY

In psychobehavioral counseling and therapy, the term "responsibility" has several meanings. The most important of these refers to the counselor-therapist's realization that he is to a significant degree responsible for the progress made in the treatment; this may be called "therapist responsibility." A second definition, seemingly more personal, but still rooted in professional role, refers to the counselor-therapist's voluntary activation of his resources to meet the needs of his clients; this may be called "responsible action."

### Therapist Responsibility

Therapist responsibility is advocated by all theorists, but close inspection of actual practice produces evidence that seems to show that it is not always present (Pierce and Schauble, 1969a). Some of the key theoretical positions are: In client-centered counseling, the counselor has the responsibility to create a certain therapeutic atmosphere, but the contents of the sessions (i.e., what is talked about), the thrust for personal growth, the goals for counseling, and the appraisal of when progress has been adequate remain the responsibility of the client; thus the name "nondirective counseling" (which has hopefully been outgrown). The existentialists assume the responsibility of "giving" to the client, but the client has the responsibility for seeking, for making all active decisions, and for directing his life style; this approach does, however, seem to have more potential for therapeutic responsibility, but it would require that the counselor-therapist accept and act on, not just give lip service to, his involvement with the client, and thus make it truly a shared responsibility for therapeutic growth. The psychoanalytically oriented counselor-therapist—despite the differences among the classic analysts, the neoanalysts, and the ego-analysts—accepts responsibility for implementing psychoanalytic theory and techniques, but he accepts no responsibility for the outcome; if the therapy is unsuccessful, it is not his fault, because he believes that the approach would work if the client were not resistant, and if it were given enough time. (It should be noted that what might seem like personal involvement by the therapist is not really that, because he is dealing with matters as a *significant other on whom the client has made transferences*.) Those using a trait-and-factor approach are able to stay almost totally out of the therapeutic responsibility arena; there is little or no personal involvement because the psychometric measures are providing the basis for directions and decision-making flows out of the data—in fact, neither the counselor-therapist nor the client has real responsibility; counseling success is viewed as the result of tests having produced accurate predictions, and failures are explained either by the client's refusal to cooperate and follow through with the directives of the data or by the poor predictive quality of the instruments. Behaviorists, of course, claim to assume full therapeutic responsibility; they accept a client and in so doing assume a role in which they use the client's acknowledged goals as the grounds for prescribing a behavioral-modification procedure; they continue treatment, reassessing and altering the techniques as might be necessary, until the initially set goals have been achieved. Certainly there is technical therapeutic responsibility within behavioral modification, but there is essentially no credence given to the concept of personal therapeutic responsibility—at least not in the classic behavior therapy research. (What goes on within the session might be quite different; as has been asserted, there may well be relationship factors working.) Therapeutic failures are explained as failures of a particular technique, or as the client's unwillingness to continue in treatment. About the closest the behavior therapist comes to acknowledging therapeutic responsibility is the admission that he must construct and adequately execute the technical program.

It would seem that the only possible way to meet therapeutic responsibility would be (1) to allow for both personal and professional involvement, and (2) to do away with the restrictive boundaries of a particular theoretical approach. As Pierce and Schauble (1969a) state:

We believe that identification with a *single, closed* theoretical system irrespective of individual client needs is—by its very nature—irresponsible and untenable behavior on the part of the therapist. We infer that an eclectic stance—where a theoretical or methods approach is chosen on the basis of client needs—is the only viable approach. . . . Once client responsibility is delineated, the counselor must determine a mode of treatment which facilitates the discharge of his own appropriate responsibility. Intrinsic to this concept is the belief that *participation in the therapy situation requires that each of the participants assume some degree of responsibility for the therapeutic process.* (p. 74)

This posture fits nicely into the psychobehavioral frame of reference.

Psychobehavioral counseling and therapy holds that the therapeutic effects are dependent, in part, on the fulfilling of therapeutic responsibility in both the personal and professional modes. In considering what takes place within the therapeutic relationship, it seems that "if the counselor looks at the behavior of his client as a probable consequence of his own behavior and if he views his own behavior as the force that may activate his client's responses, then he can understand how the client's behavior reflects the unfolding and revealing of the client's basic problem as an interpersonal process" (Kell and Mueller, 1966, p. 8). Therapeutic responsibility is thus the key to the understanding and eventual control of the interpersonal factors relevant to the client's problems. It would seem that this makes it requisite that the counselor-therapist assume technical responsibility (one of the behavioristic elements of psychobehaviorism).

It would, of course, be unscientific to assign importance to the concept of therapist responsibility solely because of subjectively derived ideas. As with so many other areas of clinical service, there is little research evidence on which to base one's views, Pierce and Schauble (1969b) have, however, conducted one cogent study. They defined the concept of "facilitative responsibility" as

the communication by the counselor of an awareness that his behavior has major consequences for the client and the therapeutic process; the counselor then discharges this responsibility in an appropriate manner. "Appropriate manner" means that the therapist brings to bear all his resources in order to help the client, but not in such a way as to obstruct the client from employing whatever resources he has of his own. In brief, facilitative responsibility is the communication by the counselor that he realizes his appropriate responsibility in the counseling relationship and that he is fulfilling it. (Pierce and Schauble, 1969a, p. 71)

Pierce and Schauble (1969b) rated recorded segments of the counseling and therapy sessions of most successful and least successful clients within a research bank of university counseling center cases and used the foregoing definition to construct a therapist responsibility scale. They found that their scale had good interjudge reliability ($r=.95$) and that the therapists of the most successful clients communicated significantly higher levels ($p< .02$) of facilitative responsibility than did the therapists whose clients were in the least successful group. They interpreted their result as showing that counseling trainees should be prepared to have an extensive repertoire of responses (i.e., that they should be prepared to use techniques from diverse theoretical orientations), and that they should be able to act on their perceptions of what the client needs from them as a professional person. Note that the term "professional person" carries the connotation of both personal and professional contributions (Woody, 1970). The Pierce-Schauble study does not adequately justify the inclusion of the concept of therapist responsibility into training programs, but it does present a valuable supportive introduction that merits further research consideration.

### Responsible Action

Responsible action is more a philosophical tenet than a scientific postulate. It is, however, extrapolated from many of the foregoing discussions about the counselor-therapist's responsibility to his recipients, and thus is based on certain scientific and professional factors.

In the discussion in Chapter 3 on the influence of the setting in which the counselor-therapist is employed, the point was made that professionals have to take action to remove barriers to optimum service to individual clients and to society. This means that the professional mental health worker, regardless of basic discipline or work setting, has to be personally prepared to assume his right and responsibility, both professional and personal, to make the system (and numerous definitions can be appropriately attached to the word) work for him (meaning to work for the mental health needs of his clients) rather than for him to have to work for the system. This equates to "responsible action."

The best justification for responsible action is found in practical needs. An excellent clarifying example can be derived from Thorne's (1961) postulates about the current status of clinical judgment:

*Postulate VII. The ethical justification for making a clinical judgment which does not have complete scientific support and validation is that it only professes to be the best that can be offered at the time and place.* The nature of practical problems is that they demand a solution. Life cannot remain in a posture of paralysed indecision but rushes inevitably onward, either carried forward blindly by its own momentum or manipulated by human decisions. . . . The clinician is not expected to be a superman, making infallible judgments, or displaying perfect efficiency in his practice. It is considered ethically sufficient simply to be able to function clinically at the level of standards of time and place. The basic point here is that society demands action from the clinician. (p. 21)

This ethical justification is applicable to counseling and therapy, which does, of course, actually involve the issue of clinical judgment. Two other postulates from Thorne (1961) seem particularly relevant:

*Postulate VIII. Clinical decisions must inevitably reflect expedience in many situations where there are no scientifically valid bases for decision or where there are conflicts of value systems all of which have some "rightness."* . . . The practical solution of such situations is to make the clinical judgment which appears to solve the largest number of considerations and is the best that can be accomplished at time and place. Such a decision carefully weighs the probable costs of alternative plans of action and supports the course which appears most advantageous from all angles. . . . The clinician must be *expedient* in everyday practice to a degree entirely unappreciated by the academician or ivory-towered theorist who can afford to stick to principles. . . . The "pure" scientist may not be interested in decisions of this type, or approve of them, but they must be made. (pp. 22–23)

*Postulate IX. Even in view of the admitted invalidity or relative inefficiency of many clinical decisions, society must depend upon clinical decisions because of the practical and economic limitations of life situations.* . . . The clinicians have the responsibility to go on making decisions in any situation where their predictions are even 1 or 2% better than common sense or pure chance choices. In cases where the differential is relatively small, then society itself must determine how much it can afford to pay for such a premium. Decisions have to be made to make the World go round, and often without adequate foundations. Let us not be afraid to make them. (p. 23)

These comments on clinical judgment are, for the most part, directly applicable to counseling and therapeutic services. The psychobehavioral position, as stated in the rationale in Chapter 1, accepts the premise that the needs of the client supersede the allegiance to a theory and that, despite the personal and professional security derived from maintaining alignment with a particular theoretical approach (even pure behaviorism), the counselor-therapist must be able to tailor his responses to the idiosyncrasies of the client and take responsible action.

To give practical grounds for professional actions may seem blasphemous, but if given more than a cursory glance, the psychobehavioral approach does place strong emphasis on scientific theory —as much or even more than most approaches; the work of Thorne (e.g., 1967), for instance, is noteworthy for the use of experimentation to justify theoretical views and applied clinical practices.

One of the dimensions that distinguishes both the psychobehavioral approach and the Thornian eclectic-integrative approach from most other approaches is the importance given to extending scientific knowledge and the concomitant investigative rigor to attempting to fulfill practical day-to-day problems that arise in the course of counseling and therapy. In other words, it is necessary to take "responsible action." In some ways, this implies that the "pure" behavior scientist (of course, many physical and natural scientists would deny that any behavioral scientist is "pure") is not taking responsible action" this is true. On the other hand, the applied clinician ing theoretical formulations, and in the complete sense of the "responsible action" this is true. On the other hand, the applied clinician who ignores behavioral science (such as some persons who hide behind a pious title like "human resources consultant" and base much of their "intervention" on social encounters) is equally irresponsible.

Psychobehaviorism goes well beyond the simple integration of behavioral and insight techniques; it emphasizes the functioning of the counselor-therapist as a *professional person*. This term has two connotations: the use of *professional* behavioral science based knowledge and skills for practical problems, and the use of the counselor-therapist's *personal* characteristics in the service of his clients' needs. This means the ability to act in the interest of clients or, more generally, society—even if it means challenging accepted views, systems, and structural limits that hinder the effectiveness of services.

Obviously, this confrontation must not be totally emotional, but must present a combined rationale of behavioral science, professionalism, and human dignity and integrity. The professional risk of such active encounters is one of the liabilities (if it is a liability— some would view it as a rewarding asset) of being a professional mental health worker: it is a societal responsibility that must be fulfilled. To shirk it is to depreciate one's claim to professional stature. Moving as a *professional person* into these encounters is the essence of *responsible action*.

## SUPERVISORY RELATIONSHIPS

The personal development of trainees for psychobehavioral counseling and therapy, like the development of the relevant psychosocial behavioral-science knowledge, is not a simple matter that can be delimited by a technical description; it is a complex process that requires flexibility in the use of the objective and subjective factors influencing the trainee. Assuming that the limited evidence justifies the inclusion in training of personal dimensions, there is little documentation as to how such dimensions as self-understanding, personal involvement, therapist responsibility, and responsible action can be implanted, cultivated, and developed. Moreover, although the dimensions of human nourishment or facilitating conditions, such as empathy and genuineness, seem to be important in the development of the professional person, training methodologies have been elusive (Carkhuff and Berenson, 1967).

Research shows that both the academic and the professional-personal aspects of developing trainees depend on supervisory factors. The facilitation level of the supervisor is one important variable. In examining the facilitative conditions of empathy, regard, genuineness, and concreteness, Pierce and Schauble (1970) found that the supervisors who were high on these dimensions had trainees who would change significantly, but those supervisors who were low on these dimensions had trainees who did not change significantly (in fact, they declined slightly). Carkhuff (1969) holds that the critical factors in counselor training are the level of trainer and trainee functioning on facilitative and action-oriented dimensions, and the type of training program. He found that programs espousing predominantly one theory or two opposing theories (such as client-centered and trait-and-factor orientations) often have low levels of facilitating conditions, whereas eclectic programs "focusing (a) upon core conditions shared by all interview-oriented processes for which there is research support complemented by a consideration of the unique contributions of the various potential preferred mcdes of treatment and (b) integrating the different critical sources of learning" (pp. 242–243) generally afford the best opportunity for growth. Further, Carkhuff, Collingwood, and Renz (1969) studied approaches to training psychology students in discrimination and communication; they conclude

that an exclusively didactic training experience focusing exclusively on discrimination yields significant improvement in discrimination but very little generalization of learning to communication. The direct implication is that to effect differences in communication, the training must emphasize a behavioristic approach providing practice in communication. (p. 460)

This underscores both the psychobehavioral integrated-theories position and the blending of academic and professional-personal aspects in training. Inherent to this is reliance upon the supervisory relationship.

There is much more lip service given to the supervisory process now than a few years ago, but the fact of the matter is that there is less one-to-one supervisor-trainee contact now than previously. Part of this is understandable, because there has been a great increase in the number of students seeking graduate-level training and no significant strides in the preparation of supervisors. One index of the decrease in direct contact is the increased reliance on group supervision of counseling practicum students. This practice may be just as effective and far more economical for the goals of a counseling practicum as the one-to-one supervision (though this has not been clearly demonstrated). However, when we note the poorly defined constructs, particularly on the personal level, that must be developed by counselors and therapists, it would seem that more tutorial-supervisory relationships in training programs are needed.

Although the "facilitating conditions" have been criticized in

this book as being too limited to constitute a comprehensive definition of the counseling-therapeutic process, the research yields sug-
gestive evidence. As summarized by Carkhuff and Berenson (1967),
college freshmen and the general public score about the same on the
facilitating-conditions scales, while graduate students in the helping
professions begin graduate school at a slightly higher level (thereby
giving support to the proposition that persons attracted to graduate
study in the mental health professions are better equipped for the
role than their contemporaries in other major areas of study). The
startling point is that following graduate training there is a decrease
in empathic understanding (which some professionals feel to be the
primary dimension). Carkhuff and Berenson (1967) interpret the
findings as follows:

> The direct suggestion is, then, that in graduate school something very
> deleterious happens to the functioning of graduate students on one of the
> critical effective ingredients of therapeutic processes. It is also important
> to note that in the Bergin and Solomon study, empathy once again related
> positively to judgments of therapeutic competence involving patient bene-
> fits, and negatively to overall and practicum grade point averages; that is,
> *those students who communicated the highest level of understanding and*
> *whose patients, in effect, had the greatest opportunity to gain or change*
> *constructively in therapy received the lowest grades in their training pro-*
> *grams.* (p. 10)

This finding would be quite distressing if there was not reason to
suspect, perhaps defensively, the rationale and design of the research
that produced them. For instance, we can ask whether the research
methodology involved was appropriate, and whether the dimensions
we have measured adequately represent what training programs need
to strive to develop. For example, perhaps a decrease in empathic
understanding is more than compensated for by an increase in other
dimensions, such as, perhaps, dissemination of behavioral science
knowledge to clients to influence their behavior (e.g., "cognitive restructuring") or responsible action that would not have been possible
without the graduate training. Is it a "rob Peter to pay Paul" situation or a stock market move of taking a loss in one holding in order
that other holdings will rise? Since the mental health professions
strive for scientific stature, the really alarming point is that we do
not know.

Thus, trainers must train not knowing exactly what factors have the most importance to the final product and not knowing what methodologies can best achieve them. Practical issues, however, require that the "weighting game" be performed, and one of the primary factors seems to be the importance of the supervisor.

There is evidence from the research on "facilitating conditions" that during training the trainees move in the direction of the functioning of their professors (Carkhuff, Kratochvil, and Friel, 1968). This finding recalls the comments made earlier on how students tend to imitate their professors—apparently the imitation is not limited to growing beards, but also includes the in-counseling responding behaviors and conditions.

There are many conflicting views as to what the supervisory relationship should encompass. In terms of a gross dichotomy, they seem to center around either: making a critical analysis of the trainee's counseling-therapy sessions (as based on tape recordings) and offering suggestions, or developing a "counseling" relationship between supervisor and trainee so that the trainee can fully experience the processes and effects of the services he aspires to offer. Kell and Mueller (1966) take a middle-of-the-road stance, asserting that "the sources of material for the supervisory sessions derives principally from the supervisee's encounters with his clients and secondarily from his supervisory relationship" (p. 129), but they emphasize that the trainee should be helped to explore how his own dynamics relate to and influence his counseling with others. This approach leaves ample opportunity to include counseling or insight-producing techniques in the supervisory relationship. Kell and Mueller (1966) further state:

Above all, the supervisor needs to believe that different counselors with varying strengths may each contribute something different to the resolution of clients' problems. What each of these different counselors contributes to a client's ability to change is partly a result of the supervisor's being able to help each different person to differentiate himself from his clients. (p. 131)

Further, we believe that ideally this relationship should become more equalitarian and consultative and less supervisory as counselor adequacy grows—the final objective being colleague status. (p. 128)

The first statement, while seemingly sound, illustrates part of the difficulty in determining criteria for selection into the profession. It is likely that there are an infinite number of combinations of personal and professional qualities, with each having the potential to make a contribution of some kind; but to accept this as a guideline for selection seems unwise, especially because more delineation is possible—even now. The second statement fits into the psychobehavioral concept of melding the professional-academic factors with the personal factors; a relationship that is characterized as consultative or as carrying colleague status would likely have such a melding effect.

In looking at whether the supervisory relationship should be didactic or counseling, Payne and Gralinski (1969) failed to find any noteworthy differences between the counseling type and the techniques (didactic) type, but both produced significantly better growth in the trainees than control (no supervision) trainees.

The discussion of these studies leads to what would seem to be the only appropriate solution, which, incidentally, is well within the psychobehavioral frame of reference: *Supervision must include a relationship between the supervisor and the trainee, and it should seek to integrate didactic and experiential approaches.*

Truax, Carkhuff, and Douds (1964) identify didactic training as "forced modification of both behavior and thinking to conform to that of the teacher-supervisor" (p. 241), and contrast it with experiential training, which they view as modification caused by social imitation of the supervisor in a model-counseling experience. They urge an integrated supervisory approach to allow for self-exploration, which they deem "one of the critical elements in superivsion" (p. 243), and for an integration of intellectual content and learning into the context of the supervisory relationship. Martin and Carkhuff (1968), in a study with acknowledged design limitations, present evidence that indicates that the integrated use of didactic and experiential techniques in training programs in counseling and therapy produces significant improvement in interpersonal functioning (such as between counselor and client) and constructive personality change for the trainees; this finding, which is compatible with the previously cited study by Carkhuff, Collingwood, and Renz (1969), underscores both the need for a supervisory relationship for clinical experiences and the need for integrally aligned academic training.

It would seem that the integration of didactic and experiential approaches to training would depend heavily upon a strong relationship between the supervisor and the trainee. The relationship might well be very much "counseling" at one point but "instructive" at another, with the potential (which many trainees might never attain) being sharing, equalitarian, and consultative. It is paradoxical that an approach like psychobehavioral counseling and therapy, which is directed at achieving professional and personal freedom for the counselor-therapist to be contemporary and even avant-garde, would espouse such a traditional relationship, one strikingly reminiscent of the relationships established centuries ago between the Oxford and Cambridge dons and their students. But this still seems like the desirable direction.

## THE FUTURE OF TRAINING

The roles, responsibilities, and functions of counselors and therapists are necessarily in constant flux. This flux cannot be eliminated, because it is the product of the needs of the recipients of the counseling and therapeutic services, both individually and societally determined. Hopefully, however, it will be reasonably well harnessed by behavioral-science knowledge and held firmly in control by professionalism.

The training of counselors and therapists must be continually altered to accommodate the changes in individual and societal needs, as manifested in the roles, responsibilities, and functions assumed by professionals. This challenge will not easily be met. It is essential that trainers be prepared to eliminate all unnecessary restrictions and be able to take "responsible action" in training, such as by modifying instructional methodologies to include technological advances, e.g., computer science.

Further, it seems that one of the main unnecessary restrictions that must be promptly confronted, eased, and then eliminated, at least in essence, is separatism among the mental health professions and the barriers constructed by unspoken but undeniably present pressures to "sign a loyalty oath" to a theoretical orientation. If such unnecessary restrictions and barriers can be eliminated, we may come closer to a never-equalled commitment to mental health: one following in many ways a public-health paradigm.

The outcomes of future training efforts depend on how the contemporary training crises are met. Hobbs (1964) cites nine objectives that he believes should guide the development of mental health training programs, regardless of discipline:

1   The changing conception of the nature of mental illness and mental retardation will require that the mental health specialist be a person of broad scientific and humanistic education, a person prepared to help make decisions not only about the welfare of an individual but also about the kind of society that must be developed to nurture the greatest human fulfillment. (p. 826)

2   The concept of the responsibility of the doctor for patient, case worker for client, so appropriately honored in traditional educational programs for the physician, social worker and clinical psychologist, must be reconceptualized to define the responsibilities of these specialists as workers with other professionals who can contribute to the development of social institutions that promote effective functioning in people. (p. 827)

3   The mental health specialist must be trained in ways to multiply his effectiveness by working through other less extensively and expensively trained people. The one-to-one model of much current practice does not provide a sound basis for a public health, mental health program. (p. 828)

4   Current developments will require that mental health training programs be revised to give attention to mental retardation commensurate with the degree of the responsibility that the mental health professions have already assumed for the retarded. Since mental retardation is a much broader problem than it is usually considered to be in those few medical, social work and psychological training programs that have given it attention, the inclusion of mental retardation in these curricula will require a substantial extension of their conceptual underpinnings. Slums are more consequential than galactosemia or phenylketonuria. (p. 828)

5   Curriculum constructors in social work, psychiatry and psychology must come to terms with the issue of the relationship between science and practice. (p. 829)

6   The main source of nourishment for the mental health professions has been clinical practice leavened and limited by research. The shift toward a public health emphasis in mental health programs will require

that the mental health specialist work through social institutions. He must acquire an appreciation of how disparate groups of people organize to achieve common goals and he must know how to encourage this process. He will need to be adept at institution building, at social intervention, at the ordering of individual and community resources in the interest of mental health. (p. 829)

7   An increased public health emphasis in mental health programs will accentuate the need for prevention and thus lead to a greater emphasis in professional training on problems of children, on childhood disorders and early indications of later difficulties and, especially, on normal patterns of development. (p. 830)

8   The new curricula should paradoxically reinstate an age-old study, that of morals and ethics, not professional ethics but classical ethics. . . . With increasing effectiveness we must become increasingly concerned with the consequences of our work. We cannot responsibly remain satisfied with vague definitions of what we mean by mental health. (p. 830)

9   Educational programs for mental specialists should anticipate an increasing obsolescence rate for knowledge and build habits of continuing scholarship and independent study. (p. 830)

With the exception of certain degrees of emphasis, e.g, on mental retardation, Hobbs' objectives for all mental health specialist training programs seem compatible with psychobehavioral counseling and therapy.

The implications of psychobehaviorism for training programs are explicit: There must be more scientific appraisal systems used to assess, restructure, and present all aspects of training. Training should give primary importance to the psychosocial behavioral sciences for the academic foundation of applied counseling and therapy. Some of the most important elements of counseling and therapeutic effectiveness are the most difficult to delineate and develop in training programs: these are the personal elements that blend in with the professionalism of the counselor-therapist. The professional person has both academic and personalized contributions to make to clients, and the nebulously formed mixture of these two ingredients leads to a need for more emphasis on preparation for continuing self-understanding and personal involvement (in a professional sense), therapeutic responsibility, and responsible action.

# REFERENCES

Arbuckle, D. S. The self of the counselor. *Personnel and Guidance Journal*, 1966, *44*, 807–812.

Arnold, D. L. Working with persons going into counseling. *Counselor Education and Supervision*, 1967, *6*, 171–178.

Bonney, W. C., and Gazda, G. Group counseling experiences: Reactions by counselor candidates. *Counselor Education and Supervision*, 1966, 5, 205–211.

Carkhuff, R. R. Critical variables in effective counselor training. *Journal of Counseling Psychology*, 1969, *16*, 238–245.

Carkhuff, R. R., and Berenson, B. G. *Beyond counseling and therapy*. New York: Holt, Rinehart and Winston, 1967.

Carkhuff, R. R., Collingwood, T., and Renz, Lauri. The effects of didactic training upon trainee level of discrimination and communication. *Journal of Clinical Psychology*, 1969, *25*, 460–461.

Carkhuff, R. R., Kratochvil, D., and Friel, T. Effects of professional training: Communication and discrimination of facilitative conditions. *Journal of Counseling Psychology*, 1968, *15*, 68–74.

Foreman, M. E. T groups: Their implications for counselor supervision and preparation. *Counselor Education and Supervision*, 1967, 7, 48–53.

Foulds, M. L. Self-actualization and the communication of facilitative conditions during counseling. *Journal of Counseling Psychology*, 1969, *16*, 132–136.

Gazda, G., and Ohlsen, M. M. The effects of short-term group counseling on prospective counselors. *Personnel and Guidance Journal*, 1961, *39*, 634–638.

Hobbs, N. Mental health's third revolution. *American Journal of Orthopsychiatry*, 1964, *34*, 822–833.

Kell, B. L., and Mueller, W. J. *Impact and change: A study of counseling relationships*. New York: Appleton-Century-Crofts, 1966.

Kirchner, Elizabeth P. Graduate education in psychology: Retrospective views of advanced degree recipients. *Journal of Clinical Psychology*, 1969, *25*, 207–213.

Klauber, J. The psychoanalyst as a person. *British Journal of Medical Psychology*, 1968, *41*, 315–322.

Martin, J. C., and Carkhuff, R. R. Changes in personality and interpersonal functioning of counselors-in-training. *Journal of Clinical Psychology*, 1968, *24*, 109–110.

Mezzano, J. Self insight of graduate students in guidance. *Counselor Education and Supervision*, 1968, 7, 397–398.

Payne, P. A., and Gralinski, D. M. Effects of supervisor style and empathy of counselor perceptions in simulated counseling. *Personnel and Guidance Journal*, 1969, *47*, 557–563.

Pierce, R. M., and Schauble, P. G. Responsibility for therapy: Counselor, client, or who? *Counseling Psychologist*, 1969, *1*, 71–77. (a)

Pierce, R. M., and Schauble, P. G. The role of therapist responsibility in the counseling relationship. Unpublished manuscript, Michigan State University, 1969. (b)

Pierce, R. M., and Schauble, P. G. Graduate training of facilitative counselors: The effects of individual supervision. *Journal of Counseling Psychology*, 1970, *17*, 210–215.

Shoben, E. J., Jr. The counseling experience as personal development. *Personnel and Guidance Journal*, 1965, *44*, 224–230.

Thorne, F. C. *Clinical judgment*. Brandon, Vt.: Journal of Clinical Psychology, 1961.

Thorne, F. C. *Integrative psychology: A systematic clinical viewpoint*. Brandon, Vt.: Clinical Psychology, 1967.

Truax, C. B., Carkhuff, R. R., and Douds, J. Toward an integration of the didactic and experiential approaches to training in counseling and psychotherapy. *Journal of Counseling Psychology*, 1964, *11*, 240–247.

Warkentin, J. An experience in teaching psychotherapy by means of group therapy. In M. Rosenbaum and M. Berger (Eds.), *Group psychotherapy and group function*. New York: Basic Books, 1963, 577–584.

Wirt, M., Betz, R., and Engle, K. The effects of group counseling on the self concepts of counselor candidates. *Counselor Education and Supervision*, 1969, *8*, 189–194.

Woody, R. H. Developing the professional person: A forgotten component of school psychology training. *School Psychologist*, 1970, *24*, 89–92.

Woody, R. H. Reactions of counselor trainees to group psychotherapy. *Counselor Education and Supervision*, 1970, *10*, in press. (a)

Woody, R. H. Self-understanding seminars: The effects of group psychotherapy in counselor training. *Counselor Education and Superivsion*, 1971, *10*, 112–119. (b)

Yamamoto, K. The "healthy person": A review. *Personnel and Guidance Journal*, 1966, *44*, 596–603.

# Name Index

# Subject Index

Accreditation and certification boards: 197

Accurate empathy: 7, 81

Affect and affectivity: 4, 10, 35

Affect simulation: 69

Alcoholism: 10, 51, 92, 93, 96, 97

American School Counselor Association: 152

American Society of Clinical Hypnosis: 86

Anxiety: 35, 37; avoidance responses, 51; behavioral vs. insight·approach, 10–11; hierarchies, 41, 68, 70–73, 86–87; sexual, 34, 35, 41, 68, 69–70; test-taking, 71–73, 132, 146, 147

Anxiety-reduction techniques: 68–77, 86–87, 124; assertion, training, 75–77; automated, 73–75, behavior reversal, 68, 76; implosive therapy, 93–96; relaxation training, 68–69;. selection, 126, 132–33; systematic desensitization, 20, 68–77, 126; treatment generalization, 102–3. *See also* Behavioral modification

Assertion and assertion training: 68, 75–77, 124, 126

Assertive practice: 140–41

Aversive conditioning and aversive therapy: 39, 51, 96–98, 126, 141; in group therapy, 145; philosophical issues, 98; setting, 150–51; therapeutic relationship, 15, 102

Avoidance conditioning: 126

Avoidance reaction paradigm: 146

Avoidance responses: 51, 94

Behavioral analysis: 120–22. *See also* Diagnosis

Behavioral counseling and behavior therapy: client resistance to, 38–39, 42; diagnosis, 39–40, 118, 120–22, 123–24; difference between, 9;

eclecticism in, 28–29; efficacy of, 11–14, 15, 34, 82; failures, 38–42; followup, 37–38; goals, 9, 21–22, 223; insight techniques in, 16–18, 42, referrals, 130–31; reinforcement conditioning principles, 32–34; relationship factors, 8, 14–18, 29–31, 37, 40–42; theoretical base, 9–18, 27–28; therapeutic responsibility, 21–23, 223; training, 40, 83. *See also* Behavioral–modification techniques, Conditioning, Counseling and therapy, Psychobehavioral counseling, *and* Therapeutic relationship

Behavioral modification and behavioral-modification techniques: 5, 49–114, 195; arguments against, 138; assertion training, 68, 75–77, 124, 126; aversive conditioning, 39, 51, 96–98, 126, 141, 150–51; behavioral reversal, 16, 35, 68, 76, 133, 140–41; clinical suggestion and hypnosis, 16–18, 34, 51, 80–87, 88, 93, 98, 126, 141, 146, 151; combinations, 86; covert sensitization, 51, 92–93; ethical and philosophical factors, 100, 103–4; in group therapy, 142–49; implosive therapy, 51, 93–96; in insight counseling-therapy, 16–21, 31, 32, 34–37, 42, 52, 61; laboratory apparatus, 50n; modeling, 51, 77–80; negative practice, 51, 98–100, 126, 127; object and social recognition rewards, 51, 65–67, 133, 135, 139; paraprofessionals, 50, 103, 202–4; public reaction to, 129; relaxation and relaxation training, 34, 35, 41, 68–69, 83, 86–87, 92, 93, 126, 147; relevant issues, 100–4; selection of, 49, 50, 117, 123–28, 132–33;